CORRIDOR CULTURES

QUALITATIVE STUDIES IN PSYCHOLOGY

This series showcases the power and possibility of qualitative work in psychology. Books feature detailed and vivid accounts of qualitative psychology research using a variety of methods, including participant observation and fieldwork, discursive and textual analyses, and critical cultural history. They probe vital issues of theory, implementation, interpretation, representation, and ethics that qualitative workers confront. The series mission is to enlarge and refine the repertoire of qualitative approaches to psychology.

GENERAL EDITORS
Michelle Fine and Jeanne Marecek

CORRIDOR CULTURES

Mapping Student Resistance at an Urban High School

MARYANN DICKAR

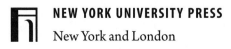

NEW YORK UNIVERSITY PRESS
New York and London

NEW YORK UNIVERSITY PRESS
New York and London
www.nyupress.org

Library of Congress Cataloging-in-Publication Data

Dickar, Maryann.
Corridor cultures : mapping student resistance at an urban high school /
Maryann Dickar.
p. cm. — (Qualitative studies in psychology)
Includes bibliographical references and index.
ISBN–13: 978–0–8147–2008–0 (cl : alk. paper)
ISBN–10: 0–8147–2008–0 (cl : alk. paper)
ISBN–13: 978–0–8147–2009–7 (pb : alk. paper)
ISBN–10: 0–8147–2009–9 (pb : alk. paper)
1. High school students—United States. 2. Urban schools—United States.
3. Classroom management—United States. 4. Educational psychology. I. Title.
LB3605.D53   2008
373.18—dc22   2008018241

Contents

■ ■ ■ ■

Acknowledgments

■   ■   ■   ■   ■

This book could not have come into being without the help of many people. First I wish to thank the co-editors of this series, Michelle Fine and Jean Maracek, and the reviewers whose names I do not know, for their astute questions that pushed my thinking and deepened my reading of school culture at Renaissance High School, and strengthened my scholarship. I also want to offer additional thanks to Michelle Fine, whose scholarly work and commitment to social justice I have long admired, and whose encouragement meant a great deal to me. Jennifer Hammer, my editor at NYU Press, was enthusiastic about this project from its inception and helped sustain it throughout its development. Despina Papazoglou Gimbel, the managing editor I worked with, paid careful attention to my writing and was infinitely patient with me.

I also am deeply grateful to the students who generously trusted me with their stories and shared their profound knowledge about schooling and their lives. I am indebted to all the students at Renaissance, many of whom I had the honor of teaching, for what they conveyed to me about urban youth, identity, and justice. Also, this project could never have been undertaken without the support of the principal of Renaissance and its teachers, the colleagues who shared my quest for a deeper understanding of our school and its limitations, and who offered support to me in more ways than I can name. And despite their generosity and my grit, this research might not have been completed without a Fellowship from the University of Minnesota and a Goddard Fellowship from the Steinhardt School of New York University which allowed the completion of the manuscript.

I also must share this accomplishment with my friends and family, who have provided me psychic and emotional support, and who have inspired me through their deep commitments to creating a more just world and their tireless devotion to their students. So a special thank you to my friends Lisa, Laurie, and Bill, who helped make Renaissance a special place despite everything, through their dedication, humor and creativity; I also could not have undertaken this work without the immeasurable support of my lifelong mentor and great friend, Carolyn, a strong, compassionate visionary who inspired me to become a teacher and who has been a constant anchor in sometimes stormy waters, while helping me to believe I could make a difference. To my husband, Ira, for his encouragement, wisdom, and sacrifices as I worked on this project, and for calming me, nagging me, inspiring me, and making me laugh all the time, I offer my deepest gratitude and love. My son, Paulo, offered uncountable hugs as he competed with the computer for my attention and my lap, and also helped make this book what it is. And to urban educators and students everywhere who take up the immense challenge of creating schools that live up to their democratic potential, thank you for compelling me to question the status quo, to imagine what might be, and to embrace the future full of hope.

Introduction

Student Resistance and the
Cultural Production of Space

The day before school started one September, I lost my classroom on the quiet south side of the building to a new Freshman Block program. My reassigned room on the noisy east side was an old computer room filled with Mac Classics bolted to the tops of tables. Though some computers worked, most needed repairs or were missing keyboards. During the summer, workers renovating the school had cut the wires, leaving no Internet access and no network, so the few working computers were essentially useless. Trying not to start the term demoralized, I dragged the old Macs into the hall and scrambled to find real desks in other rooms. When I removed the computer tables, I discovered that the floor was lined with electrical sockets that stuck up two inches and sent up sparks when I dragged a chair over them. I tried to arrange the furniture to hide these obstacles the best I could. The room was filled with an eclectic but functional mix of desks and chairs, and the sockets were reasonably concealed when the thirty Black sophomores in my first class arrived the next day.

After we introduced ourselves, I handed out two lists of rules. I labeled one "Dictatorship Rules," established by the school and district, such as "no fighting" as well as "no headphones," "no cell phones" and "no hats." I went over these rules and told students, "We don't have any say in these rules, but we have to follow them." They seemed familiar with them and indifferently turned to the second list that I had labeled "Democratic Rules," which pertained to our particular classroom and, I insisted, were things we could control. This list included such items as "no gum," the penalty for lateness, and my "three pass policy," which permitted each student to leave the room with my official hall pass three times a term. I explained that this list of rules was merely a proposal. They were to meet with their "committees" and decide if they wanted to ratify these rules, propose changes, or reject them for entirely new ones.

They met in groups of five and looked at each other awkwardly. However, slowly the groups began talking and by the end of the ten-minute discussion period were generally engaged in lively conversations. I called the class back together and asked for proposals from the floor. They immediately challenged the gum rule on the grounds that "bad breath" was an unfair burden. "You teachers want us to work in groups, but you can't work if someone's breath is stink—you got to give the brotha some gum!" a student named Tekwon argued.

"I don't care about what's in your mouth, but look at the ceiling," I instructed. They looked up at the fifteen-foot ceiling and slowly began to giggle as they noticed the wads of gum that had found their way up there. I continued, "It's the gum on the seats, the walls, the desks, and the ceiling that always causes disruptions." They debated with me fiercely as I sought to convince them that gum was not necessary to their educations. Eventually they proposed, "Students can chew gum but must dispose of it properly. If someone sits in gum, the class can't have gum for a week (even if we didn't put the gum there). If Ms. Dickar sees gum, we will clean it up." I was satisfied with these amendments because the students took responsibility for the gum in the room. With all in agreement, it became our "gum policy."

With this small victory under their belts, the students began debating how many times they could be late before I should exact a penalty. Though they had been united in their struggle for gum, they were more divided about how late was "late" and how often students needed to be late. Some argued that students should never be late, while others insisted that it was impossible to get to class on time because of the crowding in the halls. They debated this issue quite intensely, but as they were unable to create either a zero-tolerance policy or a no-penalty policy, agreed on my original proposal that three unexcused "lates" would result in a five-point deduction from their grade. With the period winding down, a student named Andrea, who had sat quietly through most of the discussion cut in, "Fine, whatever, but we got to discuss this pass rule!" She proposed that there should be no limits on when students could take the pass because they were mature enough to use it responsibly.

"What if you used your passes and you got to throw up?" Tekwon added, mocking vomiting as he spoke.

"Or you got your period?" added Belinda, lifting her head up off her desk.

"You shouldn't use the pass if you don't need it." I countered. "The idea of the rule is to get you to save it for these emergencies."

Akil shot back, "What if you got a bladder problem? You can't be limiting passes when some people got medical conditions!" Many "yeahs" followed his comment.

"Does anyone here have a medical condition?" I asked. No one raised a hand, but Akil quickly recovered, "No one want to put they business in the street like that, Miss!" Tekwon added, "I'm very sensitive about my diseases!" acting wounded as he raised his eyebrows at Belinda, whose head remained down though her eyes peered out at the class.

"Tekwon got AIDS," mumbled a male voice as students giggled.

The class was about to lose focus, so I said, "I don't want Tekwon to have to tell us about his diseases either. Let's add to the rule that if someone brings a note from home explaining why they need more passes, they can have them." Students around the room seemed to nod in agreement. "Okay, let's vote on this rule."

"Wait, Miss!" Andrea called out. "Look, it ain't about diseases. I'm gonna keep it real with you—sometimes we just don't want to be here."

"You mean, sometimes you ask for the pass when you don't have to go to the bathroom?" I asked, mocking naiveté.

"Sometimes . . . ," Andrea agreed. "Most of the time!" another voice added.

"Yeah, Miss. Sometimes I got business to attend to!" said Akil, pretending an air of importance.

"Miss, sometimes we need to go, but mostly, we just want to get out and be in the hall," Andrea clarified. "No offense, Miss," she added, a mischievous smile now breaking across her face. "Sometimes, y'all teachers can be boring!" The class laughed with agreement and added to the emphasis on boring—interjecting examples. "Mr. [X] is so boring, I feel bored just walking by his room."

"He's so boring that two periods after his class, I'm still bored!"

The class was disintegrating into joking and laughter as I yelled, "Do you mean that if I'm going to limit when you can leave the room, that I have to make the class interesting?" Their laughter died down as they seemed to think about what I had said.

Andrea broke the silence, "Interesting or boring, Miss, I still want the pass." Someone else mumbled, "Amen." I paused and said, "Now I'm going to keep it real with you—I can't let you take the pass whenever you want because everyone would take it and Ms. [Principal] would get on my case."

"Okay, Miss, but three passes is too little. We should get, like, three a marking period." Knowing there were three marking periods in a term, I offered, "Let's split the difference—how's two a marking period?" We voted and ratified our new rules as students began packing up in anticipation of the bell. I quickly handed out a reflection asking students to define "dictatorship" and "democracy" based on the activity and to discuss which they preferred.

This anecdote from my time teaching from 1996 to 2000 at Renaissance High School (pseudonym), a racially segregated public high school in New York City, contains themes that would emerge in my study of the relationship between student culture and school reform. Central to the conflicts and contradictions in everyday life at Renaissance was the on-going tension between the student-dominated halls and the teacher-dominated classrooms despite the democratic school reform effort under way at the time. As my students' desire to get the pass indicated, no matter how good or bad the class, the call of the hall loomed as a formidable spatial challenge to teaching.

The conflict between the hall and classroom was the most salient conflict shaping school life, but it was not the only spatialized struggle between students and school. Before my third period students could get in the building and its halls, they had to go through full-body scanning at the front door, a ritual designed to rid them of weapons and anti-school paraphernalia, such as markers or Wite-Out (which could be used for graffiti), scissors, sharp pencils, or hair sticks (which could be used in fights), as well as gang signs such as beads, bandanas, and colors. This border check-point imposed a notion of the good student as a disarmed, de-cultured student and constructed some street-oriented identities as inappropriate for school. Thus, the front-door scan marked the spatial division between the streets on one side and the school on the other. Once scanned, most students participated in a student-dominated hall culture derived from the very street culture the school hoped to silence when students entered. This derivative of the street thrived in the hall between classes and often well beyond, as lateness was epidemic and students took the hall passes to escape back into the halls as frequently as possible. My effort to limit the hall pass and lateness was an effort to contain students in an academic space. Their desire to get the pass was an effort to control their time, to limit my power to control their bodies, and to maintain connection to the hall spaces where their activities and agendas were central. Thus, in addition to security scanning at the front door, the halls and classrooms were daylong sites of struggle over what activities and whose values would dominate.

These conflicts are the local terms through which space was culturally produced and contested at Renaissance. By "culturally contested" I mean the conflicted ways that students and teachers performed depending on location and context. Levinson, Foley, and Holland (1996) describe the cultural production of the educated person as situated "within and against larger societal forces which instantiate themselves in schools and other in-stitutions" (14). These larger societal forces can be read in the ways spaces are occupied and challenged. Through exploring the uses of space at Re-naissance, we gain concrete images of historical, social, and ideological forces that are the implicit elements behind choices made by teachers and students. The halls, the classrooms, and the doorway scanning are where school is culturally produced as an everyday experience. These spaces are not inevitable but rather are created, allowing for the possibility of inter-ventions to change the social relations that generate conflict between stu-dents and schooling.

In the case of my classroom, space was culturally produced on several levels. The physical space was designed initially by architects and ulti-mately by the economic and political conditions that frame school expe-riences for the Black, low-income, urban students who attended Renais-sance. My efforts to create a comfortable and safe learning environment out of the dilapidated computer room couldn't mask the thoughtless indignity such conditions implied–an environmental sign from dominant society to these students that they don't count. Further, while the computers were outdated and broken, four new air conditioners installed as part of the recent renovations sat uselessly in the windows because the cord of only one could reach the designated plug. Thus, my students sat in cast-off furniture in a recently renovated though dangerous classroom and stared at three useless air conditioners witnessing both the lack and waste of resources. The casual disregard that had helped produce my classroom could be found throughout the building as doorknobs broke and pipes leaked as soon as the construction trailers left the campus. For years prior to the renovations, the wretched condition of the crumbling building conveyed the marginality of the students who attended school there. Now, the renovations reiterated that message of indifference and contempt despite a cosmetic makeover.

In this physical and social setting, a White woman in her early thirties, like me, proposed a democratic and humane pedagogy. However, I couldn't avoid representing the educational establishment despite my effort to distance myself from official policies I irreverently dubbed "dictatorship rules." Though unable to amend some of the rules they hated most, I hoped to align myself with my students (not against them). My students, all Black and Hispanic, tested my conflicted position through their humor and melodrama. They were showing friendly suspicion while I was asking them to trust me. Our implicit and explicit discourse over the rules pushed the issue—what kind of space would this classroom be? Would the teacher unilaterally control it or would they be able to shape it to better suit their agendas?

Though I asked my students to co-construct a more democratic learning environment with me, we still performed inside physical and pedagogical conditions produced by segregation and White privilege. Nonetheless, within these limits we exercised our own agency as we negotiated the nature and meaning of that classroom space. At the same time, we also were negotiating the role of the halls as students sought to increase their access and I to diminish it. Thus, the spaces through which we maneuvered were both products of structural inequality and products of our own making. Though on that particular day I had put the rules on the table for negotiation, the prevailing ethos of classrooms is, in fact, always negotiated, if only tacitly, through the degrees of cooperation and resistance students enact. Our efforts to agree on a set of classroom rules highlighted the ways classrooms and halls are always already produced when we arrive, though vulnerable to our conscious intervention through cultural exchanges and political struggles.

The upcoming chapters pursue this exploration of the ways school spaces are culturally produced, particularly when regarding urban students and schools. This book applies the insights of cultural geographers to the study of urban school cultures. The theorists from whom I will be drawing have demonstrated that social spaces are culturally produced by the history, economic systems, social relationships, and mores that define day-to-day life (Tuan 1977 and 1990; Soja 1989; Harvey 1990; Massey 1994). More specifically, daily life is informed by critical studies of the geography of childhood that recognize that "children's identities and lives are made and (re)made through the sites of everyday life" (Holloway and Valentine 2000). Like playgrounds (Gagen 2000), urban and suburban spaces (Davis 1990; Haymes 1995), and the Las Vegas strip (Venturi, Brown, and Izenour 1977) the spaces inside schools are shaped by the discourses of those who use them and who also are, in turn, shaped by these spaces.

Though many disciplines have been informed by the "spatial turn" (Massey 1993), educational studies have been slow to mine the insights of critical geographers. However, recent research on literacy practices examines space as a multiply produced environment that informs literate action within it (Leander and Sheehy 2004). More than just understanding space as a conveyor of meaning, these scholars are mapping the ways it is constantly redefined through social practices. Leander's (2004) study of a literature class, for example, demonstrates that social spaces construct individuals but also are transformed by them as the individuals appropriate these spaces for their own purposes.

Though few qualitative studies of urban schools have focused on space itself as a site of social struggle, several studies have not ignored the social geography of schools. For example, Flores-Gonzalez (2005) describes how rigid tracking at an urban high school in Chicago created two distinct social worlds of "school kids" and "street kids." Valenzuela (1999) notes how school practices create different spaces for those who possess different amounts and forms of cultural capital. Other scholars have noted the ways students become segregated even in integrated schools (Tatum 1999;

Lewis 2004; Pollock 2004). Eckert (1989) noted the different spaces occupied by "jocks" and "burnouts" in schools, and Foley (1990) charted the social geography of a high school pep rally to note the ways social locations are normalized and reinforced through the seats students occupy at school events. These studies trace out how the spaces students physically occupy reflect their social and academic identities within the school and, ultimately, their access to resources and opportunity. Though useful, such analysis focuses on relatively static conceptions of space. In this study I will argue that school spaces are constantly contested and "leaky," bleeding into one another in significant ways as parties express multiple intentions.

Other scholars have raised critical questions about spatial formation in schools, particularly probing the ways certain discourses prevail in school spaces and why. For example, Fine, Weis, and Powell (1997) trace the ways schools informed student discourses on race and racism through the policies implementing racial integration. In one high school, school officials tacitly supported the reproduction of White supremacy and the racist assumptions of White, working-class, male students, while in another high school teachers disrupted the reproduction of racist hierarchies by creating spaces for students to reflect on the meaning of race, class, and culture. Fine, Weis, and Powell's study offers an example of the ways school spaces are culturally produced, as school practices and pedagogies reflected the values and power struggles within communities and informed prevailing discourses.

Some scholars examining the production and implementation of educational policy have drawn crucial connections between the policy and physical spaces not just of schools but also of the cities in which they are embedded (Anyon 1997; Gordon, Holland, and Lahelma 2000; Lipman 2004). Lipman (2004), for example, examines the ways school policy in Chicago reflects the broad trend of globalization by sharpening geographic segregation, exacerbating social inequalities, marginalizing racial minorities, and increasing class divisions that are readily inscribed on urban space. Importantly though, she argues that these spaces are also vulnerable to change through local action. Her study of the impact of educational policies on specific Chicago schools demonstrates the complex factors, globally, nationally, and locally, that inform the cultural production of space in schools and in cities.

Expanding on this critical educational research, I explore competing discourses about who students are, what the purpose of schooling should be, and what knowledge is valuable as these discourses became spatialized in daily school life. I argue that ideologies and discourses become grafted onto specific school spaces (halls, classrooms, doorways, etc.) through social struggles, and that these spatial formations reveal the ways schools are both sites of conflict and conflicted sites. This spatial analysis calls attention to the contradictions inherent in official school discourses and those generated by students and teachers more locally. By examining the form and substance of student/school engagement, this study argues for a more nuanced and broader framework that reads multiple forms of resistance and recognizes the ways students themselves are conflicted about schooling. Rather than being staunch resistors or eager accommodationists, at the time of my study, most students moved between these positions as they often were critical of the school while believing elements of the "education gospel"(Lazerson 2005).

Renaissance in Context

Renaissance High School served a student population that was 96 percent Black and 4 percent Hispanic at the time of this study. Located in New York City in the heart of one of the largest Caribbean communities in the United States, the majority of the students were immigrants or the children of immigrants from the West Indies.[1] Of the student population, 45.7 percent who entered Renaissance were over age for their grade, as many students had repeated at least one grade prior to entering high school. Of the students who entered Renaissance as freshmen, fewer than 30 percent graduated within four years, and half never earned diplomas at all. Seventy-five percent of the students were eligible for free lunch, which indicates high levels of poverty.

Renaissance was a smaller school that had been carved from "Old School," a large, comprehensive high school that had languished on the state's list of failing schools for years. In 1994, Old School was restructured and three smaller schools (though not small by the standards of the contemporary Small Schools Movement) were opened in its place. These new entities had their own territory within the same building, their own principals, and their own reform agenda, though they shared the cafeteria and auditorium. Each served between 800 and 1000 students from the same "encatchment" area covered by Old School. The three new schools shared a similar profile, though one of the schools had a small and reputable magnet honors program and the other had a large English as a Second Language (ESL) program that served many Haitian students.

Of the three new schools, Renaissance adopted the most progressive reform strategy, including a broadly democratic school-based planning (SBP) team that gave teachers, staff, students, and family members equal voting rights. Teachers voted to make their own attendance at the weekly meetings mandatory. In addition, ten to fifteen students attended the meetings regularly, as well as a few parents. However, when controversial issues arose, such as the Police Department taking over school security, many more parents and community members came. In addition, part of the school's mission included the use of student-centered collaborative pedagogies that drew on student cultural identities to empower student voices in the classroom. Renaissance also developed sub-schools that organized teachers around students by grade and switched to a block-program that established longer class periods (100 minutes) to accommodate the time demands of student-centered, project-based pedagogy. Last, Renaissance was "detracked." No courses isolated high achievers except two AP courses (English and calculus) that some students took in their senior year. I first taught English at Old School from 1989 to 1991 and then Social Studies at the new Renaissance High School from 1996 to 2000.

Despite significant reform efforts to put students at the center, Renaissance fared only a little better than Old School in test scores and graduation rates. Old School had been hierarchically organized and prided itself on its traditional stance on education, which was echoed in its impressive neo-Gothic architecture. Once, it had an outstanding academic reputation and boasted many famous alumni drawn from an upwardly mobile, predominantly Jewish community. As Whites fled inner cities to the greener pastures of the suburbs in the 1950s through 1970s, Old School became increasingly populated by Black students, particularly Caribbean immigrants, and, at the same time, its academic reputation and the condition of its physical plant declined. Like my classroom, the physical condition of Old School was a product of more than just underfunding, it was a product of the social, economic, and political changes undermining cities across America.

By the 1980s, Old School had one of the worst reputations in the city, a demoralized teaching staff, and a dilapidated campus. However, the corps of educators who formed Renaissance believed that Old School had failed because it was unresponsive to student needs and contemptuous of student culture. Unfortunately, the well-intentioned reform efforts these educators implemented yielded only minimal results. Though the reform effort did generate a different pedagogical philosophy and modest curricular changes, its enigmatic lack of impact suggests that school experience is shaped by far more than school practices alone.

These attempts to make classrooms more student-centered met a formidable culture in the halls far more compelling than the classroom for many students. These reforms also took place amid increased top-down control of classrooms through high-stakes exams and standardized curricula, as well as school district mandates. In the chapters that follow, I examine three physical sites where students and school authority contended: the halls, the classroom, and the school entrance. Each of these contentious sites had a structure and character of its own, but the experiences in one site conditioned the terms of engagement in the others.

Method

My first teaching stint at Old School, from 1989 to 1991, awakened my interest in the spatial factors of schooling and informed my decision to go to graduate school to gain the tools to analyze what was happening in urban schools. I returned five years later to conduct scholarly research in American Studies and to teach. Trained in discourse analysis and historical research, I planned to use archival research and informant interviews to explore how the physical space of the school—the grandness of the architecture, the wretched decay of the building—informed the ways people perceived and used the school and how teachers and students spoke about their environment and experience vis-à-vis race and class in America.

However, I had left Old School a crumbling, unreformed, traditional, large school and came back to a place that was in the midst of extensive renovations and that had been restructured into new, smaller schools. Before the renovations, the degraded physical plant permeated teacher talk, but when I returned, the building had seemingly withered away as a topic of discussion. It was replaced by talk of Regents results (the state-wide exams required for high school graduation) and getting off the "SURR" list (the state's list of failing schools), about the strategies of school reform, and about the kids themselves. My experiences back at Old School (now Renaissance) changed my conception of "space." Rather than understanding it as a passive transmitter of social meanings, I realized it was actively negotiated and contested—it both produced and was produced. I needed to develop a research plan that would enable me to capture the dynamics of spatial interaction.

My desire to get at how space was constructed and constructing made my role as a teacher problematic. I was not only interested in understanding power struggles, I also was a participant in those struggles. Student resistance frustrated me—I could not pretend a dispassionate stance when many evenings I went home fuming over disruptions in my class or in the halls. My teaching and research only complicated my frustration because I saw the clash of cultures that was producing these disruptions. Being an involved teacher gave me a chance to know the situation and my limits in it. However, teaching was so consuming that I had to take a year off from it in order to conduct the research that would enable me to read the conflicts at the school more deeply.

Critics of teacher research have argued that "dual-role" conflicts may undermine the integrity of the research method or, worse, sacrifice the needs of "clients" for the sake of research (Hammock 1997). These concerns are valid and warrant being addressed. Teaching is an emotionally and intellectually engrossing activity, such that I found it very hard to slip into and out of the role of researcher. I could not conduct the kind of study I wanted while remaining a classroom teacher and, thus, seized the opportunity afforded by a fellowship to take a leave of absence, allowing me to step out of my role as teacher and focus on being a researcher. Though I was not teaching at the time I conducted my interviews, I was still known to most participants as a teacher. I sought to down play this identity by dressing as a graduate student—jeans, t-shirts, hair down, no make-up—rather than as a teacher—slacks, jacket, and hair bound in a tight, stereotypical teacher's bun. During that time, I interviewed students and teachers and hung out in the halls to try to see what I couldn't see from the teacher's role. Nonetheless, it would have been impossible to not be read as a teacher, and I never tried to pretend I was something other than what I am.

As a researcher, I followed guidelines spelled out by my university and by the school district. All students volunteered based on signs posted in halls. I did not directly recruit students in order to insure that no one felt coerced. Such recruitment was not necessary, as I was inundated with student volunteers. Though I was a White teacher, students seemed eager to talk, one saying, "its about time you teachers asked us what we thought!" No doubt my role as a teacher created methodological concerns and limited some of what students and colleagues would share, but it also provided me a familiar identity that credited my project to students. My time at the school had enabled me to develop trust with a good number of students, and my desire to understand school from their point of view validated their experiences.

In noting the dilemmas of the dual role, I do not want to undervalue the potential strengths of teachers as researchers. First, as I hope this book demonstrates, my position as a teacher enabled me to develop much deeper insight into some of the tensions in school culture. Second, the devaluing of teacher voices as legitimate ones has widened the gulf between research and practice as teachers dismiss educational research because it does not resonate with their experience. I hope this work helps bridge that gap.

More significantly, we need to rethink research paradigms that privilege the perspective of the outside observer as objective and disinterested. Critiques of the dual role of teacher/researcher are based on assumptions that as members of school communities, teachers can neither be objective nor can they avoid coercing student participants. Though certainly, both concerns must be addressed at all phases of the research process, they should not necessarily disqualify teachers as legitimate producers of knowledge about urban schools. Feminist ethnographers have raised ethical concerns about research paradigms that privilege the outsider or "watcher" as objective and the insider or watched as subjective because such models reproduce oppressive patriarchal and colonialist hierarchies (Behar 1995). Aggarwal (2000) argues for a feminist anthropology that is dialogic and shifts the traditional "looking at" to "looking out for." Rather than study a group and disappear, she calls for researchers to forge meaningful relationships with subjects and sustain those relationships after the study is over. It is in this tradition of connected and committed research for social justice that this study was forged.

Data

To address the concerns about coercion and objectivity, first, I passively recruited subjects so that students would not feel pressured. Second, I triangulated data by drawing on student interviews, teacher interviews, and my own observations. I then disaggregated student interviews by the academic orientation of students to clarify what may have been widespread and what was more specific to an academic subgroup. The central source of data used here are interviews with thirty-seven students from 10th through 12th grades who represent a spectrum of academic performance from high achieving to failing.

Student volunteers each participated in an open-ended interview conducted in school, lasting from thirty to ninety minutes. All participants were promised confidentiality and were asked about what they did in the halls and in classrooms, what mattered most to them about their school lives, and what they liked and disliked about school. As findings emerged, additional focus groups were used to check these observations. In addition, the interviews with students and focus groups were supplemented by interviews with seventeen teachers and administrators. Observations in the halls and classrooms conducted when I was a teacher from 1996 to 2000 and during the interview period (spring 1999), also provide significant data for this study. All names used are pseudonyms.

Though participants were recruited without consideration of their academic standing, gender, or cultural background, once the initial interviews were complete, they were disaggregated according to gender and their relationship to academic work. Self-reported academic achievement and attitude as well as their responses to some questions indicated that of the thirty-seven volunteers, ten (eight girls and two boys) were high achieving (HA), earning at least a B average and identifying strongly with academic success; ten others (six girls and four boys) were identified as academically oriented (AO) in that they generally passed their classes and made an effort to do well but averaged Cs and Ds. These students were at their grade level at the time of the interview and were on-track to graduate in four years. The seventeen remaining participants were nonacademically oriented. Of these, eight (three girls and five boys) were identified as ambivalent toward school (Amb) in that they sought to do just enough to pass and were making some progress toward graduation, though for half of them, it took more than four years to do so. These students chose not to make deep investments in their educational futures or did so inconsistently, but they did want to earn a high school diploma. Nine (four girls and five boys) were identified as highly alienated (AL) in that they showed little interest in academic work, were frequently late, cut classes or skipped school or were at times highly disruptive in classes. All were far behind in credits. Of these nine, only two (both boys) graduated, one taking six years to do so, the other, seven.

These multiple designations were created to more accurately capture the differing kinds of academic participation in the sample.[2] There has been a tendency to polarize urban students as either high achieving or alienated, missing the lower-performing academically oriented and ambivalent students who hover near the boundaries of these dispositions. When students are identified in the study, they will be referred to by their pseudonyms as well as by their academic orientation to help represent the ways academic identification may have framed student responses and to help clarify how some themes cut across academic orientations.

Resistance and Oppositionality

In seeking greater access to the coveted hall pass, my students suggested that the halls were more than just an escape from the classroom. The vast literature on student resistance assumes their alienation is a response to the oppressive aspects of schooling—such as boring teachers and disconnected curriculum. However, my students' desire to get into the halls where a lively nonacademic urban youth culture thrived was not only about escaping the classroom but also about affirming another identity and experience. Andrea's acknowledgment that whether class was interesting or boring she still wanted to leave the room and Akil's assertion of having "business to attend to" in the halls emphasized the allure of hall activity.

This study, then, expands two significant, though discreet, debates about student resistance and academic achievement. One debate, between reproduction and resistance theorists, probes how schools are institutions of social control and the efficacy of student resistance against them. The other debate involves an "oppositional" culture among "involuntary minorities" whose marginalized position constructs academic achievement as capitulation to dominant and racist culture. Both literatures construct students as either resistors or accommodators, a polarity inadequate in describing the multiple positions students took in the class I described above.

Though the debates about resistance offer frameworks that are too limited, they still raise important questions about student/school engagement. Reproduction theorists correctly argue that schools function to reproduce existing hierarchies in numerous and insidious ways (Bowles and Gintis 1976; Anyon 1980). Though at times quite intentional, through tracking and unequal funding for example, schooling's role in maintaining inequality is not its explicit agenda. Apple (1990) refers to the indirection of these practices as "the hidden curriculum" to emphasize the political subtext behind the apparent subject matters and learning processes. Many studies have focused on "the hidden curriculum" as it reinforces oppressive hierarchies through practices such as curriculum, advising, teacher attitudes, discipline, testing, and tracking (Katz 1971; Anyon 1980; Oakes 1985; Apple 1990; Grant and Sleeter 1996; Lipman 1998; Ferguson 2000; Kohn 2000; Lewis 2004). Reproduction theorists have emphasized the structural work schools perform in maintaining inequality over the agency of students in resisting or transforming these institutions.

In contrast, resistance theory has shifted the discussion of social control away from what schools do to students to how schools and students interact to reproduce and resist dominant culture (Willis 1977; Giroux 1983; Foley 1990; Fine 1991; Fordham 1996; Levinson, Foley, and Holland 1996). For example, Willis's exploration of the counter-school culture of "the lads," the working-class British school boys at the center of his ground-breaking study, argued that students from oppressed groups actively resisted and even mocked school efforts to socialize them into docile workers. Nevertheless, the oppositional lads eagerly marched into the factory to work, taking their masculine place in the class hierarchy. Thus, their lively resistance to schooling did not lead them to resist the reproduction of class differences. To the contrary, they embraced their social location because of patriarchal and White supremacist ideologies that enabled some identification with power. Resistance studies that followed Willis's suggest that students are not simply acted upon by institutions, but rather that social reproduction is a contention between official authority and student agency (Metz 1978; Foley 1990; Fine 1991). This notion of contested cultural production more closely represents what I recorded at Renaissance and report in this book.

Advocates of student agency within the confines of the institution construct student resistance as positive and affirming. For example, Fine (1991) noted that the most resistant students—those who dropped out of high school—exhibited a higher self-esteem than those who stayed, suggesting that resistance was a form of protection against the psychic damage caused by assimilation into the culture of the school. Fordham (1996) also notes that the high- and underachieving Black students she studied developed strategies of resistance that preserved and protected Black identity. All in all, then, resistance theorists agree that students engage schools as social actors, but theorists disagree as to how much efficacy they have in the face of structural oppression.

Shifting focus from systemic issues to cultural issues, the debate over Ogbu's (1988) "oppositional culture thesis" focuses on the extent and form of minority student identification with academic work. Ogbu explains the poor performance of Blacks and other "involuntary minorities" whose ancestors did not willingly migrate to the United States by arguing that they are participants in an oppositional culture that constructs academic success as a form of capitulation to the dominant system that devalues them. Though Ogbu defined oppositional culture as an "adaptation" to racism in the larger society, he emphasized the need to reject oppositionality over the need for social change. Fordham and Ogbu (1986) further demonstrated that Black students construct academic success as "White," requiring that those students who do well in school affirm their blackness through other means.

Ogbu's thesis has been soundly attacked by critics who argue that it is monolithic and overlooks the diversity of student subcultures and the numerous factors that inform identity (Lee 1999; Hemmings 2004). Ainsworth-Darnell and Downey (1998) found that in surveys about attitudes and academic habits, Black students, in comparison to their White and Asian peers, actually exhibit more positive attitudes toward education and more optimism about the potential outcomes of education, suggesting that claims of an oppositional culture are unfounded. Further, ethnographic studies that focus on academically successful minority students have challenged the "acting White" thesis, noting that highly successful minority students often exhibit positive attitudes toward their racial and cultural identities and are not marginalized by their peers (Flores-Gonzalez 1999; Akom 2003; Horvat and Lewis 2003; Conchas 2006). This literature proposes instead that there are multiple student identities, some clearly associated with schooling.

The debate over oppositional culture overlaps with debates about social control as both question the relationship of student resistance to academic achievement. However, resistance theorists construct resistance as an important survival tool that is potentially transformative, while participants in the oppositional culture debate generally construct resistance and oppositional identity negatively and as factors interfering with academic success. There are significant exceptions, however. Akom's (2003) study of high-achieving girls in the Nation of Islam offers an example of an oppositional identity that actually promoted academic achievement while also enabling a broad critique of schooling and White supremacy. Similarly, some high-achieving students at Renaissance, though not affiliated with the Nation of Islam, were also some of the most openly critical of school and social policies they saw as racist or unjust.

With these debates in mind, this study examines resistance and oppositionality as related yet distinct things. Not all resistance is oppositional and not all oppositionality is anti-academic. At Renaissance, the student culture in the halls was derived from the streets and articulated a notion of Black solidarity that conflicted with the mainstream culture promoted by school authorities. School practices such as scanning students for weapons or gang paraphernalia supported the construction of oppositional identities magnifying conflict rather than diminishing it. At the same time, however, many students described hall culture as irrelevant to classroom participation, others perceived them as opposed, and some described them in both terms. Thus, understanding this culture as oppositional is only partially accurate. Nonetheless, there were significant tensions between this student-defined culture and the culture that existed in the classrooms, which suggests the limits of current interpretations of student resistance.

As my students and I negotiated class rules that September morning, the students revealed many strategies they used to resist school authority, while they also sought to participate in academic culture to varying degrees. Some strategies, like asking to go the bathroom when they didn't need to, allowed a plausible deniability of any sinister intent and thus didn't seemingly disrupt the flow of the classroom enough to warrant disciplinary action. Scott (1985) refers to such everyday forms of resistance as "infrapolitical," a concept on which I will elaborate later in this book. The students also used humor to challenge my authority, to alter the relationships of power in the classroom, and to redirect the content. On the whole, their resistance in what proved to be a productive class moved from subtle nonparticipation to open mockery of teacher authority, from infrapolitical to open resistance. These shifts suggest the conflicted and contradictory nature of student and school relationships. There is a localized continuum, in any school site, between infrapolitical resistance, confrontation and oppositional culture (outright rejection of academics).

Part of the reason for these nuances of resistance was that few students who actually attend school regularly reject schooling outright. If they did, they simply would not come to school for the most part. Most students interviewed, regardless of their academic performance and orientation, wanted something from the school, whether it was merely a credential to secure a better job, academic knowledge, or access to the cultural capital needed for upward mobility. Though some students were articulately critical of school policies and teacher practices as well as suspicious of the school as a racist institution, they also sought things from the school and thus used it in conflicted ways. Theories of student agency, identity, and resistance need to account for these gradations, which is the goal of the coming chapters.

Urban Schools as Sites of Conflict and Conflicted Sites

Overall, then, public schools such as Renaissance suffer from multiple internal contradictions. On the one hand, they are grossly underfunded and racially segregated, but on the other hand, they represent "education" as the great equalizer, "euphemizing" (as Bourdieu puts it) their actual function of social reproduction with a promotional discourse of equal opportunity and the American Dream. A further internal contradiction exists in the teacher corps, many of whom enter education to be of humane service to diverse students whose learning matters to them. Yet, these same educators are officers of an unequal institution that is underfunded and overregulated. Another contradiction is enacted by students themselves, who construct a derivative of street culture in the halls to compete with the classroom and who vibrate between seizing what they can from this place and pushing away its casual indignities.

Much of the literature examining the relationship between institutional control and student agency often constructs schools as relatively simple institutions that promote the unequal status quo via practices such as tracking, teacher assumptions, curriculum, limited access to opportunity or resources, standardized testing, and other school- or district-imposed practices. However, as my negotiations with my students suggests, urban schools themselves are conflicted places, charged with contradictory responsibilities, such as social reproduction and social change, which are often implemented by well-meaning people overwhelmed by demands and mandates that at times compromise their decency. Thus, just as urban schools have proven far from successful at promoting academic achievement, the high levels of student resistance in them suggests that they have also been far from efficient at imposing dominant cultural values. These fissures provide clever students with openings enabling them to exploit the imperfect match between institutional control and staff performance that more or less defines the local possibilities for resistance in any institution.

Though the conflicts of such an urban school are evident at the doorway screening or inside the hallways, it is also visible in the classroom where the academic rubber meets the road. The classroom is the labor-intensive vortex of school as an institution. My opening anecdote suggests some of the ways these conflicts manifest themselves in classrooms. For example, I began the class by bifurcating the rules between "dictatorship" and "democracy," disavowing my own complicity in enforcing school rules. In so doing, I also destabilized the notion of authority since I was pretending I was not the only authority in the classroom. My emphasis on student input and negotiation—I kept insisting we were making these rules together even though I greatly controlled the discourse—also conflicted with more authoritarian notions of power. In line with the school's reform effort, I sought to create a democratic culture in my classroom while students tested this offer by mocking me and teachers in general. The portrait of that first day gets close to what I propose is the genuine complexity of authority, resistance, and reproduction in specific classrooms.

Students' written responses to my questions at the end of class suggested their distrust of the reform effort underway at the school and in my classroom. Asked which they preferred, democracy or dictatorship, slightly more than half the class preferred dictatorship, in part because it was "faster." Democratic negotiations took a long time, and clearly, these critics saw little substantive difference between the nonnegotiable rules and the ones on which we agreed. Other students rejected the permissiveness of the new rules. Even though they had been unanimously ratified, one student wrote, "Our rules are stupid! Students shouldn't chew gum in class and they shouldn't be late!" And another wrote that he preferred dictatorship "cause the teacher gonna do what the teacher gonna do." In supporting dictatorship over democracy, students expressed frustration with the seemingly weakened authority of the teacher (that the new rules were too lax) and with the invulnerable authority of the teacher (she'll do whatever she wants anyway).

The critiques of the new rules highlighted the multiple agendas operating for students simultaneously. Some had been vocal during our negotiations, even championing the new rules. That some of these students were angry about the rules indicated that they were willing to take whatever ground I would yield but were disappointed that I yielded it. Given the strong support for "dictatorship," students were frustrated by democratic practices that were either weak or fraudulent but that were a central component of the school reform effort. Students brought different notions of teacher authority with them; some were informed by experiences in the West Indies, where teacher authority was high profile and respected. Their responses suggested that the reform effort confronted contradictory expectations by students, whose perspective was not uniform. For example, during the debate about lateness, which was mostly a debate among students themselves, Amanda, who went on to do serious work in class, scolded her peers, "Y'all know you shouldn't be late!" She demanded that all lateness be punished, period. To her and others, some things shouldn't be negotiated—students knew better and shouldn't be held to a lower standard. At the same time that students were divided, so was the teacher within the system of mass education. I labored under restrictive mandates from the chancellor and the state that imposed a standardized curriculum, and thus I was always caught between the authorities above me and my political commitments to critical pedagogy and democratic culture. These external forces were at odds with the effort to create student-centered classrooms and curricula.

These multiple contradictions framed the cultural production of space at Renaissance and suggest that we need more nuanced theories of urban school failure and of student resistance. The chapters that follow develop such a theory by tracing out the cultural formations instantiated in the numerous spaces that locate school experiences.

Structure of This Book

This book is divided into two parts. The first section examines the physical space itself and the territories clearly controlled by the school or by the students. I begin this exploration of the cultural production of space at Renaissance with a critical reading of the physical space itself. At Renaissance, with a stunning campus that had fallen into decay and then renovated to less-than-former glory, a critical reading of the physical place helps contextualize the cultural struggles enacted inside its walls. Old School is a landmark building whose legendary status has been used to elevate, motivate, and denigrate students over time. Chapter 1 examines the hidden curriculum of the architecture and the ways the physical space itself shapes action. Chapter 2 explores the scanning ritual students go through each morning as they enter school. Here the school exhibits its full force through a security apparatus that makes student bodies fit for school. At the same time, the school constructs some student identities as outlaw, demonizing urban styles associated with the "street" or with blackness more generally. These practices indicate that oppositional cultures are not exclusively student productions but also are informed by school practices that provoke conflicts. Chapter 3 examines what I call the "exclave" culture of the halls, which constitute a spatial domain within the school itself. Students import and modify their own urban youth cultures, installing an alternative cultural economy that competes with that promoted in classrooms. Though in some ways the halls were oppositional to classroom culture, many students insisted these separate spaces were irrelevant to each other rather than opposed. Thus, the exclave in the halls operated as what Soja (1996) has theorized as a "thirdspace," a space that supported binaries between school-oriented and street-oriented identities, between academic participation and disidentification, and between group solidarity and individualism but also posited a third or "other" option as well. In this way, the exclave effect helps make visible the diverse responses of students to a similar set of circumstances and the range of influences on those decisions.

The second section focuses on the classroom as the most intense site of conflict. Chapter 4 examines the nature of school/student conflict through debates about whether students should speak Standard English or "Ebonics" in the classroom. This chapter exposes the differing stances of students toward school and local culture through their relationships to the dominant idiom and what it represents. It also clarifies how classrooms can be understood as what Pratt (1986) theorized as a "contact zone" where two cultures meet, though not on equal terms. Chapter 5 examines the infrapolitical resistance enacted to slow down or to avoid the transition from "the hall state" to the "student state." By focusing on the persistent and effective though nonconfrontational resistance at the beginning of each and every class, this analysis exposes ideological conflicts inherent in classroom work. Chapter 6 uses the framework of "hidden" and "public" transcripts (Scott 1990), discourses used within subordinate groups and those used in front of those with power, to question the extent to which students internalize dominant discourses. I examine the work of class clowns within such a context to read the political content of their activities. Finally, Chapter 7 concludes this work by exploring the ways spatial analysis allows a deeper reading of complex urban school cultures. It also explores the ways the findings reported here may influence future efforts at urban school reform.

1

■　　■　　■　　■　　■　　■　　■　　■

"The Covenant Made Visible"

The Hidden Curriculum of Space

It is no coincidence that this study of Renaissance focuses on spatial formation, because the significance of space is so overwhelming at the site itself. When I interviewed for a teaching position at Old School in 1989, I was awed by its impressive architecture as I approached from the bustling main street. When I walked through the front door I was greeted by a WPA mural and a grand marble staircase that took visitors to administrative offices on the mezzanine above. A security officer saw me and directed me to walk across the campus, the shortest way to get to where I was going. He pointed to a door that opened onto the school's courtyard, and as I stepped out of the dark foyer into the sun, I felt as if I had stepped into another place and time.

The school's limestone and brick building formed a peaceful quadrangle carpeted with a lush green lawn and lined with trees and flowers in full bloom that May afternoon. In the center sat a large wood-frame schoolhouse, the original academy. The gothic arches and terra cotta gargoyles and friezes of the main building visually transported me from the ghetto neighborhood that Old School served to an elite college campus. As I walked to the interview for my first teaching position, the campus filled me with a sense of awe at the work I hoped to undertake. On that spring afternoon, the architecture had done what it was designed to do—recall great institutions of learning and celebrate the grandness of the Western tradition.

Once I was teaching at the school, the physical plant took on different meanings. Old School was built with stationary cast-iron frame desks, the back of one seat the front of the next desk. In every classroom many of these seats were missing, leaving gaping holes like missing teeth. Plaster crumbled from ceilings that leaked in the rain, windowpanes were broken, and blackboards were cracked. The wooden desks were covered with graffiti etched in over the years. Mice and roaches were common classroom visitors. Bathrooms for students and teachers did not work; water fountains were always dry. The conditions in the building were harsh and resonated with the school's reputation, not its architecture. The physical experience of the school presented an incredible contrast—this elegant building encoded with lofty academic ideals and high expectations in a terrible state of decay. The import of these conditions framed day-to-day life at the school and no one missed this obvious irony.

On my first day of school as a teacher, a senior colleague presented me with a petition that she was circulating, demanding that the bathrooms be fixed. Seeing this as a modest request, I went to sign when another colleague, acting as a mentor, moved me away. "These people focus on the building instead of on teaching," she cautioned, encouraging me to ignore the physical conditions and focus on teaching and learning in my classroom. I quickly learned that the physical conditions in which we worked framed heated debates about what students could do and what was possible given these circumstances. They also informed discourses on race, pedagogical practice, and the curriculum. The narratives told daily in staff rooms, department and faculty meetings, and in the teachers' cafeteria, equated the school's physical and academic decline with the overwhelmingly Black population who attended at the time, while a vocal minority responded that institutional racism at all levels—the state, the city, the superintendent's office, and within the school itself—had conspired to diminish the opportunities offered to Black students. Central to understanding the meaning of space at Old School, now Renaissance, is the recognition of the role race has played in shaping educational and public policies. The spatial reorganization of Old School over its long history offers a case study of the role of race in reshaping urban geography in the postwar and post-civil rights era.

The physical plant itself informs much of the discourse on Old School prior to its restructuring and calls attention to the hidden curriculum of space. Though not carrying out any explicit policy, the physical appearance, condition, and utilization of the school's space convey powerful messages to students about the meaning of education and their place in American society. Here I offer a critical reading of the hidden curriculum of space to contextualize the issues facing reformers and students at Renaissance.

The Covenant Made Visible

Old School was one of the oldest secondary schools in the nation. Built in 1787 on land donated by the church located across the street and with funds donated by prominent New Yorkers, its original federalist-style school building is on the National Registry of Historic places. The newer structures, built between 1904 and 1939, gained landmark status in 2003. Though originally founded as an elite academy for boys, the school rapidly expanded. In 1801, girls were admitted, and in 1803, the local community funded the school, making it the first public secondary school in the nation (Landmark Preservation Commission 2003).

In 1896, Old School had 150 students, but by 1901, it had about 2000 (Board of Education 1987). This ballooning growth in population attests to a number of changes taking place at the turn of the earlier century, when New York City experienced a monumental explosion in immigration, and demands on its schools grew as well. Between 1900 and 1904, the school registers increased by 132,000 students (Landmark Preservation Commission 2003). In addition to the demand for public schooling, the demand for post-primary education increased and was not available in many parts of the city. In 1898, Old School was turned over to the City of New York on the condition that the city expand it.[1]

In the early twentieth century, G. B. Snyder, the chief architect of New York Schools, sought to establish a high school in each borough, making available to the masses a quality education beyond primary school. Each of these signature schools was designed to physically embody the vision of the high school as the "everyman's college." Snyder designed four wings for Old School, to be built as they were needed, and that, when complete, would form an enclosed quadrangle. The first wing, the front, was completed in 1904, the fourth and final wing in 1939. Though the last wing, built during the Depression, lacked the architectural flourishes of the wings designed by Snyder, all were built in brick and limestone and in the same style and scale.

The link between the physical design of the school and its educational mission is central to understanding Old School's identity. The decision to design it to look like an elite college was informed by debates on education at the turn of the century when the school's campus was planned. Surrounding both universities and public school systems expanding at this time were fierce debates between traditionalists (who supported a liberal arts and classical education) and modernists (who endorsed vocational education). Clearly, the traditionalists prevailed in the design of Old School, as Snyder encoded this commitment to the classical/liberal arts in its very walls, modeling it after the residential colleges of Oxford. From its architectural inception, Old School was aligned with conservative traditions in education representing the pursuit of knowledge as a noble pursuit in and of itself and grounded in a rejection of the demands of industrialization via vocationalism and "a nostalgia for gentlemanly elitism" (Turner 1990).

At this time, too, American institutions of higher learning embraced Medieval and Renaissance architectural styles to create a sense of scholarly tradition. Undergoing rapid development and expansion, these institutions reproduced the architectural forms of the great European universities in an effort to place themselves within that scholarly tradition. Where historical connections did not exist, American schools used exacting architectural artifice to create a visual and psychic connection to the highest intellectual traditions of the Western world (Turner 1990). This same concept informed the design of the "new" wings at Old School, which employ the Tudor style of architecture (also known as English Gothic) and reproduce elements of the English residential college such as a chapel (as the auditorium was called). The intention of the designers was to create a sense of tradition and inspire students to lofty goals (Krinsky 1987).

The decision to use such clear Anglo-Saxon forms also served other purposes, particularly the defining of an American identity for the largely first- and second-generation immigrants who would attend the school. Designers may have had one eye on the great universities but the other suspiciously considered the students enrolling in the city's schools. According to Brumberg (1986), an estimated 277,000 Jewish students attended New York City's elementary schools in the early 20th century, and in 1918 they comprised 53 percent of the city's high school population of 85,000. By the 1920s, the community surrounding Old School was a working- and middle-class Jewish community. According to the census of 1920, almost 70 percent of New York's population was either foreign born or the children of the foreign born. In the public schools, Jews comprised the largest single ethnic block followed by Italians (Brumberg 1986). By the 1920s, Old School echoed these patterns, and by the 1930s its students were predominantly Jewish.

At this time, the central role of the public schools of New York became the Americanization of this great foreign mass. Tyack (1974) suggests that one of the impulses driving turn-of-the-century "schoolmen"[2] to standardize the institution of schooling was the drive to protect patterns of Protestant socialization. In New York, this system included the teaching of the English language, punctuality, efficiency, and self-discipline, as well as manners, personal hygiene, American norms on how to set a table, clean a house, cook American food and, eventually, the Pledge of Allegiance. Brumberg argues,

> Whether the messages transmitted by New York City's public schools to its immigrant charges were accepted or rejected, they were unambiguously communicated and clearly defined. They presented an idealized America and strongly encouraged all its students to embrace that world and become active participants within it. (15)

As the identity of Old School developed, the Protestant and Anglo-Saxon forms used on the building also informed the curriculum and school rituals that reinforced strong connections between American and Anglo-Saxon culture. Thus, even at its inception, the building sent clear messages about student identity. On the one hand, it inspired and celebrated its students' upward mobility, while on the other hand, it imposed a culturally specific ideal of the scholarly tradition and American identity.

The physical campus was pivotal in defining both an explicit and a hidden curriculum and in defining what it meant to be a student at Old School. The power of the architecture to frame the way students felt about their experience was well documented in the most recent installment of the school's history, produced in celebration of its bicentennial. This volume, referred to as *The Chronicles*, focused on the years 1937 to 1987 and was the most ambitious of the school's official histories. In addition to re-telling the story of the school's founding, as earlier volumes had, this edition offered a rich social history of the school over the fifty years it covered. A team comprised of alumni and teachers sent out questionnaires to alums, culled through the school's archives, its newspapers, yearbooks, and literary magazines, and interviewed former and current school leaders. This edition offers a well-documented representation of the dominant narrative of the school's history.

The text used the campus to frame a tradition of academic excellence that carried the legacy of the greatest traditions of the Western world to New York. In each genesis of *The Chronicles,* the history of the campus is the first story retold, and this history frames the interpretation of the lived experience of the school in the 1987 volume. The first page opens with "The Memory" as an introduction to the school's history:

> The campus touched everyone who passed through it, striking chords deep in each heart. How does a place, a mass of stone and swath of green, come to mean so much? Perhaps the rich heritage of architecture and garden are the outward symbols of the inner longing for achievement. Perhaps it calls forth the veneration of the past, which enhances the present and makes it meaningful. Perhaps it is the evidence, here in stone on stone, of the continuity of human knowledge and its extension across time. Surely, for each one in each generation, it has been the heritage and the covenant of [Old School] made visible. (3)

Positing this recollection of the experience as "The Memory" and not "a" memory suggests that these are the collective memories of generations of Old Schoolers and clarifies the ways the campus informs consciousness. The powerful architecture links the rich heritage of the past with the present. Students at Old School were carrying on a grand tradition, not creating new ones. Nor were they carrying on their own cultural traditions, but rather Anglo-Protestant traditions that were more central to American identity. "The Memory" also links the architecture to academic excellence, making the school's outstanding reputation prior seem inevitable. As the campus decayed and its academic reputation plummeted, the connection between the physical space and academic performance was only strengthened. Through their appreciation of the architecture, their participation in this academic community, and their internalization of these values, the largely Jewish students who attended Old School in its hey-day (from the 1930s through the 1950s) were given access to this great tradition, to American identity, and upward mobility. The "covenant" (ironically, an Old Testament metaphor that describes God's promise to the Jews) Old School makes with its students of inclusion in elite academic and cultural traditions was not kept when students did not readily identify with the architecture.

Many alumni quoted in *The Chronicles* echo these links between academic excellence, Western civilization, and the architecture. They also document the hidden curriculum of space. For example, one alumna wrote,

> I felt privileged attending [Old School]. The buildings themselves with their Gothic architecture, arches, the lawns and pathways, the statue of [namesake of school], and the Old Building, made me feel as though I was attending a college of lasting renown. (52)

Students made the connections that architect Snyder and his colleagues had intended and linked the campus to elite, Western, academic traditions. This alumna felt elevated by the architecture, her detailed recollection of the campus indicating the centrality of the space itself in her identification with these traditions. Another alumna responded, "Every time we passed by the statue of [the school's namesake] and gazed up, we felt as if we were a part of history" (Board of Education, 52). Without the visual link to the tradition and culture encoded in the walls and statuary, she would not have perceived herself to be part of it. Such perceptions of the students' own background as outside of real history suggests the narrowness of the traditions Old School represented—traditions that were otherwise unavailable to immigrants and the children of immigrants. In inviting its students into these traditions, the school also constructs their ethnic and cultural identities as outside or marginal to them. Through the mediation of the school, students are brought into the American mainstream.

The cultural specificity of the tradition framed by the architecture was not lost on many alums. Many of the voices in *The Chronicles* noted the contradictions between their cultural identity and the culture and history celebrated by the school. One of the biggest events at the school was its Christmas concert. *The Chronicles* describes the procession:

> The Choral Club entered from the rear of the Chapel singing *Adeste Fi-delis*. They filled the stage with their red and cream robes while the Glee Clubs and the Cantata sang from the balconies with the orchestra down below. It was an emotional experience, the music rising and swelling and pouring out over the audience. With the traditional finale of Handel's *Hallelujah Chorus*, there was many a surreptitious handkerchief to wipe away an emotional tear. (151)

These Christmas concerts were overtly Christian from the musical selections to the robes of the choir, and in the setting itself (beneath a stained glass window), not the secularized fare more common in schools today. The students did not sing carols like "Deck the Halls" and "Jingle Bells." Rather, this predominantly Jewish student body awed their audiences (no doubt also predominantly Jewish) with highbrow selections that celebrated Christ as the Messiah and Christian domination.

Though these concerts, no doubt, were artistically magnificent, they were, nonetheless, problematic for many of the students:

> Now that I mention Christmas, I must add that for a predominantly Jewish school, we certainly partook of the spirit of the season, including its specific religious symbols, with a whole heartedness (more innocence) that was positively glowing. . . . The caroling and partying that took place in just about every class made the day before the holiday one long festivity—though the official Christmas concert was clearly its highlight, not only for the superior beauty of the vocal and orchestral performances, but because it gave me a chance to gaze for rapt minutes at some current "crush" in the Glee Club. Alumna, 1948 (152)

> I can still see her . . . [names music teacher], throwing herself into teaching us "There was a balm in Gilead—to heal the sin-sick soul." And I still sing it! For a naïve Jewish girl, she represented passionate, generous Christianity—and I still remember she wrote something mysterious from Isaiah in my yearbook. Alumna, 1958 (152)

These quotes suggest that these Christmas celebrations gave students a sense of inclusion in an American culture that was also a Christian culture. At the same time, the emphasis the speakers place on their naïve enthusiasm suggest that at some point, though perhaps not as students, the speakers recognized the problematic irony presented by their Jewishness and the overtly Christian festivities. The second speaker notes her fondness for a teacher who represented "passionate, generous Christianity," suggesting she had limited access to such notions of Christianity.

Another alum recalled "the thrill of singing Christmas carols on the radio with the girls especially as I came from an orthodox Jewish background" (alumna, 1948, 152). She suggests that much about these celebrations was social and at least as much about staring at boys in the glee club or singing on the radio with friends as about the Christian content. However, this alumna's sense of "thrill" was perhaps also informed by her orthodox Jewish background and suggests that these festivities at school provided access to aspects of American culture many Jewish students did not have otherwise. The speakers forgive their youthful selves for their naïveté while speaking from a distance and a mature awareness of the school's incorporation of Christian forms and their own identities as upwardly mobile Jewish students. Despite the celebratory nature of their reflections, they still suggest that their identities were in conflict with the institution. These students chose to ignore or overlook these conflicts and to embrace the school and its traditions in order to reap the benefits of such participation.

It is difficult to tell how students understood these conflicts at the time, what their families thought, and if, in fact, some students refused to participate in these activities. Certainly some students resented it, as I will discuss shortly. Within *The Chronicles*, the dominant interpretation of the Old School experience, however, was that everyone enjoyed the events.

Jewish students at Old School strategically navigated through its Christian architecture and culture. As Brumberg has pointed out, the messages sent to Jewish students by efforts to Americanize them were clear and unambiguous. American culture, as represented at Old School was clearly linked to Western European and Christian traditions. However, as Brumberg also points out, though the message was clear, it did not mean that students accepted it in its entirety. It appears, at least in *The Chronicles*, that Jewish students welcomed the opportunity to use the school to gain access to American culture. What also emerges from these quotes though, is an awareness of the symbolic violence involved in focusing Jewish students so intensely on Christian celebrations. In the dominant discourse on the school, these conflicts are ignored, but they significantly informed student experience. The erasure of these conflicts is part of the hidden curriculum.

"The Other Old School"

As a teacher at Old School, I frequently met alums. Most of the time they echoed the dominant narrative already discussed, expressing a fondness for the school and its beautiful campus as well as pride in its outstanding reputation. Such memories also were almost always followed with disgust or sorrow at the school's academic and physical decline. However, on occasion, I met alums who shared a very different experience, and even thirty years after their graduation still seemed angry. In 1991, my second year at Old School, I met a friend's mother. Brightly, the friend boasted of where I taught, noting to me that her mother had gone to Old School. Her mother narrowed her eyes at me and asked, "Do they still call the auditorium 'the Chapel?'" I told her they did. Lowering her voice for impact she said, "You know, I could never stand that! We were all Jewish and they called it "the Chapel" like it was a Christian School. I hated that!" Her quick focus on the Christian referents suggested that not all Old Schoolers welcomed the socialization into a Christian culture. She felt these practices were disrespectful to Jewish identity and her comments suggest that at least some students were uncomfortable with the contradictions between student cultural identity and the culturally specific construction of school and America.

In 1994, beginning my doctoral studies, I went to the archive that housed the records of the Board of Education hoping to see what was available on Old School. The librarian in charge of the collection interviewed me about my project, apparently making sure I had scholarly intentions. As I explained my interest, he cut me off:

> I went to [Old school]. But I didn't go to the [Old School] you're talking about. There were always two [Old Schools]: the famous one and the other one. I went to that one. We weren't the academic stars and no one wanted anything to do with us. There were a lot of us and they gave us nothing.

He felt cheated by his marginalization. Though he walked through the campus and saw the architecture, his lack of academic orientation specifically excluded him from the "covenant made visible." These two examples, though a minority perception of Old School (from what I can tell), suggest that the seemingly universal access to the tradition and to the American dream were contingent on students fitting into a specific model. Those who rejected aspects of the socialization process, resenting the Christian elements and/or rejecting the academic course, were marginalized and left outside the Old School tradition. The librarian's construction of "the other [Old School]"[3] is particularly appropriate as students like him were literally "othered" and their experiences erased from the school's official history. The willingness of students to internalize the ideal and to fit themselves into its construction of American identity would inform the school's rise and fall.

Crumbling Edifices

As noted in the introduction, though Old School had once been considered a "crown jewel" of the city's school system, by the time I came to teach there in the late 1980s, it was one of the lowest performing high schools in the city and the building was in wretched condition (Hancock 1992). Just as Old School boosters linked the physical space to academic achievement, as the school declined, the connections remained but became more problematic, particularly as the student population had become overwhelmingly Black by the 1970s. Discursively narrating the school's decline became very difficult if the traditions were timeless and the Old School experience universal. Both newspaper reports and *The Chronicles* struggled to explain the school's decline adequately.

In 1993, shortly after sorely needed renovations began on Old School, the *New York Times* (Dillon 1993) reported that the School Construction Authority (SCA) had estimated that it would cost $22 million to renovate the main building. However, shortly after the project began, it was evident that the renovation would cost at least $78 million. By the time the job was done in 1999, the cost had soared to over $100 million. One of the unexpected discoveries was that the school's massive terra cotta façade was structurally unsound and workers had to scaffold it to keep it from tumbling onto the street. These unexpected manifestations of decay and neglect bore symbolic import—the Eurocentric edifice was literally and figuratively crumbling, unable to withstand the ravages of time.

The *New York Times* also played on the irony of the school's condition as it reported on the costs of neglect and used Old School as a symbol for the entire school system:

> [Old School's] current troubles are a blemish on an illustrious history. . . . The school has always been one of the city's proudest. . . . But like many schools, [Old School] decayed rapidly after the fiscal crisis in the 1970s, (and) (b)y the 1980s, the school was badly dilapidated. . . . Its 200th anniversary, however, ignited a restoration campaign. "The 200th Birthday of [Old School] is a celebration of all that is best in American public education, and of what it can yet become," former board president Robert F. Wagner Jr. wrote in a 1987 letter to the *New York Times.* (B1)

The *New York Times* glibly explains the decline of Old School and the whole school system by conveniently collapsing the academic and physical decay. It blames the "current troubles," which included a dilapidated plant as well as a graduation rate below 50 percent, high levels of violence, and low levels of academic achievement, on the fiscal crisis of the 1970s. Such an explanation ignores the role of public policy, institutionalized racism, and the demographic and economic reorganization of cities that occurred just prior to the fiscal collapse of the city.

By the 1980s, New York's economy had recovered and some schools had been repaired in that time, but not Old School. Thus, the devastating blow to the city's schools in the fiscal crisis is not sufficient to explain the decline of some schools more than others, particularly Old School.

In addition, the newspaper also links the physical restoration of Old School with a restoration of the once-great school system. Restoring the physical space, the reporter suggests, will somehow restore everything that that space stood for—"all that is best in American education." The article alludes to the glorious past and the hopeful future, bypassing the present, excluding via silence the existing context and the students from the Old School narrative.

The *New York Times* was not alone in its inability to explain the school's collapse and to situate the Black students who attended within nostalgic notions of American education and of Old School. The rise and fall of Old School offers a case study in the limits of policies of "Americanization" designed to acculturate Southern and Eastern European immigrants into Northern and Western European traditions. Such Americanization strategies have been less effective and less welcomed by descendents of the people systematically enslaved and exploited by these Europeans. The rigid construction of American identity enshrined in such efforts was simply unable to address students whose historical experiences are not only outside the dominant culture, but also, at times, in conflict with it.

The Chronicles faced a similar rhetorical task. It sought to assert a unified narrative rooted in the timelessness and resiliency of the school's grand tradition and, like the article in the *New York Times*, posit a bright future. At the same time, *The Chronicles* had to explain the last twenty years of its scope, from 1967 to 1987. The authors employed a few revealing discursive strategies to fold these difficult years seamlessly into the master narrative. In their retelling of the years after 1965, when much of the school's demographic shifts took place, *The Chronicles* specifically separated the students attending in those years from those of the previous generation. The section titled "Urban Problems" specifically calls attention to the greatest challenge to the "tradition" of the school—the shift in Old School's student population from White to Black:

> Because of its location, [Old School] was inextricably involved in the problems of [its] neighborhood. Middle-class black families had been living in [the neighborhood] for years, but now the neighborhood was becoming home to an increasing number of poorer black families. Besides this socioeconomic change, the late 60s was a time of serious problems in maintaining racial balance in the city schools. The [Old School] district was rezoned to include children from distant neighborhoods. Along with motivated, capable students came others, who defied the rules of [Old School] education. They disrupted classes, wandered the halls, scrawled graffiti on the walls and even menaced other students. (245)

This explanation for decline separates the new arrivals from the Old School tradition asserting that "they" are not like "us," are not from "our" community, and "they" do not share "our" vision. The students who arrived in the late 60s were not like previous generations of Old Schoolers because they were both poor and Black. With no further explanation of why poor Blacks were somehow more of a problem than poor Whites (who were explicitly included in earlier sections) or middle-class Blacks,

The Chronicles relies on racist constructions of Black urban youth to blame them for the school's fall. In this way, the school's official history reproduces a narrative that links decline directly to poor Black students.

The utilization of the campus itself also reproduces this narrative. Students today are severed from the traditions earlier generations found in the architecture. As I noted earlier, many alums defined their school experience through the visual admiration of the campus. The very opening paragraph of *The Chronicles* explains, "Each [Old Schooler] remembers the first view of the campus, coming in from [the avenue], through the shadowed, echo-y arch, to be confronted by the quadrangle with [school's namesake] presiding" (3). However, in response to the increase in crime in the community, locked gates were installed across the arches in the early 1970s. Additionally, because of increased security measures, students today do not walk in "through the shadowed, echo-y arch" into the courtyard. The only arch they walk under is that of a full-body metal detector. Rather than the experience of entering an elite institution, student interviewees were much more likely to compare entering school to entering prison. Also as part of the renovations, a brick wall was installed that separates the lawn from the path students walk to go from where they are scanned to their classes; the wall blocks their view of the now-restored campus. If the visual understanding of the campus defined one's experience, students today see a brick wall that shuts them off physically and symbolically from the impressive courtyard and the traditions it represents.

The narrative on the decline of the once-great school depicts that fall as inevitable by suggesting that the newer students were simply not as committed, driven, or worthy as the students who attended in the past. However, though the narrative thrust of the authors blames the debased present on students, the authors also concede that the institution may bear some responsibility as well. Using school newspapers primarily, the authors retell significant upheavals during the 1960s. For example, students shut down Old School on several occasions during the decade. According to the front page of the May 16, 1969, issue of the school's newspaper reproduced in *The Chronicles*, the Afro-American Students Association presented a list of fifteen demands to the principal and the Board of Education. Some of those demands were "Elimination of the general course of study[,] . . . end racism in hiring," and "end use of racist literature." "Teachers who are teaching a course should have a background related to the course. (No art teachers teaching math), (No Jews teaching black history), (No Italians teaching Puerto Rican culture)." Black and Hispanic students simply did not see themselves within the Eurocentric curriculum and, thus, may have not felt such a powerful connection to the architecture and tradition.

In an attempt to synthesize the social upheavals of the 60s and 70s such as student protests, teacher strikes, the fiscal crisis of the 1970s, and the demographic shifts that drastically changed Old School, *The Chronicles* noted,

> Taken together, the outside pressures on [Old School] during 1964–1972 gravely wounded it. By 1972, along with other American institutions, [Old School] had been seriously battered by the winds of change. Because [Old School] sat in the midst of a changing borough in one of the world's largest cities, the forces of this turbulent era affected it perhaps more than other institutions. With its new black and immigrant students and its traditional stance on education, [Old School] encapsulated the tensions of the entire New York City public school system. (245–46)

Here the authors concede a crucial conflict that much of their narrative seeks to diminish. Earlier, the authors had suggested that new students outside the community had brought about decline. However, here they suggest that the school itself (and the school system as a whole) was not responsive to those students. Given that students were demanding Ethnic Studies, Black History, and Puerto Rican culture courses, there certainly was a disconnect between the school's growing minority population and its academic offerings. Not only did the new students not live within the same community, they also did not identify with the European culture that is celebrated in the architecture and in school rituals. They wanted something different from the school. Thus, the institution, so visibly linked to Western culture was unable, or at least slow, to accommodate students who did not readily identify with the traditions represented in the space.

Redefining Urban Space

Though I have rejected the explanations for the school's decline offered by *The Chronicles* and the *New York Times*, the questions remain, why did Old School decline so precipitously and what are the connections between space and the school's fate? One of the problems of these dominant discourses on Old School is that the focus remains primarily on the school itself. *The Chronicles* only references the local community to lament that it changed in a bad way and brought bad kids to the school. However, as suggested by the *New York Times*, Old School's situation was one shared by urban schools across the city. To understand its decline, we must look to the broader social conditions and public policies that informed the fates of cities and their schools in the postwar years. I argue that as urban schools served more students of color, public investment in these schools and in cities in general declined.

Beyond constructing a notion of community that is rooted in values and behaviors, the authors of *The Chronicles* sought to preserve a core community that endures to the present. The authors explain the change in population by noting zoning shifts that brought Black students from outside of the neighborhood, though they make little comment on the fact that White families were simply leaving the area. Black students did not invade Old School from far off communities—for the most part they moved into the neighborhoods abandoned by ethnic Whites who were able to move to the suburbs in the postwar years. However, it should be noted that zoning patterns did favor some schools over others as White middle-class communities close to Old School were zoned for another high school about two miles away, while poorer Black students living very near that school were zoned for Old School. Thus, the authors of *The Chronicles* were not wrong in noting such unfair public policies that preserved the White and middle-class identity of some schools at the expense of others. Their inaccuracy lies in presuming that zoning to protect White families was the only unfair public policy undermining Old School.

The emerging social geography of cities was powerfully structured by public policy that encouraged the consolidation of urban ghettoes in the cities while underwriting White flight to suburbs. Practices such as "redlining" and public policies such as the GI Bill (the benefits package offered to veterans of World War II) created segregated urban ghettos, specifically devaluing spaces defined as Black or Brown. Wilder (2000) argues that the fusion of business interests with the Home Owners Loan Corporation (HOLC), a New Deal agency established to prevent foreclosures and bank failures, in the 1930s laid the groundwork for the redlining practices of the postwar years. The HOLC developed a "Residential Security Map" that evaluated neighborhoods, noting some as good investment areas and others as bad. According to Wilder, one of the most significant criteria for assigning a rating was the racial and ethnic composition of the residents in a community. Black communities were given the lowest ratings, as were old neighborhoods with little room for new development.

This system not only specifically devalued spaces with large minority populations but also devalued urban spaces in favor of undeveloped suburban ones. Over time, redlines were drawn around neighborhoods deemed poor investments, and lenders refused to loan money to buyers in these areas. In the postwar years, the GI Bill made low-interest home loans available to veterans and thus subsidized the expansion of suburbs. Lenders would not make loans for those neighborhoods that were redlined, forcing would-be buyers to look elsewhere. Thus, the subsidized loans offered by the GI Bill pushed the aspiring middle class out of cities and into suburbs.

Because of traditional patterns of discrimination in housing and employment, fewer Black families had the capital to take advantage of the opportunity and even those who had the money often were kept out of White suburbs by restrictive covenants (statements on deeds prohibiting sale of houses to Blacks). These covenants were ruled unenforceable by the Supreme Court in 1948 but were upheld in practice nonetheless (Haynes 2001). In other cases, realtors simply didn't show Black families properties within their budgets in White communities. Of course, violence also was a tactic used to keep Blacks out, including direct intimidation and firebombing houses or the offices of realtors who showed houses in White communities to Blacks.

Ironically, Old School's neighborhood was given a low rating because it had too large a Jewish population in the 1930s. However, by the 1950s racial discourses had expanded the notion of whiteness to include Jews and other White ethnic groups, enabling them to move to White suburbs (Brodkin 1998). The segregation that exists in many American cities was bankrolled by programs such as the GI Bill and givebacks such as the tax breaks that still make homeownership viable for much of the middle class. These policies also shaped the demographic shifts at Old School as its surrounding communities slowly lost their middle-class and largely Jewish populations and became home to poorer immigrants from the Caribbean who were able to come to the United States when immigration laws changed in the 1960s (Waters 1999).

Beyond these policies, which racialized urban and suburban spaces, older patterns of housing discrimination persisted in the postwar years. Shirley Chisholm (who represented New York's 12th District in Congress from 1968 to 1983) explains what she experienced in the 1940s:

> No one knew it then, but the present-day "inner city" (to use a white eu-phemism) was being created. Black workers had to crowd into neighbor-hoods that were already black or partly so, because they could not find homes anywhere else. Buildings that had four apartments suddenly had eight, and bathrooms that had been private were shared. White building inspectors winked at housing code violations and illegal rates of occupancy, white landlords doubled and trebled their incomes on slum buildings, and the white neighborhoods in other parts of town and in the suburbs stayed white. Today's urban ghettos were being born. (Chisholm 1994)

As White families left their neighborhoods, landlords converted their for-mer dwellings to accommodate more and poorer families, creating slum-like conditions where they had not existed previously. Redlining and rac-ist practices like those Chisholm described protected the White ethnic neighborhoods that remained and informed the profound changes taking place at Old School.

Deindustrialization of New York

As upwardly mobile, ethnic Whites were able to head to greener pastures, the industrial base that had supported their dreams was deteriorating. Factories and heavy industry were also leaving for anti-union states down South and abroad. In 1954, 235,000 people worked in manufacturing in Brooklyn alone, and that number stayed as high into the 1960s when the factories began to close. The Brooklyn Navy Yard, Drake's Cakes, Piels, Schaefer and Rheingold beers, and machine makers of all sorts closed up shop. Between the mid-1960s and the mid-1970s—the ten years in which Old School's population changed from predominantly White to predomi-nantly Black—two-thirds of the city's manufacturing jobs had disappeared (Snyder-Grenier 1996).

Local and State Policies

Demographic and economic shifts underwritten by federal and state policies and by the decisions of private investors and banks altered the meaning of the spaces of different neighborhoods, devaluing them and leaving fewer opportunities for the people who now inhabited those spaces. However, the undermining of the future prospects of these communities also was ensured through the systematic underfunding of urban schools.

In 1991, Jonathan Kozol's best-selling *Savage Inequalities* chronicled the devastating contrast between struggling urban schools and the well-heeled suburban schools often within a few miles of them. Kozol used the physical conditions of schooling to viscerally demonstrate the ways urban and suburban school spaces are constructed through unjust funding policies. He noted that school funding practices that emerged in the postwar years greatly favored the rich over the poor. In particular, the practice of raising money for schools through property taxes favors more affluent communities with higher property values and residents who can afford substantial tax rates. Poorer communities often tax themselves at a higher rate but on much less valuable property and simply cannot raise the kind of funds richer communities can.

Such funding practices not only guarantee more resources for wealthier communities, but they also define communities as local geographical entities (rather than regional or national entities, for example) and allow affluent suburban communities to fund excellent schools for their children while children in urban areas are underserved. Anyon (2005) argues that focusing on local communities instead of regions perpetuates inequality. Cities and the suburbs that surround them are not the isolated communities school funding practices suggest. Cities not only provide high-income jobs for suburban workers and the services these workers use while they are at work (public transportation, emergency services, police, fire, etc.), but cities also enrich the suburbs through the many cultural resources they provide, such as museums, theaters, parks, historic sites, and universities—all often used by suburban dwellers but subsidized by the precious tax dollars of urbanites. Considering cities and suburbs regional for some funding, such as transportation and highway funds, but local for school funds systematically undermines urban schools.

Though local school taxes are often the primary source of funding for schools, states also provide a significant amount of money to schools as well. Unfortunately, school finance schemes at the state level generally reinforce trends that produce inequality. In recent years, there have been over twenty lawsuits brought on behalf of urban school children against states over inequitable funding. In New York State, these inequities are glaring. According to the Education Trust, New York City is the victim of the largest per-pupil funding gap (the gap between the wealthiest and poorest districts) in the nation (Winter 2002). Such persistent underfunding played a decisive role in the decline of Old School and public education in New York City in general.

In 1993, the Campaign for Fiscal Equity (CFE), a network of advocacy groups, filed a lawsuit against New York State on behalf on New York City's school children arguing that the state had systematically underfunded city schools. Because 60 percent of the state's poor students and 70 percent of its minority students live in the city, this underfunding constituted a violation of students' civil rights. In 2001, a judge ruled in favor of the plaintiffs insisting that the funding policies in place violated the state's constitution that promises a sound, basic education to all citizens. The judge defined such an education as one that equipped students for citizenship—to be informed voters and to serve on juries. In finding that city schools had been underfunded for decades, he wrote, "Demography is not destiny. . . . The amount of melanin in a student's skin, the home country of her antecedents, the amount of money in the family bank account, are not the inexorable determinants of academic success" (Goodnough 2001). He also attacked the unfathomable formula used by the state legislature to allocate funds, finding that the formula was "unnecessarily complex and opaque" and charged that it had "failed for more than a decade to align funding with need" (Goodnough 2001).

As of the writing of this book (spring 2008), this case has been the subject of four major decisions by a Supreme Court justice, three by the Appellate courts and three by the State Court of Appeals. Ultimately, the plaintiffs were awarded an increase of $2 billion dollars a year for city schools, a disappointing award considering that previous courts had awarded as much as $5.6 billion. However, the highest court insisted that the legislature, not the court, was to decide how school funds were allocated. In New York State, the funding of schools is more about political clout than need. The legislature, which was responsible for the funding inequalities in the first place and which has failed in session after session to correct these inequalities was charged with figuring out how to deliver these funds to the city. By not overturning the state's funding formula, the court essentially returned the henhouse to the fox.

In an effort to clarify the funding formula used by the legislature, the *New York Times* found a number of unwritten rules that greatly informed the funding gap in the state. For example, no district can receive less money than it did the previous year even if its enrollments go down or it enjoys a tax windfall, a policy that directly hurts districts that increase enrollments. Another unwritten rule guarantees that Long Island districts always enjoy a certain portion of any increase in state aid. In addition to automatically privileging Long Island districts, the rules also cap New York City's share of any increase. The *New York Times* reported that "the process works backward, with leaders determining how much money certain regions will receive and then manipulating the formulas to conform" (Medina 2006). This serpentine formula is intentionally hard to fathom in order to conceal these gross injustices in state funding to schools.

The CFE lawsuit offers a well-documented example of the systemic and long-term devaluing of urban schools and the indifference to the plight of urban students. However, even within these underfunded school districts, local policies also benefit some schools at the expense of others. Kozol (1991) documented wide funding disparities within a local school district in the Bronx. On top of state underfunding, schools serving poor and minority children were likely to receive fewer resources than their whiter and wealthier neighbors. Some of these differences come from decisions at the district level to place discretionary funds and special programs in some schools rather than others. Additionally, the ability of PTAs to raise funds, provide volunteers, and advocate for greater resources also informs the opportunities available to children attending those schools. The social and cultural capital students bring to school and that of their parents and caretakers also impacts the resources available.

For years, the city received billions less than its fair share of state aid, which left all its schools poorer, but local policies have exacerbated these inequalities. Whether in affluent suburbs favored by state funding formulas or in communities within the city favored by local policies, beneficiaries of funding systems often see that funding as a right and are unwilling to support more equitable systems.

The struggles over finances that face schools such as Old School also inform the meaning of urban school spaces. The hidden curriculum of space is designed by numerous public policies, business practices, and political maneuvering that systematically devalue some urban schools and the educational prospects of some urban school children. Time is not the only culprit in the decay and decline of Old School, nor can its post-1960s students or the fiscal crisis of the 1970s fully account for its fate. Much broader and systemic forces operate to undermine the prospects of poor, minority, urban students across the nation just as it has at Old School. All of these policies contribute to the formation of a racialized geography and the impoverishment of Black spaces. The decline of Old School must be seen as a product of these broader trends.

Toxic Schools

In light of the above discussion, the physical space at Old School can be read as a text in institutional racism, as so many of the policies that informed its physical and academic decline were designed to protect the interests of White families and students. Prophetically, in the fall of 1993, the physical decay at Old School became more than an eyesore, as a city-wide asbestos crisis enabled teachers to mobilize and place the physical condition of schools on the front pages of newspapers. That year, city schools did not open on time because of allegations that many were contaminated with asbestos and were unsafe. The city had hired a company to test schools for asbestos and remove the carcinogen, but the contractor had apparently conducted bogus tests, declared the schools safe, and then disappeared. Retests indicated that many schools had unsafe levels of asbestos, and they were closed until cleaned. At Old School, a group of teachers dubbed the Committee of Safety insisted that the school was still not safe and conducted tests of its own. Supported by the union, they refused to teach and further shut down classes through job actions and media attention.

Though the staff was divided about the safety conditions and the intentions of the committee, the struggle to have the physical conditions addressed highlighted the significance of the space in understanding school failure. To some observers, the asbestos crisis offered disgruntled teachers an opportunity to vent their frustration, but to others it was a long-needed job action to force the city to make the school a decent place to teach and learn. The disruptions brought by the asbestos crisis were extensive and forced the school into a double-session, as many classrooms were off limits. In the spring of 1994, the district superintendent announced that Old School would be broken into smaller, discreet schools.

A teacher I spoke with at the time who supported the efforts of the Committee of Safety admitted that the disruptions were really stressful. But, she explained, the Committee of Safety made "them" (Board of Education, School Maintenance) clean things they never would have bothered to. "You couldn't have guessed how dusty this place was!" Pointing to a windowsill in the hall about two feet above our heads, she said, "they [Committee of Safety] made them clean that—it was full of dust and nobody had cleaned it for years." She also believed that the restructuring was a form of punishment for the teacher activism: "that's why they're breaking us up." (However, whether the teacher disruptions in the fall accelerated the process or not, given the low performance of Old School, restructuring would have likely come anyway.)

The asbestos crisis at Old School made the toxicity of the school environment visible through the space itself. Clearly, though, the walls weren't the only toxic elements in the environment. As the discourses on the school's decline presented in the media and *The Chronicles* suggest, the institution was hostile toward its students on a number of levels. Reluctant to alter its curriculum or attempt to address the identities and experiences of its Black students, cynical about their futures through low expectations, and nostalgic about an irretrievable past when the students were White, the school also secreted poison of its own. As the school's performance worsened in comparison to other schools, heated and at times mean-spirited debates among the staff added further toxins to the environment. As the spring of 1994 approached, these battles had reached a fevered pitch and were reflected in the restructuring process.

In the fall of 1994, Old School opened as three new high schools (though all the students were simply divided among them).[4] Each school was led by its own principal and enacted its own reform agenda. At the time of the restructuring, teachers at Old School were given the opportunity to transfer to other schools or join one of the three new schools.

Many did leave, and the others divided along the ideological lines that had been in place prior to the restructuring. The principal of Renaissance had been an advocate for culturally relevant curricula and student-centered pedagogies in the debates that paralyzed Old School. Some of the teachers who helped found Renaissance were similarly minded, but some teachers were not granted their first choices and others had different reasons for selecting the school they chose. Further, all teachers were entitled to a job at one of the new schools and each school received teachers the principals did not want. Therefore, at no point were all teachers of like mind at Renaissance. Nonetheless, Renaissance enacted the most progressive slate of reforms of any of the three schools, which included student-centered pedagogies with an emphasis on collaborative instruction, block scheduling, and sub-schools, as well as forming a school-based planning team that was open to all.

Understanding the policies and funding inequities that shaped the climate at Old School and the schools it would become in the mid-1990s helps frame the frustrating conditions in which Renaissance's students and teachers worked. The hidden curriculum of space operates on many levels. The systematic underfunding of urban schools, the impoverishment of urban communities, the deindustrialization of cities, and the segregation of urban and suburban spaces all undermine the education of students. The ideology encoded in the architecture and the unconscionable decay that was tolerated at Old School also carry the messages sent by public and private policies and practices. Any analysis of spatial formation should begin by understanding what a place means and how it came to be that way. The reform effort, explored more fully in the remaining chapters, was greatly shaped by these struggles over the meaning of space at Old School. Emphasizing the need for more responsive pedagogies, the reform effort at Renaissance was forged in dialogue with this history even as it sought to negate it. But Renaissance also faced the same obstacles that Old School faced. The struggles over the meaning of spaces within school occur within this broader geography that shapes urban schools and communities and the prospects of urban students.

■　　■　　■　　■　　■　　■　　■　　■

"In a way it protects us and in a way . . . it keeps us back"

Scanning, School Space, and Student Identity

Before the first day of school, Renaissance, like most high schools, runs a freshman orientation day where new students and their parents are invited to learn about the school, procedures, what to expect the first day, and opportunities at the school. One year I was asked to attend with some of my debaters. The event was to begin with an introductory session in the cafeteria (where students enter school everyday), after which students would be brought on tours of Renaissance and then would break into groups and go into several rooms, each with a presentation on some aspect of student life. I was to be in a room on extracurricular activities.

About 100 people, new students and their families, sat at lunch tables and were introduced to the principal, guidance counselors, and some teachers. The principal defined the mission of the school and expressed her hopes for students. The guidance counselor went over graduation requirements with the audience and handed out advising sheets that showed the number and required distribution of credits as well as the required state exams. Then, two school safety officers (SSOs) introduced the students to the scanning ritual they would be subject to once school began. Standing next to a full-body metal detector and x-ray machine, one officer explained the procedures to students and clarified the long list of banned items—nothing with a blade, including scissors, razors, and box-cutters, as well as markers, highlighters and Wite-Out. "Leave 'em all home!" the SSO urged and explained further that girls went in one line and were scanned by women; boys in another line were scanned by men. She then asked a volunteer to demonstrate the process, coaching her along the way as she emptied her pockets of metal objects, placed her bag on the x-ray machine, walked through the metal detector, and then placed her hands out to be scanned by a hand-held scanner before collecting her things to go on her way. "See, it's easy," the SSO encouraged as she invited the rest to come up and try it themselves. On that orientation day, these students eagerly played the scanning game, though most would come to resent the practice.

The importance of socializing new students into the scanning process as part of their introduction to Renaissance suggests the centrality of this ritual. As students lined up to practice the new way they would enter school, their parents and families observed quietly, no one questioning the practice or raising reservations about the policy. Apparently, the need to scan Renaissance students as they entered the building was self-evident and required no extensive comment. However, though scanning appeared natural and inevitable that late August day, the practice is far from benign as it shapes student/school relationships, informs student identities, and culturally constructs school space.

Scanning and the Construction of School Space

As noted by the alumni quoted in the previous chapter, the entry ritual of walking through the school's grand front entrance that moved students from the streets into the school was central to the Old School experience. The numerous references to the experience of walking from the ordinary street, through the arch, and into a "school of lasting renown" signified by the collegiate campus nestled within ornate stone walls prove this point. For many of its alumni, the entry ritual defined the identity of the school and its students. It aligned the curriculum with Western traditions and addressed students as scholars, while it also imposed narrow constructions of American identity and marginalized their ethnic cultures.

The arches were designed to mark the threshold between street and school and in so doing, constructed both spaces. The dramatic entry created a clear visual and visceral break with streets and homes from where students had come. The massive building not only literally blocked out the streets, but the architecture also created the sensation in students of having been transported somewhere else. Thus, the inner sanctum of the school was constructed as sacred while the streets beyond the campus, from where students had come, were profane (Eliade 1961). The ideology promoted by the school was made compelling through the celebration of Western culture carved into stone and the assertion of the Anglo-Saxon foundations of American culture and identity. The entry ritual, prior to the early 1970s, when cast-iron gates closed the arches to the street, constructed both school and community space that in turn informed the ways students related to schooling.

Full-body weapon scanning is also an entry ritual, as the entry ritual of the past, which constructs the spaces of the school and the streets. And just as in earlier periods, this ritual enacts a hidden curriculum. Thus, an examination of spatial formation at Renaissance must begin where the day begins—with the first intense ideological struggle over space—the ritual of full-body weapons searches enacted at the door of Old School before students even enter the specific space allocated to Renaissance.

"Scanning" refers generically to the multiple-step process to which students were introduced at orientation and included walking through airport-style metal detectors and having their bags x-rayed. After this initial stage, students were often sent around for hand-scanning, which involved a more invasive search with an electronic handheld device that was run over a student's body (not actually touching it). Several students referred to "triple scanning," which involved going through at least one part of this process yet again and often also included having one's bags searched by hand. Though generically the whole process was referred to as "scanning," the term also was used to refer specifically to the handheld searches that were the focus of high levels of resentment (many students were less bothered by having to go through walk-through detectors). Unless otherwise specified, I use the term "scanning" to refer to the whole ritual.

Scanning Comes to Old School

Scanning greatly expanded in New York City in the early 1990s and arrived at Old School in the fall of 1991. The implementation and escalation of this policy is marked by problematic though commonsense discourses that also inform its ideological work. In New York, over fifty school sites (out of well over 200 high schools) are scanned daily, but even here, scanning occurs overwhelmingly at segregated schools serving local Black and Hispanic communities. The rhetoric that surrounded the expansion of weapons scanning in the city never explicitly raised race as an issue, but the policy has profound racial implications.

In the spring of 1991, a student at Old School was shot in the lunchroom. Within a few days of this event, a student was killed at another high school. These events, terrifying and disturbing, prompted the chancellor (the mayoral appointee who runs the entire school system) to expand an initially very small weapons-scanning program to twenty (of a total of 135) of the most troubled high schools in the city, including Old School. The initial scanning program involved a large crew (thirty SSOs) that arrived unannounced at a school in the morning and randomly scanned students with handheld scanners. Students were scanned this way about once a week (Berger 1992). However, in the spring of 1992, two students at one of the other schools targeted by scanning were shot and killed by a classmate as they walked in the halls between classes. The murder of two students at school received national and international attention and became a watershed event for the school system (Archibald 1999). Shortly after these killings, the city allocated $28 million for the installation of permanent weapons-scanning programs at five of the most dangerous schools, including Old School, with plans to expand to more schools eventually (Doyle 1992; Leavitt 1992). By the fall of 1993, forty-one high schools had daily weapons scanning with handheld scanners and an additional twenty schools were subject to occasional scanning (Olmstead 1993). In the fall of 1995, walk-through metal detectors and x-ray machines were installed in thirty-four high schools, including the newly restructured Old School campus and therefore Renaissance. Typical of the pattern that had emerged in the expansion of the handheld scanning program, this more aggressive and thorough form of weapons scanning was prompted by a shooting in a school that was already subject to daily scanning.

Hand-in-hand with the expansion of full-body weapons scanning, police presence has also increased in schools. In addition to SSOs, whose uniforms resembled that of the NYPD, police officers were placed in all schools in 1994, though they already had been present at the Old School campus and at Renaissance for a number of years. In 1998, school safety was handed directly over to the NYPD, and school safety officers became part of that system and now wear actual police uniforms.

This policy was very controversial at Renaissance, where students circulated petitions and several parents came to school-based planning meetings to complain. Many staff also opposed the change. The SSOs assured everyone that they would be the same people pre- and post-transition, but students and members of the community expressed outrage that the NYPD was penetrating into the schools. In the community surrounding Renaissance, the police were associated with racist and unfair harassment, prosecution, and even murder of Black people. At the school-based planning meeting where the issue was discussed, a parent expressed concern that the school security officers would become "part of that thin blue line" that kept secrets, covered their misdeeds, and participated in covert racist campaigns against the community. Though there was much protest and anger within the school, it was a policy implemented by the city council, and the school itself had little say. At the time of the interviews for this study, the change had already taken place and some students referred to SSOs pejoratively as "cops."

The escalation of scanning and police presence in schools followed a simple logic—extremely violent incidents were answered by an increase in surveillance. This logic was based on the assumption that students were the generators of violence and brought it to otherwise nonviolent schools. For the chancellors who ran the school system and the mayors who were called to task for safety in schools, metal detectors offered an immediate solution to a serious and pervasive problem. Though frequently peer-mediation and conflict resolution programs were also started in these schools along with weapons scanning, the money and attention went to more aggressive physical control. Militaristic solutions such as metal detectors, scanners, uniformed officers, and walkie-talkies, unlike the slow and quiet presence of antiviolence programs, create an instant sense of security. The high-profile and costly interventions gave the impression that something was being done about violence and reasserted institutional authority. Notably, too, each incident at a specific school widened the program at many other schools with similar racial profiles. Scanning not only defined violence as being inherent in certain students, but it also defined violence as inherent in Black and Hispanic communities. The continued escalation of scanning in some high schools and not in others racialized school spaces in that it targeted segregated schools and defined them as violent. These practices also normalized the criminalization of Black and Hispanic youth as they, in the words of McCormick (2004), "mimic the police surveillance" prevalent in their communities and extend racial profiling to school spaces.

Though the use of weapons scanning racialized schools, it was also a response to the serious problem presented by the proliferation of weapons in the streets that could readily enter schools. In 1993, a study by the Federal Center for Disease Control and the New York City Health Department surveyed 1400 New York City high school students and found that 20 percent of them had carried a weapon of some kind in the last thirty days. Students at schools with weapons scanning were less likely to carry a weapon to school but just as likely as nonscanned students to carry one otherwise. Further, one-third of students said they had been threatened and one-fourth had been involved in a fight. It is also worth noting that this study found that though weapons scanning did stop weapons at the doors of schools, these schools had the same rates of disciplinary incidents (fights, threats, misconduct, etc.) as other schools (Buterbaugh 1993). The study indicated that weapons scanning prevents weapons, not violence.

In exploring the impact of scanning on students at Renaissance, it is crucial to be cognizant of the seriousness of violence in student experience. Throughout the critique of scanning that follows, readers must bear in mind that the community surrounding the Old School campus was one of the more dangerous communities in New York City and that gun and gang violence was very real in student lives. In the four years I followed Renaissance, three students were murdered: one caught in a crossfire as he left an apartment, one taken by surprise in a stairwell and stabbed to death, and one fatally shot by a rival in romance. Many students also had relatives, friends, and relatives of friends who had been murdered in the streets. Additionally, several students had survived gunshot wounds or knife incidents and bore those scars, while many more had witnessed shootings or the aftermath of them. Thus, lethal violence and vulnerability to it were real anxieties for many students, and their wide acceptance of scanning suggests their fears.

Beyond the immediate issues of school safety, though, scanning and surveillance policies serve a larger symbolic purpose. The issue of school violence became politically charged in the contentious 1993 mayoral race between then-mayor David Dinkins and his challenger Rudy Giuliani (who won). Both candidates proposed aggressive policies for school safety, including pitches to station a police officer in every school and expand weapons scanning (Olmstead 1993). Thus, the use of weapons scanning in schools such as Old School has symbolic impact not just for the students who experience it daily but also for potential voters who may never set foot in such a school but who perceive inner-city schools as out of control. Scanning students who are frequently construed as violent serves to reassure the public that schools are effectively containing dangerous youth. School discipline is not merely about keeping students "safe" in school but also about representing authority and legitimating the social order. Noguera (1995) notes that heavily symbolic disciplinary policies such as metal detectors serve to restore power rather than restore order.

A number of studies of school violence have critiqued the prevailing construction of schools as neutral, nonviolent places and students and streets as intensely violent. Epp (1996) argues that when schools respond to violence the response focuses on violent children; the violence inherent in schooling practices such as tracking and labeling, confining and controlling, is normalized. Similarly, Spina (2000) argues that school practices such as tracking, standardized tests, overcrowding, and inconsistent enforcement of rules are forms of systemic violence. In fact, a large body of literature critiques the systemic violence enacted by schools through everyday school practices such as those listed above (Oakes 1985; Epp and Watkinson 1996; Watkinson 1996; Ferguson 2000; Obidah 2000; Spina 2000; Astor, Meyer, and Pitner 2001). Other studies have examined specific disciplinary policies and note the problematic constructions of children and the violence inherent in them (Webber 2003). In his ethnographic study, Casella (2001) notes the ways zero-tolerance and other rigid-discipline policies generate violence as they negatively impact the life chances of students, deflect attention away from some of the serious issues students face, and ignore the hidden violence ever present in schools.

The rhetoric around the expansion of weapons scanning and police presence in New York's schools echoed the thrust of this extensive scholarship. The problem of violence is understood as something enacted by students, particularly those attending overwhelmingly Black and Hispanic schools, often masking the ways the schools themselves and, as I will argue, scanning itself, inflict violence as well. This chapter also seeks to expand the surprisingly small body of literature on the impact of scanning. I say this is surprising because there are many studies examining the efforts to stem violence in schools but only a few that focus on weapons scanning itself (Devine 1996; Thompkins 2000; McCormick 2004).

Devine's 1996 discussion of militaristic surveillance-style security in several "scanning" high schools in New York contends that conditions in these schools have shattered the "standard concept of the school and affected the historical teacher-student bond." Devine's analysis of scanning is more theoretical than ethnographic in that he draws on little observational or interview data with students themselves. Though he relies on a nostalgic notion of the "standard concept of schools," his observation that scanning is emblematic of school failure and constructs schools as places to contain students rather than educate them raises a key issue about the symbolic impact of the practice. Despite his problematic method and hostile stance toward urban educators, he usefully notes that scanning bifurcates students (separates their bodies from their minds), denying them academic identities, which magnifies the opposition of student and school.

McCormick's 2004 study of four poets at an inner-city high school similar to Old School draws on the paramilitary apparatuses of scanning such as metal-detectors and security guards in her title metaphor of urban schools as "asylums." Like Devine, she sees scanning as representative of containing rather than educating Black school-age populations—a form of giving up on these students. She calls attention to the ways scanning symbolized the criminalization and marginalization of Black youth as it also represented racial profiling inside the school and outside of it. She also argues that on a deeper level, scanning inflicts a psychic violence that enacts students' marginality in visceral ways, particularly in the ways it makes students wait to enter school, and generally sets a hostile tone for the school day. Both Devine and McCormick argue that scanning is a dehumanizing process that undermines academic pursuits and increases student marginality. They also both contend that scanning normalizes the impoverishment of these communities as it symbolizes the failure of inner-city Black communities to take advantage of the opportunities available to them. However, neither author draws on a wide sample of students to examine how they experience scanning. In the sections that follow, I bring student voices into the critical examination of scanning.

Many critics of aggressive school policies have lumped scanning with other forms of surveillance such as zero-tolerance policies that often exact very severe penalties (including expulsion) for weapons offenses regardless of the context or the kind of weapon. Though these policies share similar assumptions about students and deflect attention away from more systemic inequalities, weapons scanning deserves particular attention because of its expense, invasiveness, symbolic power, and concentration in segregated schools. The relative silence on scanning reproduces it as a natural and unexceptional part of urban schooling, just as the demonstration of scanning procedures at Renaissance's orientation did. Given the profound impact it has on school culture at Renaissance and other schools and that such practices are expanding, examining scanning specifically is necessary. Further, since scanning is the transitioning ritual that brings students from the streets into school space, it is a crucial site of student/school conflict. This chapter seeks to further our understanding of the meaning of scanning and its role in constructing school space, student identities, and student/school relationships.

Scanning and Time

One of McCormick's critiques of scanning is that it forces students to wait to enter school, a ritual that daily confirms their marginality. A common complaint among Renaissance students (six of thirty-one interviewees) was that scanning wasted their time and made them late. McCormick's discussion of the meaning of waiting is particularly useful here because time itself was a crucial area of struggle at Renaissance. Not only did scanning require students to go through a process that took time, they often had to wait outside in the cold for their turn to pass through the scanner. Stacy (HA; see academic orientation abbreviations in the Introduction, pages 14–15) noted in her interview that the doors to the scanning area were regularly not open until eight o'clock in the morning (first period began at 8:15) and that "they [security] just don't care if you get to class on time." Thomas (HA) also complained about the guards making him wait. One of the ongoing struggles with scanning was over whose time it should be on. Students noted that some days scanning went very quickly, but on other days it could take fifteen minutes or more. They insisted on their right to arrive at the building "on time" (when their classes began) while security insisted that the students should arrive at least fifteen minutes prior to the start of class to ensure that they could be in their classroom on time. Some students suggested, with corroboration from the assistant principal (AP) in charge of security, that arriving early often would not ensure getting to class on time. One issue the AP of security noted was that the SSOs had a very high rate of absenteeism and that some days they simply were too shorthanded to get students through quickly.

When I taught second-period classes (the first class of the day for many Renaissance students), the students drifted in over the first fifteen minutes of the period with only about one-third of my students in the room when the class officially began at nine o'clock. First- and second-period classes also usually had high absence rates and students complained that if they arrived more than fifteen minutes into the period they were held in the lunchroom until the next period. Student insistence that scanning made them late emphasized their shift of this time onto school time. Thus, though generally cooperative during the actual process (there were exceptions), many students resisted the wasting of their time by refusing to accommodate the time demands of scanning.

Alice's Image and the Meaning of Time

McCormick theorizes that the disrespect projected by making students wait reinforces their marginality. "Wait repeatedly," she writes, "and, on some level, you must come to believe that you are expendable" (38). This process emphasizes "disposability"; that the students' time is not worth anything and that they are not doing anything of meaning or value. In a capitalist society in which time is money, treating people as if their time is worthless suggests that they are also worthless. McCormick's recognition of the way student time is squandered during scanning emphasizes the less obvious ways scanning inflicts psychological violence and shapes the ways students relate to schooling. To expand on her observation about scanning, I draw on an event that occurred in the "History Theater" elective class I taught in the fall of 1997. This class used Augusto Boal's technique of "Image Theater" to explore social and historical issues.

The class met second period and was an eclectic mix of academically oriented students and very popular but alienated and ambivalent students. Most mornings, it took a few minutes after the bell to have a full group, but one day the class didn't come at all. Eventually Alice and Tarika, two very vocal and alienated girls, arrived in uncharacteristically foul moods. They explained that everyone was having to go through individual hand scanning and have their bags searched, so it was taking forever for the students to get upstairs. Slowly, a few more students arrived, also angry about the morning's delays. I suggested that they design an "image" (a still scene created for critique) of scanning because it clearly was a pressing issue. Alice shot into action and dragged a table into the middle of the floor and then another, leaving a narrow passage between them. The others, picking up the visual clues, added a table to the side indicating the passage created by the walk-through metal detector and the x-ray bed next to it. Alice directed her classmates to play students on the other side of the scanners and instructed another girl to block the passage. As other students entered the room, Alice directed them to the crowded side of the image and they readily recognized the activity without instruction. When most of the class had arrived (more than thirty minutes after the class officially began) and had been placed in the image, it depicted a huge crowd of students on one side, all pushing toward a narrow passage that was blocked by another student who appeared determined to prevent them from getting through. Alice and Tarika stood on the open side of the scanners, their backs to the students, and appeared to joke with each other.

I suggested that a few students step out of the image so that they could be "spect-actors" (the audience that participates in the interpretation and enactment of images). "No!" Alice responded firmly. "Tell me what *you* see, Miss!" When groups performed images I usually led class discussion by asking the others to "tell me what you see," so she was clearly turning the tables on me, emphasizing that I was the audience for this image. I described what I saw and then asked if this was accurate—do the guards just stand around? "Yes!" the class chanted as they broke into a cacophony of stories about the indifference of the guards.

With only a few minutes remaining, I asked the class what the ideal would be—if this image was real, what would the ideal entry be? Alice, remaining in charge, immediately lined up her classmates and moved the "guard" away from the passage. She and Tarika (the guards) invited students through and appeared to be working hard at completing the scanning process quickly. Rather than the bottleneck of the previous image, this image implicated a flow of students passing through. What stood out to me was that each of the guards wore a huge smile. "Yeah," responded Alice, "it would be better if they were friendly." The critique of scanning that Alice enacted supports McCormick's analysis of the ways scanning normalizes the marginality of students. The first image suggested that the process was unnecessarily slow and that the SSOs were indifferent to student frustrations. They also openly mocked students by joking around when they knew the students were waiting. When asked to depict the ideal, Alice did not get rid of scanning but wanted it humanized. She wanted the whole procedure to be more orderly and respectful—calmer, kinder, and more efficient.

McCormick links the wasting of student time and the unproductive quality of scanning to the marginality of students in the broader society. Noting the high rates of unemployment and underemployment in their communities, the high incarceration rates, and heavy surveillance by police, she recognizes the violence inherent in imposing this marginality on students every morning. Scanning echoes the many ways poor people are disrespected, particularly through having to wait in long lines for everything. Alice's image recognized the messages the waiting sent.

Safety and Scanning

The daily scanning ritual at the Old School campus did not differentiate students by the three separate schools that operated in the building. They were all scanned in the student cafeteria, which had an entrance near the street. There, they formed two lines, girls and boys scanned separately, though some students indicated that they went in either line, so it is not clear how rigidly these gender lines were maintained. Each student began by emptying his or her pockets and walking through an airport-style metal detector. Though the ritual may initially seem similar to that which most travelers go through on airplanes, there are differences. The sensitivity of the walk-through metal detectors in schools is generally set at a much higher level than would be found at airports in order to catch "boxcutters" (generally, small plastic cases that held razor blades), which have a very low metal content (Gendar and Bode 2002). The sensitivity, however, seemed to vary from day to day according to many students, though an HA male said that he had to go for hand-scanning on most days even though he never had banned items.

Serafina (HA), in an email sent shortly after graduating, described the process: "If the radar is high in terms of metal detection you will be sent around for scanning and NYPD officers will be standing to ensure that you go around to be scanned [by handheld metal detectors]. If the radar is not high, you may proceed to class." She suggests that on "high" days, the detection was so sensitive that all students were subject to the more invasive hand-scanning, which required "arms out, legs spread apart, hands forward, etc." In addition to the physical scanning of student bodies, any contraband found in pockets or bags was seized. Serafina continued, "There is also a box where 'unlawful' items were placed; unlawful in terms of the school's regulations." Her emphasis on the word "unlawful" highlighted that the school banned many perfectly legal materials. Though school officials have little control over weapons scanning at their schools (these decisions are made by the city's Office of School Safety), they do control the additional items for which students are searched. In this sense, school officials co-opted weapons scanning to assert school authority and school protocols at the door.

Most students like Serafina accepted scanning as a safety measure but expressed anger as well:

> I felt scanning was necessary. It is the unfortunate reality of [Old School] and the neighboring schools. Scanning prevented, to a great extent, violent episodes at [Old School]. The manner in which this procedure was carried out was perhaps not very positive. Students often times felt as criminals; we were indeed treated that way.

It is interesting to note that she referred to the school as "Old School" and not "Renaissance," in part because at the door, the schools were lumped together simply as Old School. The failure to differentiate between the schools at the door inhibited each school from developing its own identity and undermined the reform effort at Renaissance that sought to distance itself from the negative reputation of Old School.

Tashona (HA) supported scanning, including the confiscation of banned items, more completely than many of her peers. Nonetheless, like most student interviewees, she was also critical of the process that equated students with criminals. To the question "Do you think scanning is necessary?" she answered,

Yes, because . . . when you come to school . . . they give you rules, "No walkmans, no hats, no beepers or pagers, no telephones." But, still students bring it, so I think that scanning is good because . . . when students do bring their stuff to school, they take it away. . . . . But, in a way, to contradict myself, um, scanning makes you feel like you're in prison because you can't go out of the school, and you see bars all over the place; what else are you to think [other than] that you're in some kind of jail.

The use of "prison" and "criminal" as a metaphor for scanning was pervasive among students and among policy makers and school leaders (Berger 1991 and 1992; Makin 1994). A popular phrase that sometimes popped up in graffiti in the neighborhood was "Schools not Prisons," a slogan demanding a greater investment in the education of Black students (particularly males) than in their incarceration. Scanning sent a different message affirming the connection between the school and the criminal justice system.

The parallels between entering school and prison were more pronounced than the mere visual imagery of the scanning apparatus. The process was also invasive and visceral. Many students complained that they didn't like having their things gone through or the scanner rubbed too close to their bodies. Students complained about the use of the scanner to invade private space. Samuel (AL) complained,

If I'm getting searched and my bag goes through the machine twice, why you gonna dig your hand in my bag, making me feel like I did a crime, like I'm doing something? If you searching up my wallet and I got my money in there. I got pictures. I got private stuff.

The breach of students' right to privacy enacted through searching their wallets and handling their personal belongings by indifferent and perhaps hostile SSOs was humiliating and caused resentment. As Samuel suggests, these searches echo the kind of aggressive search that police conduct when looking for stolen or illegal items. It doesn't just suggest his potential criminality, but it also makes him feel as if he is under arrest as a suspect of a crime.

Though many students noted that scanning made them feel like criminals, they also agreed that the practice created at least a minimal sense of security. Serafina (HA) explained, "I felt safer knowing that there was scanning, but students need not have weapons to cause harm. Nonetheless, scanning certainly impacted on my feeling safe." A high-achieving student in a focus group stated emphatically, "Do I mind scanning? Miss, I wish they scanned people before they could come on my block!" Her statement suggests that violence in the community was clearly linked to violence at school, and she, at least, felt protected from it by the process.

A number of students defined feeling safe as the absence of weapons. Daniel (AO) responded, "School is safe? Yeah, to a certain point, yeah. I never been hurt or none of that in school. I think it is safe. I never saw nobody get shot and killed and stuff like that in school." He seems to be mulling over the question on safety and concludes that because no one has been shot or killed, the school is safe. Scanning defined safety to mean no weapons, but this definition drew attention away from other forms of violence such as bullying and intimidation that Serafina hinted at as well as the violence of the SSO aggressively inspecting students' wallets and bodies.

Students, too, recognized the dilemma that violence presented. They were afraid of more severe incidents and did feel that the ability to stop weapons made them safer. However, many students were unsure of how much safer they really were. Tamara (AO) captured the ambivalence about safety felt by her peers. When asked what she liked least about school, she responded, "The violence, too much violence in school. . . . There's a lot of misunderstandings and all around this school. . . . And then again, there's another problem with all these gangs, and everyone want to prove who they are." When asked if she felt safe, however, she responded, "Yeah, I feel safe cause I know about myself. I'm not in anything. . . . You don't see any shootouts in school or anything. They could make it safer, but it's as safe as it could be." Her responses seem to contradict each other in that she focuses on violence in school and then defines the school as safe. She seems to be struggling with what safety means. On the one hand the violence around her—the fights, which she doesn't get into, the gangs, which she isn't into, create a violent environment that oppresses her, but on the other hand, she doesn't feel personally threatened. The emphasis on a personal sense of safety in the context of general violence was common.

Scanning complicated understandings of safety because it created a net at the bottom. There was a lot of violence among students at Old School, including fighting, bullying, and theft as well as verbal and psychological violence enacted through threats and taunting. Scanning, as well as the regular fights and gang presence, may have concealed what Casella (2001) described as "hidden" forms of violence because school officials were unaware of their existence. Scanning created a limit to what could happen in the school itself, but it also may have shaped what students and teachers defined as violence by emphasizing dangerous violence with weapons. Scanning created a sense of safety at the same time that students were unsure of how much it ultimately protected them and from what. Shelly (HA) explained,

> In a way it protects us and in a way it's bad because it keeps us back. . . . I'm a student that's always running late and to have to go through constant scanning. . . . And then on top of it, I find scanning in a way, like, biased because they do it on what you look like or what you wearing that day. I see people they will come just because you will have like big baggy pants on, your hat's on, you look like you're not in a good mood today. They go through triple scanning which is unfair because most of the time you don't have anything on you. But, I think in a way it's biased, but then again it protects us. . . . We haven't heard that much about someone getting stabbed or somebody getting shot."

Shelly's uncertainty about scanning's ultimate impact echoes the ambivalence of many students. In fact, of the students who spoke about scanning, violence, or security issues, only one (of thirty-one) was completely positive and only two defined it as completely wrong. Like Shelly, most students felt it was a necessary practice, but they too were critical of its symbolic and material impact. Shelly called attention to two of the biggest frustrations with scanning: the targeting of certain ways of dressing for "triple" or more extensive scanning and the ways scanning wasted time. The "bias" she notes was a central issue in the ways scanning racialized school spaces.

Racializing Space

As Shelly suggested, students frequently complained about the "bias" of targeting specific fashions. John (Amb) described the ways scanning was implemented day to day to reward certain styles and harass others:

When you come in in the morning and you wearing Timbs and your baggy jeans, and you have, you could either have a book bag or have no book bag, you got the do-rag on, you jacket unzipped and you got your hat on, whatever, and you come through the machine and you beep, automatically, they gonna send you around through the whole phase. And then, like for me, for instance, I come here with my shoes, my slacks, and I dress my preppy prep and I come through and the thing beeps, they don't send me around. They just like, you could go upstairs. They figure, ah, look at the way he dress, he not gonna kill nobody. Like that.

Harold (AO) shared a similar critique:

MD: Are there things that bother you about school?
Harold: That scanning business. I don't like that. I understand that we need it, but . . . I don't like it because I feel they're invading my privacy and . . .
MD: You mean they go through your bags?
Harold: Yeah.
MD: Everybody's?
Harold: No, sometimes they choose randomly, or if you ring through the machine then you definitely have to go around, but sometimes they just judge you by the way you look and tell you to go get [hand] scanned.
MD: And what kind of judgment is that?
Harold: People that dress with like, hoodies and dark clothes. People that dress . . . casual [gestures to his own clothes, which included a polo shirt and jeans], they don't really get it, even if they do ring. They don't, the guards don't tell them.

Though the issue of safety is accepted by most students, something more than the removal of weapons and banned paraphernalia is going on. At the moment when students meet the school, the institution insists on a culturally narrow notion of the good student. In some ways scanning is a cleansing ritual that makes student bodies fit for the institution by removing the elements of the street. Such a practice clearly identifies certain items and cultural markers as "unclean." As the students above describe, styles overly identified with the street and hip-hop culture were negatively constructed through scanning. Students from across the academic spectrum who donned a wide range of styles all noted that students (males particularly) wearing baggy jeans, hoodies, and other Black-identified styles always came under intense scrutiny. However, occasionally girls were sent home for wearing skirts too short or for wearing too much red or blue (the colors of the two biggest street gangs, the Bloods and the Crips).

Tashona (HA), who generally endorsed weapons scanning, complained that one thing she didn't like was the physical invasiveness of the scanner:

> Tashona: And they're sitting there scanning you and they want to scale up on you and take all your stuff and go through your hair and stuff like that.
>
> MD: Have they done that, have they gone through people's hair?
>
> Tashona: Like if you have a scarf on, like if your religion is Muslim or something like that, they be all up in your scarf with the scanning thing.

Tashona's suggestion that the head coverings worn by Muslim women were inappropriately scanned is interesting. There were extremely few visibly Muslim girls (none of which I was aware) who wore a scarf/veil every day at Renaissance. However, many girls wore head wraps that they linked to African culture and style but which were not permitted in school. Students often claimed the right to wear hats and head wraps on religious grounds, perhaps because such arguments seemed more valid than asserting cultural traditions. Tashona may have felt less confident asserting the cultural value of head wraps and thus referred to the more institutionally legitimate headwear of Muslim women. Though not a Muslim, she probably resented the aggressive searching of head wraps because she often wore one. A serious student who wanted rules enforced, her desire to wear a head wrap presented a dilemma posed specifically by scanning. Her example suggests one of the subtle ways scanning constructs oppositional student identities as it created a tension between following school rules and maintaining an overt connection to Black identity. I will return to this point shortly.

Students widespread criticism of the targeting of specific fashions suggests that Black cultural identity is attacked during scanning, setting the tone for the distrust of the school that permeates student culture. What is also notable in several of the student descriptions of the ritual, "preppy-prep" styles or "casual" dress were rewarded with easy passing through scanning. These styles were implicitly connected to White culture—preppy, nonstreet identified, mainstream catalog and store styles—particularly in contrast to clothing that was linked to the street, hip-hop and Black culture.

One of the symbolic roles of scanning is to clearly differentiate school space from street space by coercing students to remove such styles, at least at the entry point. Most students responded with the symbolic gesture of taking off their hats and do-rags to move through scanning more quickly. Samuel (AL) noted that he didn't get hand-scanned as much as he used to: "If I had my do-rag on my head, or my hat, I would get searched. . . . I just take it off. I wear it when I'm over here [referring to Renaissance's space]." However, this ritual of cleansing students of street elements also differentiated the school from local cultures and student identities. In assaulting styles linked to Black identity (including head wraps and beads, discussed further below) scanning also constructed the school as "White space" where Black cultural styles were not appropriate.

Scanning racializes school space in a number of ways. As noted by Devine and McCormick, it is a practice that marks segregated schools. Recognizing the racial component of the policy, Samuel (AL) observed, "I wonder if these White kids get searched like we get searched." Thus, scanning marks a clear distinction between schools serving large minority populations and those serving White students. Though teachers were not asked about their perceptions of scanning and its impact on students, and generally teachers did not witness scanning at all, a few noted its impact. One teacher, David, echoed Samuel's critique explaining what he liked least about working at Renaissance:

> I think what I like least is that a lot of people kinda get down on the kids, you know. And it comes from, like, the metal detectors; I really don't like that. That to me is really abusive, and you know, if you're not going to put it in every school in the city then, you know, its just not fair to do that to our kids.

David links people getting "down on the kids," having low expectations, for example, to scanning, which constructs students as "criminals," another way of being down on them. He concludes the process is "definitely racist; whether the guns are going in, it doesn't matter, it still makes kids . . . feel like criminals." In this way, scanning marked Renaissance as a Black school and criminalized its students.

While scanning marked the school as a Black school, within the building scanning defined school space as implicitly White by privileging mainstream "preppy-prep" styles and attacking styles linked to Black identity. Many scholars have examined the extent to which Black students construct academics as "White" (Ogbu 1988; Horvat and Lewis 2003; Foley 2005), however, little attention has been paid to the ways schools themselves reinforce this construction. Scanning is one such site through which schooling is linked to whiteness and separated from blackness, and importantly, the school itself is establishing these boundaries.

Constructing Oppositional Identities

One of the debates at the center of understanding the achievement gap has questioned whether Black students (and other involuntary minorities), responding to their historical and lived experiences, construct schooling as a project of White domination and therefore antithetical to Black identity. The rich literature within this debate, discussed in the introduction, focuses primarily on student perceptions and behaviors. Some studies have suggested that schools also participate in this process. Particularly, Flores-Gonzalez (2005) notes that school policies that bar low-performing students from after-school activities and teams help create oppositional identities. Here, I argue that through scanning, the school plays a far greater role in constructing such identities as it explicitly excludes certain cultural identities and questions academic identities.

To examine the ways scanning operated to attack aspects of student identities, I draw on one incident that is worth exploring at length. In this incident, Serafina (HA) was arrested during scanning because she refused to accept the stripping of her academic and her cultural identity. She described this incident in an email a year after it happened:

Backdrop: At [Old School] there was a list of restricted items that students were not allowed to bring into the building. For example, bandannas, markers, knives of course, beads, and highlighters. Most of these items, if not weapons, were signs of gang activity. For example, if a student is wearing all blue clothing, blue beads, blue marker, etc., he/she is most likely a "Crip." Students often used the markers to write graffiti on the walls so those items were prohibited.

Incident: The scalpel is to a doctor as the marker is to a debater. I would come to school with yellow markers for debate and other school oriented purposes. This was a restricted item, however [principal] wrote a note to the security officers for me to be permitted to bring these items into school. On one particular morning I did not have the note with me but the security guards knew very well who I was and they also knew of the note. They said it didn't matter, but they needed to see the actual note. As a result my highlighters were confiscated and placed into the box. This incident is twofold; it also involves my beads. The beads I wore were of African colors, yellow, green, black, and red, they were in no way gang related which the officers knew very well. I wore these beads for cultural reasons. I think at times they felt the need to exert their "authority" but in unnecessary ways. I was told to relinquish my beads and I refused to do so. In protest, I popped the necklace, placed the beads in my mouth and dropped the string on the floor (I laugh at my action now, ha-ha, a progressive rebel in the making). The guards were already not pleased with what I did. I then proceeded to go into the box to retrieve my highlighters. Immediately, approximately 7 NYPD police officers began to push me down onto the lunchroom table. The force was not needed, as I was very fragile and some of the guards were much heavier and stronger than myself. My neck was jammed and I was taken to the security office. At that time I realized that I had bruises on my arm as the cuffs were forced on too hard. I took pictures of these but have lost them. . . . I was given a notice to appear in court on the charge of misconduct and the judge immediately dropped the charges.

I quote Serafina here extensively because this one incident so clearly demonstrates what many of her peers hinted at—that through scanning, the school constructed Black cultural identity (not just street identity) as opposed to schooling at the same time that the incident implies that students are nonacademic by nature.

Two key aspects of Serafina's identity were assaulted that day at scanning: her identity as a debater, a scholastic activity, was denied as they removed her highlighters (the symbol of debaters, as the scalpel is the symbol of the surgeon), and her identity as a Black woman through confiscating her beads. Usually she carried a note that gave her permission, authorizing her to carry contraband highlighters. Though the guards knew her and knew she was a debater, they refused to recognize her legitimacy as a student/scholar without the letter that conferred that identity on her.[1] At scanning, her academic identity did not reside in her body but was vouched for by the principal via a note. Without external acknowledgement, her academic seriousness was not recognized—it was not part of her but was something that must be signified externally. Her insistence on her right to her highlighters expressed by diving into the box to retrieve them suggests the depth of their symbolic value. The failure of the SSOs to recognize her status as a debater and student despite knowing who she was underscores the ways that scanning, in an effort to prevent graffiti and other mischief, constructed students as lacking an academic orientation and therefore having no legitimate use for such things. Taken as they are, without special passes, visas really, students at Renaissance were not academic.

At the same time that Serafina's academic identity was denied, the symbols of her Black identity were also taken from her. In the earlier examples of profiling, the styles students noted as those targeted at scanning were often styles that could also be associated with street and "thug" identities—hoodies, baggy jeans, and braids. The targeting of these styles, despite their popularity among many nongang members, might be justified as part of an effort to keep gangs out of school. Serafina's beads, though, were clearly symbols of Black identity. But these, too, were equated with gangs, thus degrading powerful aspects of student cultural identity.

Though many researchers have sought to put Ogbu's oppositional culture thesis to rest, it must be reconsidered in light of the cultural and symbolic work that scanning Black students does. At scanning, it is the school itself that constructs schooling as a White project in opposition to Black cultural identities. Scanning further opposes blackness and schooling through denying students an academic identity that would make them legitimate carriers of things such as highlighters, magic markers, and compasses with points. Sarafina's experience captured all these tensions and, perhaps what made it notable, was her refusal to passively accept these rules despite her general commitment to schooling.

Sarafina's experience is not unique. The New York City Civil Liberties Union has received hundreds of complaints about rough treatment of students and unwarranted arrests at front-door scanning (Medina 2007a). In 2005 and again in 2007, principals were arrested for interfering with an attempted arrest. In the 2007 case, an honors student arrived at school about fifteen minutes early and expected to be admitted so she could study and speak with her teachers. She was told to come back later, and when she insisted she be admitted, an altercation broke out between the student and two SSOs (Medina 2007a; Medina 2007b). This more recent incident is strikingly similar to Sarafina's story in that in both cases high-achieving young women found their academic identities denied as they entered school. In both cases, the young women were arrested, though at Renaissance the SSOs were content to issue a summons and bring her to the principal. In the 2007 incident, the student and her principal were marched out in handcuffs.

In Sarafina's story, she repeatedly insists that "the security guards knew very well" that she was a debater, that she had a note, that she was not in a gang, and her beads were not gang signifiers. In insisting that the security officers knew but acted contrary to this knowledge, she calls attention to the multiple regimes of truth in operation at scanning and that are in play throughout the school day. The SSOs are in a very difficult position—they both know and don't know who she is. As individuals, the SSOs know her and about her academic activity. But as functionaries of the institution, they do not know who she is. She is a generic student, any student, and must be treated exactly as all the others are. The SSOs must carry out policies even when they know individual students and cases. The local and immediate face-to-face knowledge that they possess is negated by the institution's construction of students. Thus, the SSOs know who Sarafina is, but the institution does not know, or, rather, the institution knows that it is easier to establish and enforce blanket policies for generic students. Part of Sarafina's actions are informed by her anger at the rejection of local knowledge in favor of the impersonal and demeaning practices of scanning, which in her case, assaulted two deeply valued facets of her identity. Samuel (AL), an astute critic of schooling, recognized that the security officers were not attacking him personally when they searched through his wallet: "Yo man, it's they job. Someone else is making them do it." His separation of the individuals from the role they fill recognizes this double-knowledge that Serafina rebelled against the morning she was clapped in handcuffs.

The depersonalization of knowledge and the imposition of generic and stereotyped identities onto students, regardless of their accomplishments, also impacted the reform effort at Renaissance. Jim, a former dean, familiar with the ritual of scanning, described what he saw as systemic violence enacted through scanning:

> The biggest problem facing our school is the fact that we . . . are split into three schools, but it is one physical space. I've always said that even though we have three separate schools . . . still, it feels like one building with 3,000 kids. It feels like one of the old, big, dinosaur schools, and security is run like the Gestapo. In one sense we are doing some progressive stuff in the classroom, but we are limited in how far we can go. If we had our own building, everything would change. . . . Right now, a lot of what's happening in the hallways, a lot of the feeling of the school, a lot of the kids' perceptions of this place, are still based on one building.
>
> MD: Can you give me any examples of that?
>
> Jim: Um, I guess a single thing that stands out for me is security. They come in such huge numbers getting scanned in an airport style. Metal detectors, it's really not, you know, you go through something like that, you're a number. And you're being treated, you know, processed.

His recognition of the violence inherent in seeing people as mere numbers validates Serafina's rejection of this dehumanizing process. He sees this impersonal, undifferentiated morning ritual in conflict with the "progressive stuff" going on in classrooms and suggests that this contradiction limits the effectiveness of Renaissance's reform agenda. The morning scanning lumps students together, failing to see them as students at different schools, debaters, proud Black people, scholars, athletes, and so on. Such a practice is at odds with a reform effort that claims to be student centered. A guidance counselor who attended scanning sporadically also emphasized this dehumanizing aspect of the ritual: "I try to go to scanning just to say 'good morning,' you know, just so someone smiles at them and says good morning because otherwise, no one does and that's no way to start the day."

Serafina's story also highlights that scanning was a   violent ritual. Though such direct scuffles were not everyday occurrences, they did happen despite the impossibility of student victory. Students are scanned one-by-one and are well outnumbered by uniformed police officers. Though students are not generally physically abused, the potential for such handling is always visibly represented through uniformed police officers with their handcuffs at the ready to restrain uncooperative students. Jim's comparison of security to the Gestapo is telling. The Gestapo was so terrifying not only because of the intense violence the officers inflicted but also because of the intense fear they inspired. At scanning, school security takes on this profile. Even on days when no student is arrested or physically restrained, both physical and symbolic violence are present.

Bringing in the Cops

The transfer of school security to the New York Police Department bears further elaboration in this discussion of the ways schools structure oppositional identities. Though school security officers had long worn policelike uniforms and their day-to-day activities changed little, the subtle shift in their identities also had significant symbolic impact because it further connected the school to an institution viewed suspiciously by students. Twenty percent of the students who addressed security issues (six of thirty-one) criticized the presence of "cops" in school, and all thirty-one students brought up the issue when asked either what they disliked or found unfair at school. Many felt that the "cops" were more aggressive than security officers had been because, as Marie (HA) noted, "they feel, well, 'we're cops and we're higher than you.'" Derek (Amb) described cops as more aggressive and less respectful than security guards. He explained the distinctions,

> Some of them don't act like cops. Some of them act like regular people; some of them act like regular security guards that just clear the hallway. Some of them want to be cops and they act bad and they gonna tell you this and they tell you that . . . and they be like, "I'm gonna arrest you" and all this.

Acting like a cop, Derek suggests, means bullying students for no apparent reason. Like him, several students called attention to the threat of "arrest" that seemed to become part of security vocabulary after the transition. Interestingly, he also was aware that the transition to the NYPD did not really change the status of SSOs but did change their mentality, explaining, "They [school security] say they not cops, they just getting trained by them. If you getting trained by them, that's even worse!"

Students perceived that police officers were less respectful and more hostile to them. Samuel (AL) explained the connection clearly: "I been searched by the cops. The same way I get searched by the cops, I get searched up at school." The NYPD has a problematic relationship with Black urban youth in the city. During the period of these interviews, they engaged in a "stop and frisk" program in which they randomly stopped Black and Hispanic young men not suspected of a specific crime and frisked them for drugs or guns. Many of the young men interviewed said they had experienced such harassment by the police. Further, in 1997, a Haitian immigrant was tortured and sodomized by police and, in 1999, Amadou Diallo, a young, unarmed, Black immigrant was gunned down in front of his apartment building by police officers who mistook him for a rape suspect. Both victims in these high-profile cases had not committed a crime. The officers in the Diallo shooting were exonerated as I was completing this study. Such events increased student distrust of police and the sense that there was nothing they could do about police brutality. The linking of school security to the NYPD symbolically connected the school to an institution many students feared and distrusted. The high profile of SSOs, now NYPD, at scanning problematically links school authority with police authority.

In this chapter, I argue that scanning itself exerts psychic and symbolic violence in the process of insuring that the school is less physically violent. This entry ritual, which defines who and in what manner individuals can enter school, impacts the ways students relate to schooling because the ritual generates specific ideologies about what it means to be a good student. Others have noted the ways scanning negatively marks Black schools as dangerous, which links race to violence (Devine 1996; McCormick 2004). More than this, I argue scanning structures school spaces and frames school in opposition to student identities, particularly negating academic identities. Scanning also undermined the reform process that was underway at Renaissance by dehumanizing students, negating the identities of individual schools, and contradicting the student-centered rhetoric of the reform effort.

However, recognizing the intense symbolic violence of scanning and its ideological work cannot be the end of our analysis. Scanning is only one facet of the school and does not exhaust its identity. Both McCormick and Devine rely on scanning to frame the schools they study, but even as scanning frames the school day, it does not frame the full experience of school. Rather, it is one site where specific discourses, though powerful and aggressively promoted, are circulated, but at no other site within the school can school authority assert this much control over students. It is a mistake to limit our understanding of schools as merely the institution represented at scanning. Despite the aggressive show of strength, Renaissance is a complex and dynamic school, not a simple and static one. Just as the SSOs who arrested Serafina navigated through multiple knowledge regimes, multiple ways of knowing circulate in the halls and classrooms as well.

Despite the forceful show at scanning, students reinhabited the styles that were targeted at scanning as they, like Samuel, put their do-rags and hats back on once they got "over here." Students also aggressively occupied the school and offered a counter-balance to scanning in the ways they claimed the halls. McCormick and Devine both assume that the level of force at scanning is maintained throughout the school, but, as the next chapter will demonstrate, this is not the case. We need to recognize the powerful symbolic and physical violence enacted by scanning but must not over-determine the nature of urban schools.

3

. . . .

"It's just all about being popular"

Hallways as Thirdspace

During the four minutes between periods, I usually stood in the hallway to help move students along to class. Though this was a general expectation of all teachers, many did not do it, perhaps because standing in the halls—the nexus of student culture—was an exercise in futility. Because I spent two years teaching in a classroom on the corridor that was the center of student social life, I became intensely aware of my powerlessness in the face of this assertive student hall culture. Students taunted, teased, insulted, and sometimes came near blows (on rare occasions, fights actually began), and my efforts to contain such volatile behavior were met with indifference and even laughter. I could often see more than half my class hanging out within ten feet of my classroom door, and yet most would still enter the room five to ten minutes late. To try to hasten them in, I would go around and tell them directly that the bell had rung, an effort usually politely ignored, though occasionally met with hostility.

One student particularly resented my nudging and yelled at me one day, "I'm not done yet!" At other times my intrusions into their hall activity were met with disrespectful commands to "Mind your own business, Miss!" Students who rushed into class in the first few minutes after the bell were usually not marked late. Several teachers I interviewed admitted the same gap in their vigilance and many students reported this assumption as well (see chapter 5). Student rejection of my authority until they had entered my room and their insistence on finishing their "business" before coming to class successfully extended "passing" time—the time students were allowed to be at large in the halls as they passed from one class to the next—by about five minutes beyond the official late bell.

More than just an effort to extend the time they were not in class, the defiant lateness I regularly encountered indicated that students felt in possession of the halls. One group of boys who ignored my command to go to class sneered, "We in the halls Miss. You ain't got no weight." I use these anecdotes to clarify the significant ownership students took of the halls and the marginality of teachers in that space. I also use them to note my own partisanship in the struggles over the halls. As a classroom teacher I contended with the struggles daily. I wanted to be able to begin my lessons on time, not to have to step into the halls in response to rowdiness during my lessons, and not to have my lessons constantly interrupted by students entering throughout the period. The lively activity of the halls undermined my efforts. As a teacher, I did not see them as a space of equal significance to the classroom. They were a distraction—something kids enjoyed more than class but that offered them little. The fierceness with which students insisted on their right to control the halls for as long as possible suggests that there was much going on, but I was not able to see it. Thus, when I began interviewing students about what they did in the halls, I was surprised by the logical, rule-bound space they described. As a teacher I experienced the halls as chaos, but, in fact, they were a meaningful cosmos.

The formidable assertion of the halls as a student-controlled space must be understood in relationship to the high profile of school authority at scanning and teacher control in the classrooms. Once students passed through scanning, the school was unable to sustain such an intense display of power. As students dispersed into the hallways, their numerical advantage and their collective insistence on freedom in the halls enabled them to exercise far more autonomy. In these spaces, students installed a derivative of their local street cultures that affirmed local identities as well as broader notions of Black identity. As the anecdotes above attest, school personnel were socialized, as I was, into an acceptance of this spatial regime. At least during the extended passing time, students ruled the halls, and school personnel made minimal effort to enforce school rules.

Most students, including high-achieving and academically oriented students, participated in this hall culture. By participate, I mean that they at least stopped and socialized between classes. It should be noted that Renaissance occupied a small portion of a larger school building and that the east corridor, about 150 feet long, was the central hangout for Renaissance students and often also hosted "visitors" from the other two schools as well. "The halls" were generally this one hallway that many students packed into between periods, even if their classes were not nearby. This chapter explores how students appropriated hall space and there created a community "exclave" of local youth culture. I call attention to what I term "the exclave effect" (the ways students import and adapt local cultures into schools) to move beyond the limits of debates over oppositional culture and make the complex interactions between local and dominant cultures more visible.

Reconsidering the Oppositional Culture Thesis

As I have noted in chapter 2, debates about oppositional culture have focused on John Ogbu's contention that oppositionality in urban education emerges historically from the subordinate position of involuntary minorities (Fordham and Ogbu 1986; Ogbu 1988). Black students bring this culture with them to class and reject schooling as a project of domination and denigration. However, Ogbu's critics have claimed that many high-achieving involuntary minorities strongly identify with their cultural and racial groups. (Flores-Gonzalez 1999; Conchas 2001; Horvat and Lewis 2003). This literature focuses on high-performing students to negate Ogbu's monolithic construction of oppositional culture. Previous works have not adequately addressed the role of local cultures in shaping responses to schooling, particularly the role of local cultures across the spectrum of academic performance.

Ogbu's assumption that the culture some adolescent students create in schools is a replication of their racial and ethnic cultures has obscured the complex ways these students contend with schooling. The exclave effect corrects Ogbu's theories because it emphasizes that the culture students install in the halls draws on their local and street cultures but is also adapted in significant ways to suit the school and student context. At the same time, it does not reduce the substance of those local cultures to what students bring into schools.

While the exclave in the halls is an adaptation of local cultures, it does not mirror the streets and it is not simply an inversion of the classroom. It pushes the limits of school policies but is not merely what the classroom is not. It is different, an alternative produced by students for themselves. In this sense, the exclave is what Soja (1996) has termed a "thirdspace," which responds to binaries without reproducing or negating them. In other words, the ethos of the halls highlights tensions between school-oriented and street-oriented identities, between academic participation and disidentification, and between group solidarity and individualism, but "thirdspace" also posits a third or alternative option as well. It allows that students move along a continuum of resistance and that while they are informed by these binaries they are not limited to them. Composing the exclave of the halls as a thirdspace helps explain the wide range of student responses to hall and academic culture, but it is important to emphasize that the halls are not a magical or idyllic space where students are free to explore a range of possibilities. It is part of the real world with rigid codes, social hierarchies, and symbolic and physical violence.

Recently, Akom (2007) has argued for the possibility of "free spaces" within schools. Free spaces, he explains, are places that affirm and value shared cultures and historical experiences and enable democratic or radical possibilities. In his words, free spaces are "places to recover and enjoy group identity, places to cultivate self and communal respect, cooperation, and community uplift" (613). Though I would welcome such a phenomenon, the halls must not be mistaken for such a free space because though students exercise more agency and affirm shared cultural and racial identities in the halls, students also impose rigid hierarchies amplifying oppressive social relationships. The halls offer students more freedom in some regards but restrict and limit students in others. Thirdspace is a more useful framework through which to explore these spaces.

The value of thirdspace as a theoretical framework as well as inadequacies of current theories on student resistance became apparent when I tried to determine to what extent the halls operated as an oppositional space. Many students (twenty of thirty-seven: six HA, six AO, four Amb, and four AL) insisted that participation in the classroom and the halls were unrelated, that good grades did not prevent popularity (the central prize of the halls), and that the halls and classrooms, though parallel places, were somewhat irrelevant to each other. However, eleven other students constructed the two spaces as opposed (two HA, four AO, one Amb, and four AL). Three of these students admitted that they used to walk the halls regularly but stopped when they realized they might not graduate. They felt that it was not possible to be a notable presence in the halls while also passing classes. Two high achievers also noted that full participation in the hall culture required a rejection of academics and vice versa. In addition, six students expressed both positions, sometimes noting the oppositional qualities and other times emphasizing the parallel nature of classes and halls (one HA, two AO, one Amb, two AL). No students suggested that the two were complimentary spaces—that success in one promoted success in the other.

Further adding to the difficulty of defining the halls, sixteen students in the sample (four claiming parallel, three uncertain, and nine claiming opposition) indicated that peer pressure was a major factor informing cutting class and other nonacademic behavior. Of these sixteen, six described direct experiences when peer pressure negatively affected them—either making them cut class or making them feel badly about their academic success. Two others described ostracizing students one termed "teachers pets"—those too eager to please the teacher. Seven students (four claiming parallel, one uncertain, and two claiming opposition) also explicitly explained that though good grades themselves did not undermine popularity, there were limits to an individual's popularity if he or she was too focused on school work. Behavior that placed academic work over the peer group—wanting to complete an assignment instead of gossiping in class, not allowing peers to cheat from one's work, choosing to do homework instead of hanging out with friends—marked one as a "nerd" and destroyed one's social status. In these ways exclave culture and academic culture were parallel only to a point and were in opposition to each other only to a point. Both constructions of the halls (as parallel or as oppositional) bled into each other, which suggests the limits of binary constructions and the efficacy of the concept of thirdspace to recognize the multiple ways students relate to both the halls and classrooms.

In the remaining sections of this chapter I sketch the general description of the exclave hall culture that emerged across the interviews and around which there was clear consensus. I then deconstruct some of the assumptions and values circulated in this culture to explore the ways the constructions of race, class, sexuality, and gender informed exclave and academic culture. I also explore some of the key values in the halls that conflict with those promoted by the school and complicate and often limit student engagement with schooling. Through this reading of exclave culture I argue for thirdspace as a framework that captures the complexity and fluidity of the halls.

The Exclave Effect

As I have been suggesting, inner-city schools can be constructed as official enclaves of dominant culture operating as outposts of authority in marginalized communities. Financed and regulated by city- and state-based authorities outside the community, schools promote and project a mainstream culture to a nonmainstream community. School staff rarely live in these neighborhoods, and schools employ a discourse widely associated with White, middle-class society, not that of the local community (Delpit 1995; Stanton-Salazar 1997). Further, the meritocratic values promoted by public schooling—that any one can succeed if she or he works hard—are often contradicted by local knowledge. Structural inequalities of race and class dramatically circumscribe lives in this community. Though many students and their families want to participate in mainstream, middle-class American culture, their experiences of racism and poverty inform a deep ambivalence toward schooling.

Studies of the West Indian experience have noted that though the immigrant generation is hopeful about their future in America, by the second generation, West Indian immigrants experience a decline in status as they become more generically Black and less marked as immigrants. They become assimilated into the reality of American racism, which contradicts their aspirations. This contradiction between aspiration and reality is particularly true for males of West Indian descent (Waters 1999; Lopez 2002). Thus, as a mainstream enclave, Renaissance brings the meritocratic myths of dominant culture into a marginalized community that gives it a tepid reception. While the school as mass education imports dominant culture into the community, students import local culture into the school, especially into the halls, where school authority holds the least sway, enabling this space to emerge as an exclave of the street. While contending with authority in all school spaces, the students' strongest agency is exerted in the halls.

The culture students import into the halls is most notably informed by "the code of the streets," which is defined by Elijah Anderson (1999) as a set of informal rules governing public behavior, at the heart of which is respect. Respect is gained through not allowing oneself to be "dissed" (disrespected) by others, and this is often achieved by fighting anyone who does not "give props" (pay proper deference). This social ritual is informed by the "profound sense of alienation from mainstream society and institutions felt by many poor inner-city black people, particularly the young" (33–34). The high profile of respect, imported from street culture, clarifies the steep tension between street and academic rituals as examined by Flores-Gonzalez (2002) in her study of "street kids" and "school kids."

Though hall rituals are derivative of street culture, they are also altered from street rituals in important ways. Though diminished in numbers compared to their force at scanning, security officers, teachers, deans, and the school aides who circulate in the halls do manage to alter the terms of student engagement. In a study of violent girls at an urban high school, Dickar and Klann (1997) found that the girls they studied preferred to fight at school rather than in the street because at school they were confident no one would pull out weapons and security or teachers would break up fights before they got out of hand. Anything could happen in the street, but in the halls, there were limits precisely because they were inside a school. Nonetheless, what happened in the halls was talked about in the streets, so status gained in the halls enhanced status outside. Further, the halls were spatially small compared to the neighborhood making them a much more densely teenage social space than outside. Thus, the outside was more dangerous and less concentrated with a ready audience for displays of status. Students could count on the security officers to limit the consequences of status games, making the halls attractive as a safer and exclusively adolescent version of the street.

Hall culture diverges from street culture in other ways, too. For example, hall culture constructed a generically Black youth culture though the community itself is clearly marked as immigrant and West Indian. Outside Renaissance, Jamaican and Guyanese restaurants and bakeries compete effectively with fast-food chains. Hair salons and West Indian travel agencies fill the business district. The greengrocers and butchers sold foods such as breadfruit, goat meat, and oxtail, which are unavailable in other parts of the city. Street vendors hawked sugarcane and mangoes along with coconuts, all freshly chopped with a machete. Music vendors blared Caribbean hip-hop and reggae while patois and West Indian accents were frequently heard on the streets. And everywhere—dangling from the rearview mirrors of cars, stamped on bumpers, hung in stores, posted on telephone poles, and blazoned across t-shirts—were the flags and colors of various Caribbean nations. However, back in school, West Indian culture was muted. Students wore pendants, key-chains, and beads that announced their West Indian and national identities but used more Americanized idioms and styles to express themselves.

By referring to hall culture as Black, I seek to emphasize the ways this culture leveled the great ethnic diversity of students through a political and social identification with North American blackness. Though most students claimed West Indian roots, many, in fact, had only loose connections to the Caribbean. Of the thirty-seven students interviewed for this study, eleven were first-generation immigrants who had recent and vivid memories of their home country and were often marked by their accents. Fourteen either were very young when they arrived and have, at best, only distant recollections of their home country and no perceptible accent, or they are second-generation immigrants, having been born in the United States. Twelve students identified themselves as Black, their families having been in the United States for more than two generations. Many of these students referred to being from "down South," though some claimed a West Indian heritage, which suggests that their ancestors may have arrived in earlier waves of West Indian immigration or that their families were culturally mixed. The diversity among students favored a homogenized Blackness in the halls that was grounded in group solidarity and emphasized shared identities.

Students drew on commonly shared cultural experiences, particularly popular Black youth culture, designer fashions, and the culture of the streets, which included gang identification and tough posturing. West Indian culture did have a profile, but it was submerged amid other swirling influences on student identities. For example, the dominant idiom in the halls was what students referred to as "slang," "street," or "street slang" (Black Vernacular English or Ebonics), not island dialects, which many students could not speak. Further, though students said they listened to a wide range of music including reggae and Jamaican hip-hop, the music with which most identified at school was African American hip-hop and R&B such as NAZ, JayZee, and Genuwine.

Even while referring to student culture at Renaissance as a Black culture, it must be noted that Haitian students were specially marked as outside this English-language–dominant Black culture and were marginalized in the widely shared hall culture. They often did not participate in the consumer culture popular among American Blacks and West Indian immigrants. They were perceived as poorer than other students and their use of Haitian Creole, not English, was viewed with suspicion by their English-speaking peers. Many Haitian students were in the ESL program with separate courses often taught by Haitian teachers that further segregated them from the others. Among the anglophone population, "Haitian" was used as a putdown, and Haitian students who were not in the ESL program often hid their cultural identity. However, on Haitian Flag Day (May 18), with some resentment but more resignation, the mainstream student body yielded dominance in the halls to their Haitian peers who ran through them all day shouting proclamations of Haitian pride while waving Haitian flags. Despite generally disparaging Haitian students, the majority of non-Haitians tolerated their right to national pride on that special day.

Though several students like Andrea described their activity in the hall as "chillin'," it was not so relaxed and easygoing as such a term suggests, because hall culture centered on the circulation of social and symbolic capital understood in terms of respect. Students enforced strict codes of dress, conduct, and attitude, based in a social hierarchy around popularity (a cognate of respect). Because popularity and respect were much more defined for boys, I will begin with those rules, which promote oppressive constructions of gender, sexuality, and class.

Defining Masculinity

Jamal (AL), a sophomore, laid out the rules for popularity very clearly. He described the hall scene as "the politics of what they have":

> Jamal: Like, clothes, everybody in competition right now in school. That's what really people come to school for, girls and clothes. . . . 'Cause some people, I know, they won't even come to school . . . [if] they don't know what to wear or if they don't have no money.
> MD: So what is it about money? If you have nice clothes then you'll look like you have money?

Jamal: That's about what it is, cause once people see that, you get girls, you get this and that. It's just all about being popular, basically.

MD: Being popular means what?

Jamal: Like, everybody know you, everybody know who you is, you just like a famous person in school. . . .

MD: What else do you get popular for?

Jamal: Another thing is like, all right, fights. If you have a certain amount of fights and you win them, people will respect you if they fear you. That's another thing people in this school be about. People want to act the hardest and toughest, you know, for what, I don't know.

Almost every student interviewed touched on the same key points in explaining male popularity in the halls suggesting the centrality of boys in the hall.

The Guys with the Gear: Name Brand and Social Rank

"Gear" (expensive clothes with brand names such as Tommy Hilfiger, DKNY, Polo, Guess, etc.) proved that the wearer had money, which gave him access to girls and a higher social rank. Darrell (AO), a senior, explained, "If one person has more money than you that means they're gonna get something else that you want and you can't get 'cause you don't have the money for it." "Something else" was clearly defined by other students as girls and friends. George (AO) commented, "If a person, like, you, have the money, then you be able to get a lot of things and the girls see that. And they like, yeah, I could get any girl, or whatever, because they got money." Beyond the immediate satisfaction of being able to get girls, gear also indicated a higher place in the social hierarchy.

Students often located themselves within hierarchies, whether it was teachers over students, adults over children, or seniors over freshmen. At Renaissance, the cosmos of the hall is also hierarchically ordered, and the boys who have gear are at the top. Daniel (AO) illustrates the hierarchy:

You know, most, for me, I cannot be with nobody that looks bad, tore up and everything. I cannot hang out with them. . . . I just cannot, I just don't know. I feel like they lower than me. They lower than me, financial-wise. I mean, they down here and I'm up here. I don't like . . . it's like your peers, you with the clothes, look good, more presentable. . . . You see kids who got on $100 clothes and everything; you don't see no one who looks like a bum and everything. We all look more, you know, presentable.

Students frequently denigrated those lacking expensive clothes calling them "bummy" or "bums," the bottom of the status hierarchy. The boys had some reason to avoid bummy looks as a number of girls from all academic categories admitted they would not go out with a guy who was not wearing "gear" because, as Loretta (AO) and Tameeka (Amb), both using the same phrase, explained, "You don't want to go out with anybody that look like a bum!" Though most students at Renaissance were poor or working class, looking poor by lacking expensive clothes (especially for young men) led to social marginalization.

The consumer marketplace is a generalized force in child development. In consumerist manner, the students validated oppressive notions of class by denigrating poverty and emphasizing the importance of possessions (the symbolic marker for "money").

Good Girls, Bad Boys: Maintaining Reputations

While gear for boys reproduced a market ethos of conspicuous consumption, it also increased their ability to seduce girls, as the girls above confirm. Many students pointed out that the more "conquests" a boy brags about, the more respected and popular he becomes—a predictable ritual of patriarchy fully embedded in this corridor culture. Camille, an ambivalent senior, reported that

Boys will get respect, by, first of all, saying, okay, they will say, who girl I slept with, who girl I been with, (mockingly) "Oh, son! You did that, Son, oh son! You is my boy, son!" you know. I have been there, because I hang out with a lot of guys, I have heard them talk before. They talk about who girl they have had, who girl did this to them, and they get enough respect too. "Yo, son. I didn't know you had it like that." And they will get that, and it will be no problem for them, because they did whatever they feel like doing. Boys will look up to them.

Though girls were more critical of this practice, all the students acknowledged that boys known to be sexually promiscuous were well respected by both genders.

This familiar gender pattern encourages boys to pursue as many girls as they can. Typically, though, the risks of sexual activity rest largely on girls. Not only can they get pregnant and more easily infected by STDs, but girls also face a pervasive double standard. Beth (AL), a second-year student, explained the traditional gender roles: "Like, girls, if they mess with a certain boy, they called a ho. Boys can mess with everybody in the world, I mean, and they get props for it. So, boys get treated very different than girls." Like Beth, other girls expressed anger over this double standard but also acknowledged that they themselves participated in ostracizing their wayward sisters. Referring to a girl who foolishly went to a boy's house and was sexually ambushed by the boy and his friends, Sharon (AL) noted, "You know, its like, don't none of the girls want to be around her cause its like, you know, you're gonna be with her, you gonna get that name. . . . Everybody's like, 'so that's her primmie to get some head.'" She and her friends ostracize those with bad reputations to protect their own. Girls are held solely responsible for their own reputations even if boys assaulted them against their will.

Fighting and Dominance: Demanding Respect

Fighting was also a way that students gained respect from their peers because it established a student's ability to control how others treated him or her. George (AO) describes the tie between fighting and respect:

> 'Cause some people could come up to you and say, "Ah, he's a herb, he can't fight. He's nothing." And you know, I think, once you fight that person and you beat him, he'll look at himself and, like, "I don't believe he just beat me." You know, and I guess, like, he gets some respect for you. I think, you know, once you finish fighting a person, I think you get respect from that person. That person don't think of you as, you know, somebody low. Once you beat him, he'll look up to you, you know, he's kind of cool, he beat me. He's all right.

Students having the ability to fight well were respected and not picked on by others. A number of students defined respect similarly to Jamal (AL), when he said, "People don't diss you, put it like that . . . basically, people not stepping out of line with you."

Fighting confers respect, but more than this, it confers dominance over other boys and, of course, over girls. Dominance is the ultimate goal of the gear, the sex, and the fighting. Anderson (AL) explains,

> Everybody has it, even animals, you know, down to animals. If a dog stare a dog down, they gonna bark to fight. Exactly how a male and a male stare each other down, they gonna bark to fight. . . . It's like, you know, men, men always do this. You know, it's like, something you have in you, a system of blood, you know, like, you have to be more dominant than somebody else, than the other men, you know. This is something that's been happening for years in every aspect, in everything.

Such assumptions about patriarchy and human nature were reinforced in the halls. Hall culture naturalized social constructions of gender, race, sexuality, and class by exaggerating differences. The emphasis on dominance also suggests a masculine conception of power that conflicts with expectations of submission in the classroom (often requiring submission to a woman).

The key status markers in the halls are also key markers of gang identity. The gang member is able to wear the latest clothes due to the spoils of gang life, is able to seduce more girls because of his money and his cachet as "a thug," and he inspires significant fear in his peers. Patrick (Amb) states, "If you're in a gang, you got respect or whatever, and if you're not in a gang, you're, like, just there. You're one of the other ones." While acknowledging that gang membership did bring popularity, students disliked the violent imposition won by gang status. Melissa (AL) describes, "Its not that people think you really cool, but you know that no one is gonna mess with you cause you down with this and this person." Basically, then, gangs oppress students who lack the power to erase the threat. But most students traded in the gang economy, a stylized version of patriarchal consumerism of violent fighting and displays of dominance in strut-worthy name-brand gear.

During the period of my observation and interviews, the local police department had identified Renaissance as a "Crip school." However, open gang activity was effectively driven underground in the halls as gang colors and other visible gang markers were barred at scanning, and any open signs of gang identity led to suspension or expulsion. None of the students interviewed admitted to being in a gang, though it seemed that at least a few were. Moreover, the dominance of the Crips at the time limited gang violence, since, as Craig (AL) put it, "there's no Bloods to fight." School security once again made the space a protected zone of social life because gang activity was held in check, unlike in the streets themselves.

Dance (2002) notes that in addition to gang membership, there are other levels of gang identification, such as "wannabes" who are not "hard" enough for gang membership but are fascinated by it. Though I could not confirm the number of students actually in gangs, I observed much interest in gangs, particularly in the Crips, the gang that was dominant in the local area. For example, some students frequently crossed out the "B"s on signs around the halls, a popular way of disrespecting the Bloods, rivals to the Crips. I also observed students teaching each other Crip handshakes and signs, suggesting their interest in the gang. However, this does not indicate actual gang membership, as students even offered to teach me the latest signs. The high status accorded to gang identity coexisted with a majority of interviewees being critical of gangs (at least in their conversation with me), describing members as "stupid" (Marie, HA), "clowns" (Sharon, AL), "cowards" (Samuel, AL), and "punks" who can't fight their own battles (Derek, Amb; Tameeka, Amb). Nonetheless, when I asked students what percentage of their classmates were in gangs, their estimates were generally very high.

Though it is hard to tell the extent or nature of gang activity, it is clear that in the streets and in the halls gang culture sits at the top of all the social markers. Anderson (AL) explained how gang culture caused him "stress" because of the competition for dominance:

So they think they higher by being in gangs. . . . It [gangs] makes your mind think, like, I'm really dominant. . . . That's, like, the stupid thing about it, like, that's like the most stupid thing in school right now. . . . Because of the people who's in it . . . they make people angry. And, it get to your head. . . . I'm not even gonna make this stress me, but, I have to see this person everyday and, you know, he . . . acting like . . . they have some kind of power or they god and that really stress you out.

Anderson was "hard enough," meaning he didn't need to prove himself (Dance 2002) and was not in a gang as far as I could tell. Street savvy, well dressed, funny, and a great flirt, he resented being displaced at the top of the social hierarchy by those he didn't look up to but had to fear. Other students noted that gang members got undeserved status because of their gang connections. The gang hierarchy dominating hall culture frustrated Anderson, but his frustration only clarifies the ruling ethos of student culture—male domination based on physical power, sexual prowess, and material display, and solidified by gang membership.

Girls Contending for Respect: Silenced Critical Voices

The decidedly masculine nature of hall culture becomes even more evident when one examines the competing notions of how girls get respect. Though student after student could rattle off the rules for boys to gain popularity, they were less certain on the rules for girls. Apparently, what girls didn't do was as important as what they did do. Nina (HA) explains,

> I'm nice to everyone. Everybody likes me because I'm a nice person. I don't be screaming and cursing. I be myself, I don't want to be like them, like kissing up on people and . . . like they touching and stuff. No, I'm not that kind of girl!

Nina focuses on "niceness," which she defines both as a soft-spoken demeanor as well as not behaving in a sluttish manner, kissing or rubbing up on others. Beth (AL) also highlighted the importance of avoiding sexual behavior while focusing on cultivating coolness:

> Like, you don't do things that you know people gonna talk about you. . . . Like if you hanging out with a whole bunch of boys that's all right. But if you leave school with a whole bunch of boys people are gonna say something. Like, you gain respect by doing certain things . . . like smoking, hanging with cool people.

As these students suggest, girls have to fit themselves into very traditional notions of femininity. They must be friendly and nice to others and they cannot be sluttish.

While gear was important for boys, girls were not expected to wear name brands. The male gaze that dominates girls' choices in clothes and behavior was well articulated by John (Amb), who was very critical of the sexist nature of the hall culture:

> Girls don't get judged by name brand, they get judged by what they have on. They have like them really short, short skirts, and they have on them really tall boots or whatever and tight shirts, they immediately say, "Oh, she's a ho. She's stupid." And like if you see a girl who's wearing jeans and sneakers and like a regular, loose shirt, and they be like, okay, she's not a ho, she's mmm.

Though boys and girls both judged girls negatively for overly revealing clothing, many girls still chose to wear it. Though endangering their reputations, such clothes enabled them to assert their sexuality and get attention from boys. Here again, girls had to navigate through the contradictions of hall culture—sexy clothes made them more attractive to boys but also tainted them as potential hos.

Just as clothes have a different meaning for girls (sexiness/sluttiness rather than status marker), so too does sexual activity. As I have already discussed, girls cannot exercise their sexuality as freely as boys can, a situation consistent with the dominant patriarchy. Girls' sexuality is contained by a traditional heterosexuality. They can be sexually active but, to maintain respect, their activity must be confined to one young man. Though only a few students said it was important for a girl to have a boyfriend, the amount of fighting that went on over boys suggests that it was very important. Camille (Amb) explained that "they [boys] totally different from girls. It's like the only way [girls] can get respect is, like, 'look, that's my man, that boy.' If she find out her man cheatin' on her with her best friend, they'll start fighting, just like that." As a number of students have already pointed out, boys tend to fight to prove themselves and to establish dominance, but for girls, its "guys they fight over" (Nina, HA). In addition to Camille and Nina, five other girls noted boys as a major cause of fights.

The code of the halls contains the sexuality of girls in monogamous relationships because they are ostracized for sexual activity outside of such relationships even though boys are free to play the field. In fact, cheating on girlfriends brought boys only greater public respect. Girls often attacked the rivals who had moved in on their men. Camille (Amb) observed, "The guys can just sit there and chill. And they love it and they get more props like that. It happens, I have seen it in the lunchroom. . . . Two girls, they fought over the same guy and the guy was just sitting there. He didn't say nothing."

Though many students asserted that fighting was usually over "stupid things," girls may have fought for more sensible reasons. On the one hand, many students admitted that having a reputation as a good fighter, male or female, got respect. Girls who have been cheated on can restore some of their lost status by fighting. By fighting, girls publicly claim their young men, proving their physical dominance and asserting that they are not sluts or hos. They did not simply "give it up like that," but rather they were in a legitimate relationship worth fighting over. In a number of ways these fights were public performances of status preservation and, at the same time, they reinforced group norms.

Because the culture of the halls is highly patriarchal and hierarchical, girls navigate a very difficult terrain as they are pressured to have sex and yet the community exacts tough penalties for such behavior. The code of the halls favors young men's broad freedoms, rewarding aggressive, abusive, and sometimes illegal behavior while girls must fit themselves into uncomfortable and subordinate roles. However, girls are aware of much of the disrespect they experience and can be vocal about sexism in the halls as Shelly (HA) explains,

I think every guy picks up how a girl is supposed to be. Everybody has their own idea and, like, they give respect to the ones who show those qualities, and the ones that don't have these qualities, they're the ones who they call "chicken heads" or whatever. But, I would say, I learned how to communicate with other people on a different level. . . . Yeah, even though at times I wore my skirts short, I had respect for myself. . . . It doesn't matter what I wear, it's what's in my brain. But there some times I sit in classes and I notice guys they just be lookin' at the girls, for, you know, what they're wearing. And I be like, that's wrong, you don't look at a girl for how they present themselves, it's how they present themselves intellectually. So, in a way, they's a lot of guys out there, and especially in this school, who have no respect for women, they just talk to you like you trash or something. They grab on you like they own you. . . . They used to grab me and I was like, "do you know me?" That's how my mother raised me! You don't grab me; you don't own me!

Shelly criticizes the sexism of her peers insisting on her right to define her own sexuality. Here, she offers an alternative and feminist discourse on the meaning of her clothes and her identity though such a posture was rare.

The "B-Word"

Though few girls were as outspokenly critical of the limits placed on them as Shelly was, many were critical of sexism in the halls. Girls were quick to point to the widespread use of the "B-word" (bitch), which they would rarely utter. The word conveys so much sexism that most girls considered it unacceptable to repeat, though boys use it frequently. Beth (AL) explained, "Like, if a boy try to talk to you and he calling you then you ignore him, he's gonna be like, 'I don't want you anyway you B!' And he gonna curse you out or whatever." Florence (AO) felt that the "B-word" was used too widely among girls and boys:

> And another thing I don't like, you know some girls they call each other Bs and hos and stuff like that. I think that is so disrespectful even for you to say, and some girls tolerate guys saying that, and I find that so disrespectful. You're trying to get connected with a girl, you do not come out there calling her one of those things and expect her to turn around like "yes?" . . . And girls use it on each other and I be like, how can you discriminate yourself like that, put yourself down so low?

Many girls resented the sexism embedded in these derogatory words that were commonly used in the halls.

Boys and some girls admitted that they used the B-word to discipline girls who did not conform to the rigid gender codes of the halls. Andrea (Amb) explained that at times she felt it was appropriate to use the word to bring erring girls back into line:

> Okay, one way is the way she carry herself and if she's too easy, then she'll get abused both by girls and by guys. So at times, I think, calling girls bitches is for them to really realize that the way they carry themselves is, like, dreadful. . . .

However, she added, sometimes guys call girls bitches "because they feel like they gotta have they way, and if they can't get that way, they call you a bitch and that's supposed to downsize you in your mind." Andrea's ambivalence toward the use of the word "bitch" is indicative of the ways girls both accepted and resisted the gender hierarchy of the halls.

Michael (Amb) told me that just prior to arriving at the interview he and a friend had had to "discipline a female." "If one shout and it gets out of hand then you got to put them in they place." In this case, a girl had yelled at them, gave his friend dirty looks, and came "up to his face and we snuffed her." "Snuffing" is shoving someone's face with an open hand, expressing disrespect. Girls who resisted their subordinate status or challenged boys who betrayed them were subject to physical and verbal abuse. Many girls were outspoken, competitive, and assertive in the halls, but they rarely openly challenged the way they were treated by young men. The boys' comfortable hold on gendered authority put the girls in conflicted positions, disliking while participating in the reinforcement of hierarchical gender relationships.

Parallel Universes?

In students' descriptions of the codes of the halls they noted the actions and markers that enhanced or limited popularity. The salient silence about academic work when explaining popularity certainly reinforces the perception that halls and classrooms were separate, even parallel, and peculiarly irrelevant to each other. However, the parallel locations were not equal to students in appeal, consequence, or experience. George, an academically oriented junior who also was attuned to the hall scene, explained,

> It's like you go to school and just want to present yourself out. You know, wear something nice and flashy, everybody sees you, you know, you go to class, everybody sees you in the classroom. You go to the classroom, *do absolutely nothing*. Go back in the hallway, you know, flash around.

He raised his voice when he said "do absolutely nothing" to call attention to the irony that the classroom is supposed to be the place where students do "something," at least in official school discourse. He suggests an inversion of purposes students have established through their creation of a hall culture of greater importance than academics. Though George was a student who took classroom work seriously and graduated in four years, he describes what he experiences as a typical male student in the school. He highlights the flat, empty substance of class time compared to the rich, vibrant life of the halls. Time in class is simply an intermission to the more important theater of peer relations and postures.

Other students agreed that academic work was marginal compared to hall activity. Andrea (Amb), a third-year student well behind in credits said, "School is chill; you know what I'm saying? Basically, what I think is if you do what you got to do then you could have time to chill in the hallway or basically *parlez*." Class work or being in a classroom was a required activity, "what you got to do," while "chilling," was what students wanted to do. Andrea clearly defines a commonly held position that class work is a parallel, subordinate obligation to the central allure of representing and jockeying for position in the hall. John (Amb), who passed most of his classes with little effort but was content with Cs and Ds explained his opinion:

> MD: What is school to you?
>
> John: A social club. . . . I mean, I know a lot of people that come to school, the only really reason that we come is to meet people and you do work, meanwhile, in the background.
>
> MD: Is that how you feel about your own work here?
>
> John: Yeah, I'm just here to talk to people and make friends and hang out and stuff like that, and then decide what to do for the weekend. In the meantime, my work happens to get done.

Like Andrea, John described school work as "the background" and what "happens to get done." John is active as he describes himself talking to people, making friends, and hanging out. But he shifts to a passive posture when discussing schoolwork: it happens to get done; he doesn't actively do it. Like Andrea, who described school work as "what you got to do," he distances himself from academic work. George, who was more academically oriented than either Andrea or John, also emphasized the insignificance of academic work in relation to the halls.

The twenty students who interpreted the halls and classrooms as parallel spaces insisted that good grades did not interfere with popularity because the two sites were separate domains. However, the stunning void of their descriptions of classroom life in contrast to the rich allure of the halls gives them an unavoidable structural relation. The six students who moved between oppositional and parallel constructions of hall culture often recognized these tensions. For example, Nina (HA) said she liked to talk in the halls between classes and say hello to people. She also admitted that she took the hall pass sometimes to finish gossip begun during passing time. However, she also felt that the ethos and lure of the halls prevented most students from achieving academically and described being harassed because she would "come to class on time and be different." Nina negotiated her hall time (gossiping between classes and occasionally letting that spill over to class time) so that it did not interfere with her academic success, but she perceived that this choice was not one made by most others.

Her remarks also call attention to the place of high achievers and academically oriented students within this culture. To be sure, Nina and students like her did not participate in the halls to the level of those who failed their classes, but for five academically oriented and one high achieving student, socializing in the hall was more of a central part of school than academic work. Four other high achievers identified socializing in the hall as important, though not as important as their academic work. Not surprisingly, all the ambivalent and highly alienated students preferred the halls to the classroom. However, it was not that easy for high achievers to be key players in the halls, which suggests that success in one space restricted success in the other.

Academic Culture and Hall Culture

Tensions between academic culture and hall culture were often implicit in many of the interviews. Camille (Amb) made these tensions explicit in her description of what she did in the halls:

We talk about what classes, yo, I'm failing this class. We talking about our boyfriends. We talk about which teacher we don't like, what we doin' after school, what we wanna eat. What we be buying, who got a car, whose car we going somewhere in, music, parties, that's what we talk about in the hallway.

School-related items are intermixed with other aspects of Camille's social life, but the school references are all negative—"the classes we're failing" and "the teachers we don't like"—suggesting the hostile relationship between students and academic culture. She did graduate, but she had to give up her hall walking to do so. Thus, though students insisted that academic success wasn't a barrier to popularity in and of itself, it required less presence in the halls and a different orientation toward class work. Andrea (Amb), who was very popular, assured me that students could do well academically and still be popular, but "when you get into being popular, your school work doesn't matter to you no more, just being popular right now so." Though good grades themselves are not bad, she also explained,

> You could be into it [school work], but up to a certain level. You just can't be all about school, school, school. Like, okay, when you in a group [referring to cooperative learning groups] and they want to talk to you about . . . they boyfriend or friend and then you're talking about [school] work, and you're, like, bothering people, like, what am I hanging out with you for?

The "certain level" of acceptable academic participation requires that loyalty to the peer group not be compromised. Andrea's example highlights how students sought to co-opt classroom activities for their own purposes. Those who resisted such co-option by insisting on "talking about work" had gone too far. In these subtle ways, academic and hall culture had a problematic relationship to each other.

Several high achieving and academically oriented students shared this understanding of expressing solidarity. Daniel (AO) explained that students could get good grades, but they couldn't be "stuck up about it." He praised a high-achieving friend who "helped" her peers by allowing them to copy from her as a way to express her solidarity. Laura (AO) criticized another high-achieving peer for answering too many questions, explaining, "I know my limits." Answering too many questions in class would make others look bad. Daniel (AO) and Nina (HA) complained that sometimes they were harassed for thinking they were "better than us." However, Daniel and Nina were also popular. Daniel was a school celebrity known for his big mouth and for being a class clown, and Nina was a student leader who often confronted school authorities on behalf of students. Despite her efforts to advocate for her peers and her general popularity, she did feel picked on by a rival group of girls who used her academic performance as a marker of her difference. These students suggest that the halls and classrooms were parallel and unrelated environments only to a point. Solidarity with the peer group was an absolute requirement for social acceptance, and academic achievement cast doubt on one's loyalty to the peer group.

A small number of high achieving and academically oriented students rejected exclave culture outright, referring to it as "ghetto" (Thomas, HA) and dismissing the possible futures of their peers. These students stuck with a similar peer group, formed close relationships with teachers, and spent little time in the halls. Similar to the "school kids" in a study by Flores-Gonzalez (2002), these high-achieving and academically oriented students were generally left alone by their street-identified peers as long as they did not seek to be part of the "street" social scene. The decision of this small group to reject the culture of the halls underscored the larger assumptions circulating there—they did not identify with their peers and were not in solidarity with them, at least around issues of academics and identity. In fact, they were often highly critical of the behavior of their peers. However, as many studies of high-achieving minority students have noted, these students articulated alternative notions of Black identity (Fordham 1996; Akom 2003; Horvat and Lewis 2003). Thomas (HA) went as far as criticizing student hall culture for promoting demeaning stereotypes of Black people. He embraced a middle-class Black identity that enabled him to express racial pride while also pursuing academic excellence.

Very few students at Renaissance found such alternative ways of seeing themselves and their academic work. In contrast to Thomas, who comfortably ignored his peer group, Ann (HA) was constantly plagued by an aching desire to fit in. She did not slack off on her grades to win acceptance, but she sought to gain a toehold in social status by pursuing high-status boys as beaus. She was not successful and was often abused and humiliated in the process. She paid a high psychic and social cost for her desire to be a star pupil and be socially included.

Coding the Halls

To further understand the relationship of hall culture to academic culture it is useful also to examine the ways cultural understandings of gender, race, and sexuality are imposed on school spaces. Spaces become gendered, racialized, or sexualized when specific activities or values are promoted or enacted in them and others excluded or ostracized. Because there are tensions between halls and the classroom, the way one space is socially constructed informs the other and may impact student academic achievement, particularly undermining the achievement of young men.

In addition to the social dominance of young men and the subordination of young women in the halls, many practices further inscribed the halls as male space. For example, terms used to describe weakness and cowardice in the halls were often feminine references. One day at lunchtime, a group of apparent Crips (who were not students at the school) attacked Jamal (AL) in the hall outside my classroom (many students preferred it to the lunchroom). Jamal ran out to the street, where, he assured me later, he and his friends "took care of that situation." His best friend did not come to his aid but stood by and watched. A group of girls circled him in the hall yelling, "You pussy! Pussy! Pussy!" Derek (Amb) referred to running away from a fight as being "a girl." One of the vilest insults students would hurl at boys was the term "bunger clot," which was a West Indian reference to menses. These insults all constructed femaleness as weak and even disgusting. Through the widespread use of such putdowns, the use of the "B-word," and the aggressive double standard and importance of gear for boys but not girls, the halls were coded masculine, and maleness was a status marker. Not surprisingly, however, girls at Renaissance as at high schools everywhere outperform boys academically, graduate at a higher rate, and are more likely to go on to college.

The coding of the halls as male implicitly codes the classrooms as female and boys who participate in academic work as effeminate. For example, Oliver (AO) was regularly called a "nerd" by some of his peers, an insult that suggests a debased masculinity. In later discussions of classroom culture I will further expand on the ways the classroom explicitly becomes feminized.

Compulsory Heterosexuality and Hall Culture

In addition to being gendered, the halls are also defined as heterosexual space. The fighting over boys among girls, the importance of sexual activity, and the dominance of boys all suggest what Adrienne Rich (1986) referred to as "compulsory heterosexuality." Just as student culture exaggerates gender differences into a hierarchy, it also imposes a hyper-heterosexuality on its members. Gay students at Renaissance hid their identity from peers because such identities were aggressively denigrated and at times verbally and physically assaulted. Homophobic remarks were heard frequently in the halls and classrooms and students often expressed violent hostility toward homosexuality. Accusing someone of being gay could, and often did, lead to fights, and putdowns like "faggot" were common assertions of this widespread antigay climate. In a lunchtime conversation, a group of students applauded a gay-bashing incident that had been reported in the papers.

The high level of homophobic remarks and attitudes created a very unfriendly climate for gay students. Despite this, during the 1999 to 2000 school year, a small but visible subculture of openly gay and bisexual students emerged for the first time at Renaissance. This group of fifteen students from all grades hung out together in the halls and formed a very tight friendship group. Though a strong support group for one another, these students were highly marginalized by other students, made to feel unwelcome in the classroom, and ostracized in the halls. Most of these students cut classes regularly and failed their courses. Though creating a space for themselves in the school, it was not one that promoted their academic success or challenged negative perceptions of gay identity.

That same year, a group of seniors insisted on the right of same-sex couples to attend the prom and eventually prevailed. However, no same-sex couples actually attended. These incidents suggest that attitudinal shifts may have been underway, but the hall was still an environment where performances of heterosexuality (getting numbers, flirting, physical play, kissing, and bragging) were required to secure popularity. Though the male dominance in the halls supported female dominance in the classroom, gay students did not benefit by such a bifurcation. Often subject to isolation and harassment, openly gay students were marginalized in classrooms as well as the hallways. Though the halls were coded masculine and classrooms feminine, both spaces were "straight" spaces.

The male-privileged heterosexuality promoted in the halls enacts a "silenced discourse of desire" (Fine and McClelland 2006) that constrains the sexuality of girls, as well as gay and bisexual students. It forces them into very narrow and traditional boundaries that deny them the agency straight boys enjoy. Thus, the halls as a space of peer solidarity are not necessarily more egalitarian than the classrooms. As scholars of student resistance have noted, student resistance to aspects of dominant culture often reproduces other oppressive hierarchies (Willis 1977; MacLeod 1995). In the halls at Renaissance a similar phenomenon exists as well. The alternatives installed in the exclave are not necessarily libratory as they often magnify oppressive hierarchies rather than deconstruct them.

Racializing Space

In addition to imposing notions of gender and sexuality, hall culture also encoded race onto school spaces. As I've already noted, the halls were spaces where Black identity was celebrated, implicitly suggesting that classrooms were places where it was marginalized, particularly in light of the ways Black identity was assaulted at scanning. In a number of ways, participation in hall culture was understood as an expression of both racial and peer solidarity, while over-identification with academic culture could cast suspicion on a student's loyalties.

Though the connection between academic identity and whiteness (nonblackness) was implicit in attitudes and practices within hall culture, occasionally this link was made explicit. For example, I surveyed a class to determine who owned a computer. About one-third of the class raised their hands even as one student protested that Black people didn't own computers. Referring to the students who had raised their hands (all Black), he exclaimed, "See! It's the White kids!" The students admitting computer ownership were generally high-achieving and academically oriented students and were publicly constructed as "White" because of their academic identity. In this example, a flag of racial solidarity was planted in the halls by defining participation in classroom activities as White, thus attacking the racial identities of academic students.

Students further enacted their ascribed racial distinctions between the halls and classrooms in their linguistic choices. As will be discussed in chapter 4, all students felt it was okay to use "Ebonics" and "slang" in the halls but were split about whether such language should be used in the classroom. The halls were the spaces of the school where expressions of blackness were expected and encouraged, while in the classroom these styles were subordinate to Standard English (Dickar 2004).

As discussed in chapter 2, school officials also reinforced the construction of hall culture as Black and nonacademic when tropes of blackness were removed from student bodies as they entered each morning. Such practices widened the chasm between street culture and academic culture by turning the ritual of entering the school into a full-scale border checkpoint. Other practices in the school may have further placed academic culture and local culture in opposition to each other, such as disciplinary policies, the "hat rule" (the rule banning baseball caps from the heads of boys, particularly, discussed in chapter 5), the largely White administration, and the state-mandated Eurocentric curriculum. Thus, though the school was informed by a progressive reform agenda and valued a culturally relevant curriculum and pedagogy, it still appeared as a White institution in many ways. Lewis (2004) found a similar phenomenon in her study of three schools in California, where, despite overwhelmingly Black and Hispanic student populations, the schools were still perceived as White institutions.

Importantly, though Black-identified styles were frequently targeted at scanning, students persisted in wearing them. To evade confiscation, students temporarily removed hats, do-rags, and head wraps before they entered the school but quickly put these items back on once they successfully passed through scanning and entered the halls. The explicitly Black-identified, masculine, youth culture that circulates defiantly in the halls and the academic culture implicitly coded as White and feminine suggest a dialectical tension between the two spaces.

Dual Economies of Social, Cultural, and Symbolic Capital

The coding of the halls as Black, male, and straight suggest that alternative notions of social, cultural, and symbolic capital circulate in them as well. One function of public schools is the socialization of youth into the mores and ideology of the dominant society in preparation for their entry into occupational and civic roles. In addition to learning specific skills such as mathematics and literacy in Standard English and a knowledge of national and world history, schools also socialize students into work-discipline behaviors such as promptness, cooperation, deference to superiors, and individual responsibility. In this way schools provide access to the multiple forms of capital theorized by Bourdieu and Passeron (1977). They particularly provide (1) cultural capital, or the knowledge and behaviors students will need to function in dominant culture; (2) social capital, or social networks through their peer groups as well as through school-organized opportunities such as internships; and (3) symbolic capital, or status markers. Bourdieu and Passeron conceptualize these forms of knowledge and networks as capital because each can be exchanged for other forms of capital. For example, social networks can open access to better jobs. Many of the young Caribbean women Lopez (2003) interviewed had gotten jobs or assistance in obtaining them through former teachers. Similarly, knowing how to read and write well and speak the dominant idiom, all forms of cultural capital, also enhances individual competitiveness for college and jobs. In addition to the social networks and cultural skills students acquire at school, they also receive a credential—their diploma, a form of symbolic capital—which they can use to enhance their earning capacity and their potential to further their educations. Students at Renaissance were well aware of the symbolic value of the diploma; the vast majority of students admitted that they wanted one even if their behaviors did not support that desire.

A significant body of scholarship has used Bourdieu's theories of multiple economies to examine how schools distribute social, symbolic, and cultural capital to marginalized youth (Lamont and Lareau 1988; Stanton-Salazar 1997; Arriaza 2003; Carter 2003; Lewis 2004; Monkman, Ronald, and Theramene 2005). However, an alternative economy exists in the halls in which students circulate their own symbols and discourses. This hall capital draws from and feeds back into their community lives allowing them to accumulate "street credit," though they may be rejecting dominant forms of capital accumulation. Students choose to develop some forms of social and cultural capital while consciously "not learning" others (Kohl 1994).

Highlighting some of the underlying tensions at play in student rejections of dominant forms of capital, Samuel (AL) explained, "The diploma means you got their deal. You got their deal and then you got your street." He went on to describe the kinds of lessons the older men who gathered on stoops and street corners taught him about history and being a

Black man. School is about getting "their deal"—their cultural, social, and symbolic capital—which is something not of or belonging to an implied "us" (Black people, the local community, or students at the school) but to "them" (the dominant society, Whites). However, the real deal, what Samuel perceives as closer to the truth, is the knowledge and capital available on the streets. He clearly constructs a dual economy from which he selectively chooses what he will integrate into his being and how he will integrate it. His selectivity was evident in his academic career. Samuel chose to fail many classes because he found them useless, insulting, or full of "lies," a decision made by many of his peers. However, unlike many alienated students, he hung on for seven years and ultimately earned a diploma. Similarly, many high-achieving and academically oriented students also recognized dual forms of capital but were more interested in gaining access to the capital the school could provide than were their peers who felt more rooted in the local community.

Samuel's division between "their deal" and the "street" suggests a dialectical relationship between the halls and classrooms. But exclave culture is not merely in opposition to or a negation of academic culture. As has already been examined, hall culture reproduced many elements of dominant culture, sometimes in more extreme form, as in its denigration of public poverty (not having gear, for example), its hyper-consumerism, or its acute form of patriarchy. In this sense again, the exclave in the hall must be seen as a thirdspace that includes oppositional elements but is not defined by that oppositionality alone.

Conclusion

This exploration of exclave culture at Renaissance suggests that student life in the hall establishes values and perceptions that conflict with values and perceptions promoted by the classroom. Students must negotiate both spaces. In this way, the exclave effect is a useful framework to move beyond the limits of the oppositional-culture thesis. Exclave theory represents student/school conflicts by recognizing the ways that local culture influences academic orientations without completely defining them. It also calls attention to the crucial relationship between locally generated identities and academic identities and exposes contradictions embedded in students' own cultural spaces as well as the spaces of the school.

At Renaissance, academic achievement was rarely defined as White (as Fordham and Ogbu (1986) have argued), but academically oriented students nonetheless faced the burden of questioned loyalties. Those who sought both popularity among their peers and academic achievement were caught in the contradictions between two value systems. Despite this, most high-achieving and academically oriented students participated in the same hall culture as their more alienated and ambivalent peers, even though their participation was limited. Thus, we need to reconsider literature that suggests that students with different academic identifications participate in separate and distinct student cultures (Horvat and Lewis 2003; Flores-Gonzalez 2005; Gibson 2005). Students with differing attitudes toward school generally participated in the same social scene (though not to the same degree and with the significant exceptions of excluded gay and Haitian students). However, it is important to note that the lack of an honors track at Renaissance (detracking was part of the reform effort) meant that there were no bracketed spaces segregating high achievers from others. Also, in comparison to many urban schools, Renaissance was relatively homogeneous with the overwhelming majority of students identifying as Black. Other studies have often focused on schools that spatially separated students by academic track or that were more racially diverse (Valenzuela 1999; Flores-Gonzalez 2002; Pollock 2004). It is unclear if such a coherent hall culture would emerge in more racially diverse schools, particularly given the marginalization of the relatively small Haitian population seen at Renaissance. The relative homogeneity of straight, Black, anglophone Renaissance students offers a useful case study to understand ways local cultures are brought into and altered in school spaces.

Understanding the exclave of the halls as a thirdspace captures the greater nuance and complexity of these spaces and opens new ways of reading school cultures. It allows us to recognize the opposing relationships between student hall culture and academic culture without defining student/school relationships as inherently oppositional. It also supports the notion that oppositionality, resistance, and academic identification and accommodation exist along a continuum and that students move along it throughout the day and throughout their academic careers (Hemmings 2002; 2004).

Hall culture undermines the academic efficacy of the school, but this same academic culture invites the construction of alternatives to itself.

The events at scanning inform the ways students inhabit the halls in that some of the very markers that are targeted at scanning (styles of dress and hats, for example) are rewarded in the halls. The ways school authority represents itself at the boundary between the streets and the school and the ways students claim school space for themselves suggest that some of the oppositional aspects of hall culture are co-created by both students and schools. In the classrooms, student/school tensions come into greatest sustained dispute. Classrooms are the sites of contact-zone conflicts because unlike the daily scanning and activity in the halls, where it is clear who is in control, students and school authority contend in the classrooms. I turn to the contested classrooms in the next chapters.

4

■　　■　　■　　■　　■　　■　　■　　■

"If I can't be myself, what's the point of being here?"

Language and Contested Classroom Space

One day during lunchtime I sat grading assignments in my classroom when Natalia and her friend Clarissa stopped by. Natalia was an insightful student in my class though marginally engaged in school. Her attendance was spotty and she was quiet in class, though outside of class she was boisterous and witty—a leader. The girls joined me at the table where I was working. I continued as they amiably shared gossip about other students. Natalia became curious about the mystery of grading and began carefully watching what I was doing. Suddenly she erupted with laughter. Referring to the particular work I was grading, apparently by a friend of hers, she exclaimed, "Susannah is so ghetto! She doin' her class work in Ebonics!" "So what?" Clarissa responded with a shrug, "I do too. Why should she change?"

Natalia's outburst revealed the complexity of student linguistic choices. Natalia did indeed write well in Standard English and used it in her written work. However, she generally spoke what she called Ebonics, except while class was in session. She had been speaking "Black language" while chatting with me but perceived that it was absurdly inappropriate during class and constructed that behavior as "ghetto." "Ghetto" was a term that often indicated the low-class status and degenerate values derisively equated with residents of public housing projects or the "ghetto." To Natalia, the inappropriateness of Ebonics or what Alim and Baugh (2007) term "Black language" (BL) for schoolwork was so obvious that she found Susannah's use of it funny. However, like Susannah and Clarissa, many students did not code-switch from Black language to Standard English (SE) when they entered the classroom or in completing their written work. As a teacher, I offered no clarity on the issue. I focused on the substance of what students said and did not comment on the linguistic choices students made if I understood their meaning. But Natalia made me aware that my preference to accept any dialect of English I could understand was not necessarily what all my students wanted or expected and was not necessarily in their best interest. In one utterance, she challenged my language policy. She and her friends revealed that language choices carried meaning and that though she had a clear opinion of those who did not code-switch in class, there was no consensus among students.

The uncertain status of BL and SE dialects in the classroom demonstrated that the classroom was a contested space. Unlike at the front door, where school authority was high profile, or in the halls where student culture prevailed, the classrooms were not clearly controlled by teachers, administrators, or students. The site of the vast majority of the school's formal work, the worksite for teachers, and the space where both students and teachers spent the majority of their time at school, the classroom was the space where the most significant struggles over the meaning and purpose of schooling took place. It was also where important connections between student and school were forged. Language politics reflected numerous conflicts inherent in classroom culture, and these conflicts speak to broad contradictions embedded within urban schools that directly impact the academic aspirations and outcomes of their students. In this and the next two chapters I explore the very nuanced and complex nature of the struggle between students and schooling that played out in the classroom. I begin this discussion of the construction of classroom space with an examination of language politics because these positions reveal the contested and conflicted nature of the classroom.

The clash over language choice that emerged briefly during lunch also emerged in the interviews I conducted. Of thirty-seven interviewees, only three were not specific enough about language to determine a position. Of the thirty-four remaining, twelve agreed with Natalia that Standard

ACADEMIC DISPOSITION	SE AS IDIOM OF CLASSROOM	OPEN LANGUAGE	UNCERTAIN	NON-SPECIFIC	TOTAL
High Achieving (HA)	5	1	3	0	9
Academically Oriented (AO)	5	2	3	1	11
Ambivalent (Amb)	1	4	1	2	8
Alienated (AL)	1	5	3	0	9
Total	12	12	10	3	37

English was the only appropriate idiom for class work, both written and verbal. Twelve students advocated a more open policy, similar to Clarissa's, noting that students should use the language of their choice in the classroom, which generally meant BL. Ten others were ambivalent toward language, either admitting they were not sure or expressing aspects of both positions so that it was impossible to place them in one camp or the other.

Though students appeared to diverge significantly on language, there are a number of patterns and areas of consensus worth noting. Significantly, there was a strong correlation between academic disposition and language preference. Students who identified with school in that they were accumulating credits in a timely manner and sought to do well overwhelmingly endorsed the use of Standard English as the lingua franca of the classroom. Only three of these students endorsed an open policy. Conversely, ambivalent and alienated students generally opposed the imposition of Standard English; nine of them endorsed an open classroom, while only one from each group supported Standard English as the dominant language of the classroom.

Students who were generally more oriented toward schooling and academic success were far more likely to want Standard English to prevail in the classroom. Gender did not appear to be significant in determining language policy, as eight of twelve SE supporters were girls and seven of twelve open-policy advocates were girls. Given that girls represented two-thirds of the overall sample, these numbers are consistent. Far more significant is the strong correlation between academic identity and language policy. The divergent opinions about language policy reveal the competing perceptions of what kind of space classrooms should be and what and whose purposes they should serve.

In addition to alerting us to a significant attitudinal distinction between those who identify with schooling and those who do not, striking consistencies across these positions also emerged that highlight the significance of classroom space as contested terrain. Particularly, thirty-six of the thirty-seven respondents thought that it was acceptable to use Black language in the streets and with friends. Thirty-four of thirty-seven also thought that in more formal places, such as at a job interview, Standard English was required. Most students felt that they needed to know and use Standard English and, as several stated, "There's a time and place for everything," indicating a consensus around the need to code-switch.

Though code-switching itself was widely accepted, it carried different meanings for a number of students. Proponents of SE felt students should code-switch to SE in the classroom; others noted that they modified their language in the classroom but did not necessarily use SE. Some students explained that when they entered the classroom they "dropped the slang" (Darrel, AO) or stopped using curses (a regular augmentation of language in the halls and streets), but that such code-switching did not necessarily mean they attempted to use Standard English. Some students emphasized "tone" over syntax or grammar as what needed to change in classrooms. Thus, though some students were not willing to insist on Standard English, their general consensus that aspects of language should change suggests that the classroom was a different kind of space than the hall. This finding also suggests complex understandings of code-switching that have been overlooked in the literature on language politics. Most students marked classroom space as more formal than the halls and shifted to more neutral language (no curses) and a more polite tone. Some proponents of an SE language policy perceived that some students do not "know better" (Ricky, Amb), and if they did not practice code-switching at school, they would not do it in situations when they absolutely should. Others rejected that perception and insisted on their capacity to code-switch, emphasizing that they choose not to. Students widely endorsed changing aspects of their language in the classroom but differed over the idiom to which they should switch.

In addition to generally agreeing that some form of code-switching should occur in the classroom, students also agreed on the language of the world beyond the classroom. In settings that were more formal—for example, in which one was being judged—students agreed that Standard

English was the appropriate idiom. In clearly informal settings where power relationships were far more horizontal—among friends, in teenage spaces like the halls and familiar places like the streets—local vernacular and slang were expected. Students' lack of agreement on language use in the classroom problematized the nature of classroom space specifically. Is the classroom a space of student self-expression or a space reproducing societal norms? Is it a place where students are directly prepared for the job market or a place where they can explore their own identities and make their own paths? Are teachers at school like bosses at work who should be addressed in Standard English or are they more familiar "caregivers" who can be addressed in familiar language?

The uncertainty about language use in the classroom marks it as a unique contact zone where cultural struggles spill across borders of multiple purposes and parallel authorities. Pratt (1986) defines the contact zone as social spaces "where cultures meet, clash, and grapple with each other, often in contexts of highly asymmetrical relations of power, such as colonialism, slavery, or their aftermaths as they are lived out in many parts of the world today" (34). It is important to note that contact zones are not places where two cultures meet on equal terms. Rather, such zones are specifically places where the terms of domination and resistance are worked out. They are indeterminate in that they are spaces where neither side has been completely victorious. The struggle over linguistic practices in classrooms is a contact-zone struggle over the meaning of schooling and of classroom space.

Clarification of Terms

Defining student positions on language presented dilemmas worth discussing here. Though I focused my questions on whether students felt they needed to know Standard English and if they felt they should code-switch, students employed a far wider range of understandings of their languages. They saw themselves as speakers of many dialects. "Proper" English, as students most commonly termed Standard English, was one idiom most insisted they could use. They also saw themselves as speakers of "slang" and of Black vernacular languages that some recognized by vocabulary, grammar, and syntax. Many students also seemed to use "slang" to refer to both the informal and group-specific words they used (such as "crib" for "house," "my bad" for "I'm sorry," etc.) as well as what some called Ebonics, referring to a larger language system with grammar and syntax rules. Additionally, many also referenced the wide use of curses within their informal language and drew distinctions between cursing and slang. In addition, a few students also noted that they spoke languages from the Caribbean, referencing Caribbean slang, Jamaican, Trinidadian, and Creole.

In this study, I refer to all the languages described above, which were generally created and used by Black people as Black language (BL). BL includes what has become widely understood as Ebonics or Black vernacular English, which Smitherman (1977; 1998) notes refers to grammatical rules, vocabulary, and style. BL also includes Caribbean dialects such as Jamaican or Trinidadian patois and what some students referred to as "Caribbean slang." Alim (2007) explains,

> While the Black population in the United States is far more diverse than is often noted, the languages of most Black slave descendants in the Americas do share two very important points. First, all of the "New World" hybrid languages are the result of contact between African and European languages (Ibo and English, for example). Second, all these languages, without exception, have been viewed as lesser versions of their European counterparts, to put it mildly, or have suffered under the laws, practices, and ideologies of linguistic supremacy and White racism. (4)

Students generally linked their local idioms to Black identity while seeing SE as something outside of their own culture. They also overwhelmingly used BL even if they endorsed the development of SE proficiency at school. Student discussions of their languages echoed Alim's definition of BL making it particularly useful in this discussion of language politics.

I also include in this broad category of Black language what students referred to as "slang" or "ghetto slang." One reason for this inclusion was that it was unclear what students meant by "slang," since some students referred to SE as "proper" and all BL as "slang." Another reason for this inclusion is that scholars of Black language have noted the integral relationship of slang to Black language. Smitherman (1977) explains, "Slang suggests a highly specialized vocabulary used only by a certain group of people. . . . Yet in the Black community, the vocabulary of soul crosses generational and class lines and is grounded in Black people's common linguistic and cultural history" (43). She further notes that slang phrases often are widely embraced within the community and become part of the language. In this discussion, I refer to the broad range of languages students described as their own as Black language.

I use the term Standard English (SE) to refer to the dominant idiom that is used in most television news reports, newspapers, business transactions, and by those in power. Many students, as I note above, often referred to this as "proper English" or simply "proper," underscoring the ways their own dialects were implicitly constructed as "improper" or "incorrect." A few students also constructed SE as "White" language. Oliver (AO) connected the notion of correctness and whiteness: "If you speak perfect English, they'll say, 'what are you, White?'" Samuel (AL) saw the imposition of SE as a project of White domination: "White language, you got the state of mind. They enslaved your brain."

Standard English is the language of the White middle class and of dominant culture and the language that is often considered correct in terms of vocabulary, syntax, and grammar. I am writing this book in Standard English and it is the language I generally use. It is also the language I myself was forced to internalize as a student in the public schools of New York City. My elementary school teachers regularly corrected our New York accents, forcing us to repeat (and implicitly correct) ourselves when we did things like "aks a question" or if we used "can" instead of "may," "bathroom" instead of "lavatory," and "good" instead of "well." Criticizing our poor use of Standard English on essays on an exam, one of my high school teachers mockingly noted, "None a yous talk good!" There is a long tradition of imposing the dominant idiom over the ethnically and class-inflected dialects that flourish in the city. I approached language in my classroom and in this discussion through my own mixed feelings about the denigration of the working-class argot of my childhood that I was regularly told, and believed, was wrong.

Student Descriptions of Black Language and Standard English

Whether students approved of the use of Black language in the classroom or not, they generally saw it as a valued part of their culture. Many students saw BL as a dynamic and expressive language, in contrast to SE, which some viewed as limited, clumsy, and inefficient. Samuel (AL) described

BL as a set of codes constantly in flux that could not be taught. His description helps set up how students defined their languages.

> Words is changing every day. . . . Most people who listen to rap, they can't understand it. I am hip-hop. I used to be into reggae stuff. Now, Ebonics is changing everyday. New words, I made up words, people made up words. I bring new words to people they didn't even know about. Ebonics, it's just people's little code, it's a whole 'nother language, yeah, but don't make that a class. You can't because it changes everyday.

Ebonics or BL is dynamic, improvisational, and truly democratic. Samuel makes up words, rap music adds words, and many people broadly participate in creating the language. It is a language of the moment, constantly changing to meet new discursive needs.

Samuel echoes what Spears (2007) argues are specific elements of BL, particularly the creative performance of utterances or "improvisation" and "semantic license," which "refers to the freedom AAL [African American Language] speakers exercise in creating . . . new words" (101). Samuel also implicates Black popular culture, youth culture, and his own agency in the ever-evolving quality of Black language. In contrast, other languages, such as Standard English, are more fixed and lack this playful and egalitarian quality. To amplify the significance of the fluidity of BL, Jennie (HA) who saw SE as the appropriate language of the classroom, corrected her use of the word "conversatin" noting, "'conversatin' is not a word, it's a word we use, but it's not a word. . . . It's not in the dictionary; I looked it up." There appears to be little room to alter SE, or at least she does not have the authority to do so. With her friends, the word was not problematic ("we" use it) but with me, it was. Samuel rejects this rigidity. In BL, he is powerful and a producer of neologisms, but in SE, like Jennie, he is trapped in a much more rigid idiom. Samuel was one of the few students who rejected using SE at all.

Sheena (AO) also emphasized the role of Black popular culture in shaping a unique language that unites Black communities all over America:

> Sheena: Okay, it is somewhat, I don't really know the definition for Ebonics, but say for instance, I be with my friends, but some of them, the words that they use, I'm like, "what does that mean?" But they say, "Hello [Sheena], wake up, don't you know what that

means?" I'm like, no, because, you know, I'm not outside 24-7, and you know I don't watch the TV that much so I don't know.

MD: So do students get words from TV?

Sheena: From the movies . . . in general meaning the Black movies, so they get all that stuff, you know, Ebonics, and all that stuff is from people coming from other parts of the country, like, you know, from the west side, you know, like Los Angeles and people moving from there to here and people going there to there, down South.

Like Samuel who made up words, Sheena also acknowledged that the language changes all the time. She couldn't keep up, in fact.

Gilroy (1993) argues that Black culture is transatlantic as influences circulate from Africa to the Caribbean to Black communities in the United States and Europe, particularly England. He called this transatlantic community the "Black Atlantic." Similarly, Sheena recognized that Black American culture is national in character, not local. Language is developed in Los Angeles, New York, and down South and is disseminated by the movement of people and by Black movies, music, and television. It is also shared and taught on the streets, which is why some students may have referred to the language as "street talk" and "street slang." Samuel referred to both hip-hop and reggae as sources of language linking the Caribbean to this Black culture. Black popular culture exposes even more people to new words and expressions.

Many students saw the use of Black languages as expressions of Black identity. Sheena went further and explained that language was just one, but perhaps the most obvious, marker of blackness and that things associated with Black people were not present in formal places like offices. She echoed the typical mantra about needing to know Standard English to get a job, but she broadened this observation into a far-reaching critique of the denigration of blackness:

MD: Is it useful to know Standard English?

Sheena: Yeah, it is. Because suppose, they have kids out there that are real smart, but they use Ebonics or whatever. It's good if they know the Ebonics from the standardized English because they go out there to get a job and . . . you know, and all of a sudden they start speaking Ebonics. The man is gonna be like, the man, or woman, is gonna be like, "We can't hire him because of the way he speaks."

MD: So people judge you by the way you speak?

Sheena: They do, because, I mean, like, for instance, you apply, you have an application. Applications say they're not gonna use race or sexuality or whatever whatever because, you know. But that's how things are in life. You know, you go out there to get a job, I mean, I'm gonna use an example. I'm not trying to put anybody down or be a racist or anything, but if a Black guy goes out there to get a job and he wears certain clothing, I mean, he could be, like, pants off his butt or . . . baggy, you know. It could be that the man that's interviewing you, or the woman, could be a Black person also. They wouldn't hire you because they would be, like, this is not what we want in our workplace, you know. In a business place it's not appropriate because you go out there to work in an office they don't want you walking around like that because suppose someone comes in to look around and say . . . "That's what we have working here?" you know.

MD: Why do people look down on that (the baggy pants look)?

Sheena: I guess it's the way that, you know, the way I look at it, I guess it's the way that Black people do things, you know. . . . I guess it's the way they do things, people, like, you can't have that, they're not allowing it.

In addition to BL as unacceptable, Sheena referred to fashions popular among Black youths as also forbidden in office environments. Echoing student criticisms of scanning, which targeted such fashions, she perceives that Black culture is just not proper: "they're not allowing it." She was reluctant to call this discrimination racism, in part because she sensed that Black interviewers (like the Black SSOs at scanning) would also reject candidates in baggy pants who spoke BL. Perhaps, too, she did not want to offend me. Nonetheless, she perceived that discrimination is part of the game and that if someone is too visibly Black, it will count against him or her in the job market. Sheena was uncertain about language policy because she felt students needed to learn SE and didn't know it but also felt the imposition of SE was part of a broad societal marginalization of Black people.

Student descriptions of BL highlight the ways it reflects their historical and cultural experiences and empowers their voices, which are implicitly silenced in SE. Though students defined a dynamic sense of BL, they also recognized distinctions within this very broad category that complicates notions of code-switching. Their assertions that they did change how they spoke in the classroom without necessarily using SE emphasizes the broadness of BL and the importance of self-expression. As Alim (2007) notes as well, most students were aware that the broader society looked down on BL, which informed the decisions around language of both those who advocated open language and those who advocated SE policies.

Many students seemed to recognize the dilemma posed by the need to know and use SE in the broader society and their commitment to their own idioms and cultures. Most notably, twenty-four students named a job interview, specifically, as a place where Standard English was necessary. Camille (Amb), who was uncertain of language policy in the classroom, explained, "I'm saying, you can't come to a job interview and say, 'yo, son, give me an application.' That's how he's going to be talking to his boss or manager like that?" In addition to the casual vocabulary such as "yo" and the informal address, "son," she also focused on the tone of the utterance. She explained, "This country is based on the way you are, your attitude, your respect, and the way you conduct yourself, and your intelligence, and that's what you need." Camille argues that Standard English is the dominant idiom, part of the way things are done in this country, and part of a cluster of behaviors and aptitudes that frame the way one is judged. The use of Black language in the search for employment, particularly its overly familiar vocabulary (yo, son) and the style in which it is often presented, demonstrated a lack of respect for the status of the boss, showed a poor attitude toward work, and indicated a lack of education. The centrality of SE to the ways one is perceived by others, particularly those with power, is a theme that permeated many of the interviews.

Like Camille, a number of students noted that in addition to changing vocabulary and syntax, SE required a different tone. When several students, all opposed to the imposition of SE, sought to prove their mastery of it, they shifted to a deferential and overly polite tone. For example, John (Amb) slowed his speech to say, "Hello, how are you today? I am fine. How are the wife and kids?" He constructed SE as formal, deliberate, and deferential by his purposeful pronunciation. He presented SE as part of an adult exchange removed from his experience (he did not have a wife and kids). Tina (AL) further highlighted this remoteness by shifting to a mock British accent to demonstrate her ability to speak SE. Further magnifying the remoteness of SE, she explained, "When I win the Noble Prize, I can't say, 'Yo, what up? I wanna thank my peeps!'" Students often manipulated both word choice and tone of address to define the boundaries between SE and BL. This distinction clearly marks SE as a formal language appropriate for addressing authorities in formal situations but not appropriate for familiar exchanges.

Given that most students felt they needed to know SE, their expectations of teachers in this regard also defined clear boundaries between SE and BL. Most students, regardless of their position on classroom language, felt teachers should not publicly correct students. Sharon (AL), who was opposed to the imposition of SE in the classroom, admitted,

> If my teachers told me that you can't talk your street language, or whatever whatever, first, I wouldn't want her to just come out and say, "Oh you can't talk the way you talking, shut up." I would want her to say, "Well, you know, we're in class and I would like for you to speak properly. Just for the future, you know what I'm saying, for future references, just in case of a job or whatever."

There was a dominant language that Sharon chose not to speak. She rejected the construction of "street language" as inappropriate for the classroom though she would respect a teacher's desire to promote Standard English if there were reasons stated. Nonetheless, she wanted her language respected and not simply dismissed, which she equated with being told to "shut up," or being silenced. Again, the theme of power and agency through linguistic virtuosity emerges as an important aspect of the language debate.

Dilemmas around Language Policies:
Teacher Perspectives

Just as no clear language policy preference emerged among students, teachers, too, found language policies to be a dilemma. Susan, a White teacher from a working-class background admitted that she is offended when people correct her colloquial expressions, particularly when they insult her further by adding, "And you're an English teacher?!" She recognized in these exchanges that the person correcting her used Standard English as a tool to gain power. By insulting her use of the English language they diminished her by implying that she was inadequate. Students also recognized that being corrected or insulted regarding language use was disempowering and silencing, as Sharon above indicated.

Thomas (HA), who was hostile to BL, nonetheless did not think teachers should correct students in front of class:

> When students come into class, they should speak proper English. If they can't, they should try. Teachers shouldn't just go up and say, "You're wrong." That will offend them. It is part of our culture.

For him, this demand for respect spilled into writing as well. He cautioned that teachers should not "pull out the big red marker and you know, say it's wrong." He asserts that BL is part of a shared legacy and recognizes, as Susan did, that correcting language is a way that teachers deploy their power. Several students cautioned teachers about how they should respond to language. Latisha (AO), who advocated an open policy toward language, felt teachers should only correct language if it offended them. "I think if they don't feel somehow disrespected by that, they shouldn't try to correct them, but if they do, they should say, 'Could you please approach me a different way?'" Latisha suggests that rather than correct their use of language, teachers should instruct students to code-switch instead—to ask students to speak to them in a different manner rather than dismiss their language as wrong.

Teachers were also mindful of the cultural significance of language and this may have also discouraged clear language policies. Because of her own struggles to rise from poverty, Susan felt sympathetic to students who do not want to change their language. She described her own struggles to become fluent in Standard English:

> For example, instead of "should've gone," I grew up saying "shoulda went." And so I went through a period in college where, like, my roommate had told me, "Why do you say, 'shoulda went?'" . . . So, I had to teach myself not to say it and it was incredibly hard, and I was so embarrassed. Maybe other people were around or something. But I would say

to myself, "Should have gone, should have gone, should have gone," until I internalized it and that was kind of weird. So I was code-switching; getting my ear to recognize that. And now when I go home and my mom says, "Well, You shoulda went to the store." I go, "Ooo."

Susan describes ridding herself of "shoulda went" and other phrases from her childhood as part of becoming college educated. She no longer can talk like her mother, and every time these local phrases come up she is reminded of the changes and choices she has made. These experiences and the sense of loss she feels over giving up such expressions has made her sensitive to her students' relationship to their dialects. She did not correct their spoken language because she felt that to do so would be to humiliate a child as she had been humiliated. Also, she pointed out that "if you correct their language in front of their peers and correct it even when they're speaking—even when they are saying something they are passionate about—it becomes about how they're doing it instead of what they're saying."

Susan's solution to the code-switching dilemma was to encourage students to write and to focus on specific problems individually but not to correct their spoken English. Even in correcting their writing she had the students focus on their biggest problems only. As they mastered each concept, she then had them focus on the next. She pointed out that many students have a fear of writing, and if she were to correct every error, they would be more afraid. She sought to encourage her students to express their ideas and to create a safe environment for them to do so. Her language policy was a way of allowing students to feel comfortable speaking and writing about their ideas while supporting their development of skills. These open policies echoed the concerns of students supporting an open classroom: that first and foremost the classroom was a space for self-expression. Similarly, few teachers simply forbade the use of Black language in their classrooms. Instead, most tolerated a polyglot environment where numerous dialects of English were simultaneously used and generally understood.

Susan was not the only White teacher who struggled with her own code-switching history and with promoting SE. Another White teacher admitted that he did not feel secure enough in his own use of SE to require it of students. Having grown up near Renaissance, he, too, was more comfortable using much of the language his students used and did not feel he had mastered SE. Though SE is often constructed as the language of White people, several White teachers felt uncomfortable promoting it, particularly if they were from working-class, immigrant, or ethnic communities and struggled with code-switching themselves.

Susan's narrative suggests that in mastering SE, she actually lost parts of her original dialect. In some cases, she doesn't really code-switch anymore but rather has "internalized it," making the change permanent and automatic. She no longer consciously corrects "shoulda went" but automatically says "should have gone." Susan wanted to fit in with her more middle-class peers in college, and in forcing herself to adopt their dialect, she reproduced the assumption that her own dialect was lesser or wrong. Despite her significant accomplishment in becoming fluent in SE, she admitted feeling stung when other people corrected her language. Her transformation, from working to middle class, is perhaps always incomplete as she still experiences anxiety about code-switching. Some students at Renaissance may also have been influenced by a similar anxiety that no matter what, their language use will always be scrutinized.

The reluctance of many teachers to establish a language policy essentially meant that the policy was an open one by default, not intention. However, as Natalia suggested that day at lunch, many students perceived that it was disrespectful, or "ghetto," to use BL in the classroom, particularly in front of the teacher. The lack of a clear language policy or of meaningful dialog about language choices left such decisions to students. This lack was an abdication of teacher responsibility.

Anderson (AL) noted that this abdication undermined teacher authority. He explained how "students used that slang language to their advantage." He felt he was openly disrespectful to his teachers by using "street" expressions that they permitted but that he himself felt were inappropriate. For example, he described his use of the expression "good lookin'," which was a term he would use to flirt with a peer. However, when his female teachers gave him work to do, he would say, "Thanks, good lookin'," and his teachers seemed flattered by it. Anderson felt it was a disrespectful remark that should have been corrected. A class clown generally, he regularly sought ways to mock authority, and many of his antics were often met with laughter from his peers. He told this story in a focus group and one of his friends began laughing about the event Anderson described, confirming his point that his peers recognized his verbal game though the teachers may not have. He consciously undermined teacher authority through his manipulation of the lack of any clear language policy. Such policies represented real dilemmas for teachers. On one hand, not having a clear policy was a way teachers may have felt they were respecting Black culture. On the other hand, it was also one of the many ways that school authority became weakened and left some students feeling that they were denied crucial knowledge.

The Case for an Open and Pro-BL Classroom

Students who endorsed a pro-BL classroom constructed the classroom as a space of self-expression and cultural affirmation. They saw Standard English as a language that was inauthentic and limited their expressive capacities and their power over language. John (Amb) highlighted many of the issues raised by those who preferred to use BL in the classroom:

MD: Do you use different language then when you're in class?

John: Yeah it's like you're two totally different people but not with everybody. Like, 'cause, one way, when you in the hallway with your friends, you speak, basically you speak in Ebonics, like that, and you talkin' slang with your friends, and they understand what you sayin'. And then when you in the classroom, you know you can't say, "'Nah, nah,' 'know what I mean,' 'word up,' and whatever." The teacher don't really be understandin' you, so you got to, like, well, okay, "You see this is the problem I have?" and stuff like that.

MD: Do students tend to drop the slang when they come into the room?

John: Me, I don't drop the slang when I'm in the classroom. That's how I talk and that's the way I write. 'Cause I know, 'cause most of the time I know if I change, if I write the way that they want me to write, they gonna be like, "you didn't write this. You a totally different person, somebody else wrote this for you." So, I don't even waste my time.

MD: If you write in Standard English, teachers will think you copied it from somewhere?

John: . . . 'Cause they don't, I think it's they think you can't speak Standard English, and me, I really see that there's no point in this 'cause instead of somebody sayin' it in Standard English, "Well, how are you doin' today." "Oh, I'm doing fine, everything is good." And they tell you, "how's the kids?" And, like, with me, I could say that all in one, all in one movement. Like, when I see [friend], I be like, I could either say, "What up?" and he be like, "Nothin'" so I know everything is good, or I could just give him a pound and we just said everything that they said in a pound! And I know like if I go to give him a pound and he doesn't give me a pound, then I know there's something wrong. So that way, I don't have to say, "Well, what's wrong?" when we go through that whole conversation, like that. It's a whole lot quicker then just doin' Standard English.

MD: Do you think you need to know Standard English?

John: I don't think, well, I think you do need to know Standard English 'cause you might get into situations where that's the only way you gonna get out. But mainly, and it also depends on where you live. Like where I live and like where [friend] lives, you don't have no use for Standard English. It doesn't really, nobody really cares if you speak Standard English or not.

John addresses a number of key values expressed by students who felt that local languages should be allowed in the classroom: authenticity and wholeness, efficiency, and community.

First, he felt that school required him to be two different people, his real self in the hall and someone else in the classroom. Over 100 years ago, W. E. B. Du Bois (1903) discussed the "two-ness" of being African American and of being American while wishing to be one, whole, undivided person (364). For several students advocating BL, the need to shift between the language of the dominant society and their home idioms was an example of this forced two-ness. John rejects this double-consciousness by refusing to speak Standard English. Using SE undermines his authenticity because it is a language imposed on him by the school and the White establishment and because he will be accused of copying or cheating for using it. His sense that the teachers wouldn't believe he wrote Standard English even if he used it also suggests the double bind SE represented and the great suspicion students hold toward the school they fear ultimately distrusts them.

The importance of authenticity, of being who you are and not having to change, was echoed frequently. Florence (AO) asserted, "You should be yourself." Derek (Amb) felt, "They should speak the way how they speak, they shouldn't change for nobody." Students who defended BL as part of their culture also echoed the sense that language reflected a core part of a person's identity.

Tina (AL) and Sharon (AL) defended their preference for BL by focusing on the significance of their authentic selves:

> Tina: Sometimes, it's just hard for some people, like they, teenagers now, like, you know, us urban teens, like, we been speakin' this way for so long, its just hard, like, to just turn around and change it. . . . It's not hard, like, you could do it when you need to, but I mean, like, when you in school, you want to express yourself.
> Sharon: A habit.
> Tina: Yeah it's like a habit. You know, like, you just can't stop.
> Sharon: I see it this way. If I act one way when I'm at one place, when I get to the next place, my attitude's gonna be the same.
> MD: You don't like to have to change?
> Sharon: No.
> Tina: Like, I gotta just be myself, if I can't be myself, you know, what's the use of being here.

Similar to John, who also did not want to divide himself, Tina and Sharon point to the difficulty of switching. Using SE means losing an ability to express who they are. The shift is uncomfortable and difficult though, they insist, doable. They are explicit that the classroom is a space of self-expression. Tina's assertion, "If I can't be myself, what's the use of being here?" clearly links the use of language to understandings of her true and whole self. Code-switching between BL and SE forced Tina and Sharon to become "two totally different people," as John put it, and those committed to BL rejected this double-consciousness.

The second issue John raised was that BL was so much more efficient. He includes as part of his language "a pound," a gesture that is much more expressive then many words in Standard English. He imitates an overly formal and polite conversation to point out how much must be said to achieve the information shared in a single gesture. Several students justified their preference for BL by emphasizing its immediacy and efficiency. Diane (AO), for example, said simply, "Slang is a shorter way." Even those who endorsed the use of SE echoed this sense of efficiency, which really speaks to BL's effectiveness to communicate emotion and self-expression. Shelly (HA), who supported an SE policy, noted,

> Shelly: I notice that when I'm angry or when I get mad, people say I break out my dialect; it actually come out. . . . The only time I could say I am not speaking Standard English is when I'm angry.
> MD: Why do you think that is?
> Shelly: I think it's shorter because you get your point across and you just say it shortly and you don't really have to get into, like, "Well, this is how I feel." Well, you just get it all out.

Though she identified as someone who spoke SE regularly, she admitted that in the heat of emotion, SE just didn't pass muster. In SE, one explains, describes, and narrates what one feels. In her local dialect, one just expresses feeling. She, too, perceived Standard English to be more alien to her immediate experiences. Expressing herself in Standard English required a lot of talking around what she feels and was inefficient for this reason. When she was angry, she reverts to a language that is naturally hers and does not require her to translate. In this sense, John's insistence on efficiency speaks to feeling powerful in one's mastery of language and ability to express inner feelings.

Finally, John also emphasizes the importance of his community in his rejection of SE. If he is going to stay in his community, he doesn't need to use SE. His aspirations inform his language politics, as would also be the case among those advocating SE. His use of BL and his resistance to SE solidified his commitment to his community. Many students, regardless of language preference, affirmed John's position that BL indicated immediate and communal relationships while SE was for more alien and hostile contexts.

Students frequently expressed the sense that the language with which they spoke with others established their distance or closeness. SE emphasized the diminished position of students in a school hierarchy, a vertical orientation of relationships, in contrast to the more horizontal relationships noted by the use of BL. Daniel (AO), who felt students should use SE in class explained,

> When you in the class, you're around teachers and everything. Like, you got to understand that they high and they know a little more—how to speak and everything. But when you around your peers, they're just like you. That's like my sister and brother; they know that I feel more comfortable talking around my peers than I'd feel by a teacher. . . . You change with your teachers; you change for your peers.

Daniel saw himself as lower than his teachers and marked that hierarchy by code-switching. However, his closeness to his peers enabled him to speak more comfortably. He compares his peers to "brother and sister" to indicate the closeness he felt to them. BL signifies this closeness and ease of manner. He went on to explain that in front of peers, "you just say what you want to say" but in the presence of a teacher "you try to switch; you don't want them thinking bad about you." Standard English is the language one uses to impress potentially hostile figures who are in a position to judge you. It is not a language shared among equals. Proponents of BL in the class sought to emphasize horizontal relationships and group solidarity through their language preference.

Geography of Language

One way the connection between the local community and BL was clarified was the ways students linked language to specific spaces to define their community and what is outside of it. An interesting geography of language emerged which highlights the conflicted location of the classroom within it. John focused on his neighborhood to insist he did not need to know SE. His argument suggests that he sees his neighborhood as his world—it is where he wants to or expects to stay and it is his discursive audience. Other students referenced specific spaces to expand this linguistic geography. Florence (AO) who was uncertain of which language policy was best, observed, "If you go to Harvard, most of the kids in Harvard, I don't think any of them even talk Ebonics." Keeping things closer to home, Jason (AL) echoed John's notion of neighborhood in explaining,

See how we's from [Renaissance's neighborhood], right. But if you go in Manhattan, you know, you supposed to change the way you speak. You just can't go out there and start giving the slang to the people out there because you know how they civilized and upper classes. And they don't understand where you comin' from and think we bad kids. So we can't just go out there and speak how we speak.

Jason, who was also uncertain of the language policies that should prevail in classrooms, nonetheless notes that in Manhattan, a center of culture and power, BL is inappropriate and the people there will judge them negatively for using it. Manhattan is also located "out there," distant, even though it is part of his city and only a subway ride away. He, like John, links BL to his local community but perceives, as Florence does, that elites do not use that language and probably can't understand it. Idiom marks space and defines power relationships within it. Students who rejected the use of SE in the classroom were marking the classroom as part of their local community and as a space where they could feel powerful. They rejected it as a space linked to the broader society in which they are negatively judged.

In fact, several students noted that though in the broader world they were negatively judged by the way they used or failed to use SE, among peers, it was the use of SE that was negatively valued. Some students confirmed the powerful link between BL and local community through their negative experiences using SE. Some admitted that they spoke BL around their peers to avoid their teasing. Ann (HA) was the only student who insisted she always spoke SE, and she felt hopelessly outside the community of her peers. "Like, even when I'm in school, most people think I speak a certain way or something like that. And I am usually being picked on for it a lot, but this is the way I always am. . . . This is how I speak to any- and everybody [in Standard English]." The use of BL creates a community of ease and acceptance among equals, but SE generally indicates the subordinate status of students and the broader Black community. Ann's exclusive use of SE carried significant social consequences, particularly as it marked her disconnection from the local Black community. It is also worth noting that Ann was a relatively recent West Indian immigrant (having been in the country less than two years) from a middle-class background, and she may not have had significant street or local affinities. Her refusal to pick up the local "slang" was read as snobbishness and identification with the dominant culture. The tension about using SE is deeply rooted in African American struggles in the United States. Smitherman (1977) writes,

> Historically, Black speech has been demanded of those who wish to retain close affinities with the Black community, and intrusions of White English are likely to be frowned upon and any Black users thereof promptly ostracized by the group. Talkin' proper (trying to sound White) just ain' considered cool. On the other hand, White America has insisted upon White English as the price of admission into its economic and social mainstream. (12)

The struggle over language policies at Renaissance echoed these historic struggles, which were also embedded in understandings of space. Students who preferred to use BL in the classroom, as John noted, sought to maintain these close connections to their racial and cultural communities and wanted classroom space to be an extension of that geography.

The Case for Standard English

Students who valued horizontal relationships over hierarchical ones preferred the language of solidarity with their racial and peer group. They resisted having to use an idiom that emphasized vertical relationships and, generally, their relatively low status within social hierarchies. Conversely, proponents of SE valued knowing SE because they sought to move up that vertical axis. References to hierarchies abounded in the rhetoric on language used by SE advocates who often saw themselves as having the agency to alter their class positions. These students endorsed SE as a "proper" and "higher-class" language while challenging constructions of blackness implicit in the connection of Black solidarity to BL. They sought to separate Black identity from BL to open up avenues for themselves in which they could be middle class, upwardly mobile, and Black.

The tension between these two orientations (vertical versus horizontal) was evident in the experiences of SE users. Though in the broader society students were economically marginalized for their use of BL, in the halls of Renaissance (and classrooms too), students were socially marginalized for using SE, as Ann suggested. Laura (AO) explained of her experiences using SE, "Okay, they will make remarks, such as 'she thinks she's better than us.' You know, so I believe most students, they try to come down to their classmates' level in order to stop the teasing and the taunting." Laura suggests, as did many others, that SE is above BL in the vertical structure of the school and society. In order to affirm solidarity with peers, or at least to avoid their teasing, those who would speak SE must "come down" to the level of their peers through using BL. Importantly though, as Laura admits, most SE proponents (except Ann) did use BL with their peers, in part because they were punished for not doing so and, perhaps, in part because they also valued these relationships.

Standard English supporters were attuned to hierarchies of social and economic class and articulated alternative notions of blackness to claim middle-class aspirations. Thomas (HA), the most ardent and explicit defender of SE, was critical of BL because it reinforced racist stereotypes of Black people. His critique is instructive because although advocates of BL often constructed speakers of Standard English as traitors and occasionally as "White" (even if they weren't), those who preferred SE were often equally motivated by group solidarity:

Thomas: I'm the bomb student, not like these ghetto heads!

MD: What do you mean by "ghetto heads?"

Thomas: Ghetto, welfare. They talk "ghetto," not Black. Like, "is," "ain't no nigga," "ain't got that son," "illin'," "chillin'," "buggin'," "what is you doin." People think that Black people talk like the students in this school, but they don't—that is ghetto! Ebonics is crap! It's ghetto. People think Black people can't speak better. . . . It's that White people perceive that that's how all Black people speak. That's how ghetto people speak. To your friends, you can talk any way, but you have to know the boundaries.

Thomas is a user of BL, using it to define himself, but criticized its use in public settings because he feared it defined Black people negatively. Though his peers identified BL with Black identity, Thomas specifically separated it, identifying the language widely used by students as "ghetto," not Black. His use of the term "ghetto" associates BL with "welfare," low socio-economic status and other negative stereotypes of Black people. In separating the Black community from "ghetto," Thomas preserves a positive Black identity that transcended these stereotypes. He creates a different geography of language that marginalizes BL as a product of "the ghetto," narrowing the scope of its appropriateness. Thomas insists that the refusal to code-switch, particularly in spaces where there are White people, denigrates Black identity by linking it to lower-class status.

The separation of "ghetto" from Black is a class-based division. Ghetto Blacks are poor, while others are not. Such a division may be a response to those who define academically successful students as the "other" or "White." In a class I was teaching, a student accused Thomas and a few others of being White because they owned computers and were good students. I asked Thomas to interpret this event for me. He felt the remark was more aimed at the economic class of high achievers and offered a class-based analysis of the animosity between serious academic students and those who attack them as breaking solidarity with their race:

> They just most of the times, you know, they're, like, offended, no, they're mad at you because you have a better upbringing you know. You're more fortunate than they are. You have, like, a house instead of an apartment and stuff like that . . . a computer at home. . . . Most of the time, you know, it's like kids who have, like, a secure financial place for them to live in or whatever, usually those students do better you know, that's a fact. Not that it's necessary, you know, you must have a house or a computer, or whatever, but for the most part if you have a secure home, a mother and a father, for the most part, these are the kids that do well.

Access to computers, intact families, and home ownership all support high academic achievement, and for Thomas, to a great extent, academic success and failure are products of socio-economic class. The student in class equated middle-class tropes, such as computer ownership, with whiteness. Thomas identifies as middle class but does not identify with whiteness. By separating Black identity from a subordinate class position, he promotes a competing notion of blackness that includes academic achievement and middle-class goals without compromising Black identity.

Thomas's support for Standard English ties into his perception that lower-class status is wrongly affixed to Black identity: "White people think that's how all Black people speak. That's how ghetto people speak." The role of language connects directly to his core identity just as it did for those who advocated a pro-BL policy. Separating BL from Black identity frees it from marginalization. Thomas's critique also highlights how race and class have become so closely linked in the construction of White and Black identities that blackness is inextricably connected to poverty and middle-class status automatically commuted to whiteness. Thomas attacks this equation, making room for his own aspirations and inclinations.

Fordham (1996) has pointed out that African American students often construct academic success as "White" and refuse to strive for it because such actions are perceived as an assault on blackness. Success in school requires submission and buying in to dominant values that often negatively construct blackness. The discussion in this chapter and elsewhere in this book certainly note a problematic tension between the cultural identities of Black students and academic success. However, Fordham argues that high-achieving African American students often resist these very same negative constructions of blackness by challenging racist stereotypes. Students who felt strongly about the use of Standard English were generally high-achieving or academically oriented students and some, like Thomas, exhibited the kind of resistance Fordham and others have found (Akom 2003). Students supporting SE expressed a strong sense of racial pride in resisting the stereotypes they felt were perpetuated by some of their peers.

Resisting the equation of BL and racial solidarity, Tanisha (AO), an advocate of SE, charged that failing to teach SE to Black students kept the race down:

> It is very important because the students, in this world, you cannot use Ebonics to speak to your should-be or might-be boss. You have to speak proper English, 'cause that's what we were taught when we came to America. I mean, we don't speak African or Latin, you know, Spanish; we speak English. That's the language that we were taught and we need to speak it. Ebonics, I feel, is just a trick to make most people, you know, people can't get a job with that language. So when it's taught to people who already don't know how to speak better, you know, then they gonna go into the world not knowing how to speak proper at all, and people are not going to understand you. You're not gonna get anywhere, pretty much.

Tanisha identified the widespread use of BL and the lack of knowledge of Standard English as detrimental to the upward mobility of Black people. Several students echoed this idea—that the school must teach students to speak and write Standard English because it is crucial to future success. Tashona (HA) commented, "If you want to excel in life, you have to speak Standard English." Beyond just a job or job interview, these students saw Standard English as the language of success and ambition. For them, the classroom should be a space where students are prepared to participate in the world of more powerful people. Its primary purpose was to provide them with the cultural capital necessary for upward mobility. Class-inflected understandings of race and language permeated much of the support for teaching Standard English and using it in the classroom.

Several pro-SE students felt that some of their peers, and sometimes they themselves, could not speak Standard English and negatively viewed such inability. Tanisha again charged,

> A lot of them still speak the slang; they don't learn any better even at home. Some of the parents now, they don't know better themselves. They teach their kids what they know, and the kids come in the school not knowing any better but carrying what they know from home to school. But, you know, I for instance, I know better.

She links the use of BL to lower-class status by pointing to the family as having failed to teach Standard English because "the parents . . . don't know better themselves." Insisting that she does know better, she defines herself as superior to those that don't. Like Thomas, she, too, creates a division based on upbringing and aspirations. She went on to explain,

> What you say is a lot about you. It shows where your head is at. If you say, "Yo, this and that," most people will think you don't have much on your mind. And you don't have much; you know, you want nothing, goals in life, whatever.

Using BL outside of one's immediate community suggests that the speaker is not seeking upward mobility. Not speaking Standard English tells others, "you don't have much," and "you want nothing." The emphasis on what you have and to what you aspire reflects a class-based construction of language use.

Similar to several other supporters of SE, Tanisha emphasized the connection of the classroom to future aspirations by constructing it as a staging ground for those desires. Jamal (AL) was one of the most emphatic that the school should teach SE. He expressed anger over what he felt was the school's great failure to teach him what he really needed to know:

> I think English is a waste of my time. They don't teach you how to speak proper English. They teach you mythology. Nothing is wrong with that, but I think Americans should have their English down pat before they go to that. A lot of people cannot speak proper English for nothin.' I ain't saying I'm perfect at it, but just because you speak it don't mean you know it. . . . People say, "I got a dollar," it's "I have a dollar." You know what I mean? A lot of people don't know how to speak English; they speak broken-down English. A lot of Columbians and people from other countries come here, learn our language. They can speak it better than us. But they got they slang, but they speak proper English.

Like other students who supported the use of SE, Jamal suspects a plot against the Black community. The school is not teaching him the basic linguistic tools he will need to move up in American society, leaving him to watch immigrants come in and move up ahead of him because they learn the language. By giving him literature instead of specific instruction in Standard English usage, the school was wasting his time.

Solomon (1992) points out that the school is the key to upward mobility for West Indian immigrants. For many Caribbean students, immigration to America offers educational opportunities denied them in their home countries. Proponents of Standard English hoped that the school would deliver the educational goods they need to attain access to greater opportunity. Delpit (1995) has argued that by not teaching minority and marginalized children the dominant language, the school is withholding crucial tools for future advancement and survival. These students, too, echo Delpit's demand that the school help them develop fluency in the codes of power that they will need to compete in a market often hostile to them.

Not only did proponents of SE feel that failing to provide them this linguistic competence kept their people down, but they also constructed many hierarchies that almost always favored Standard English. For example, Tashona (HA) explained what her use of SE meant to her,

Well, I speak differently around my peers than I do in front of adults. So, I want to be perceived as an intelligent intellectual, so I'll speak with dignity, and I'll speak with pride, and I speak with some intelligence. I know something. So that they'll know that.

For Tashona, SE represents intelligence, pride, and dignity. By implication, BL does not convey these things. In addition to equating SE with these positive attributes, many students perceived BL as a language for children but not for adults, establishing another hierarchy.

Though Tashona admitted that she enjoys using BL with her friends, she claimed she does not use it around adults. When asked if she spoke BL with her mother, she explained, "No, only when we're joking around, but other than that I talk to her with respect." Here, again, she indicates that SE is the language of respect and deference but when she and her mother are kidding around, BL is fine. Sounding the same connection between SE and adulthood, Tameeka, the only ambivalent student to endorse SE in the classroom, explained,

Yeah, they should teach us Standard English. They should, because, like, if we go to a job interview for example, we have to dress nice and all. And the person talking to you, you want to talk on a mature adult level, not on a, you know, you want to be up there, not coming in there, "Yo, what's up?". . . They'll look at you as "Hmm, they don't really want this job." They would think they in the street somewhere, they wouldn't look at you as a mature professional. They would look at you as in, "grow up!"

Tameeka reiterated that students should use SE in the classroom because when "you're talking to an adult, which is the teacher, talk on an adult level." Both Tameeka and Vera link the use of BL to childhood and youth culture, which they need to grow out of as they near their own efforts to enter the workforce. The classroom for them represents preparation for this process.

Students established hierarchies that placed SE over BL and gave students who were competent in SE a sense of power and efficacy. Echoing Vera's sense that SE was the language of "respect" and "intelligence," Shelly (HA) described her pride in her verbal accomplishments:

I find that's one thing I put a lot of emphasis on, having a strong vocabulary. That's how I push myself, 'cause you could, say, use one word to explain a lot of little words, so it's like, the stronger your vocabulary the easier to get, to put yourself out there because people could understand you. And it shows people that you have a level of intelligence, you know. It's like, I'm not like everybody else, don't put me in the level of everybody else, but you could have a little bit more respect for me because I could understand you. And like talking to adults if you can convey information to them real well—big words, not really big words, but, like, you know, could talk in their tone, not really in their tone, using words in their vocabulary, they'll look at you in a different light. They won't shut you down, like, "okay, his Mama didn't teach him English."

Shelly's mastery over SE through the development of a large vocabulary made her feel powerful. She also perceived that she gained the respect of potentially hostile assessors by being able to draw on their language, which she recognized as more than just big words and tone but also using their vocabulary effectively. Tellingly, she also insisted that her use of language should separate her from the pack—that she is worthy of more respect. At the heart of the tension between vertical and horizontal orientations is the conflict between individual advancement and group solidarity.

Students who endorsed SE understood the classroom as part of a vertically oriented world in which they had to negotiate their way up in a hierarchy. They saw SE as a higher language—that of adults, bosses, people with power—and those who couldn't use it were lower in this hierarchy. The classroom was a space in which they were preparing for participation in the broader society outside of their own community. Students who endorsed SE generally identified with middle-class aspirations but rejected the equation of Black solidarity with BL asserting, instead, that the failure to master SE was keeping the race down.

The Eyes of the "Other"

Deep tensions about racial identity and solidarity informed the differences on language policy. Those who aspired to inhabit places such as Harvard or Manhattan were much more receptive to learning the language they would need in those places. Other students constructed a far more local geography in which relationships were familiar and level. Despite these striking differences about language and worldview, students, generally, regardless of their language preferences, noted what Delpit (2002) refers to as "the eyes of 'the other'" that judge and condemn. John (Amb), Thomas (HA), Daniel (AO), Sheena (AO), and Tanisha (AO), though having different opinions about what classroom language policy should be, all allude to the potentially hostile gaze of others, particularly teachers and White people. Thomas's critique of Ebonics was that it gave White people the wrong impression and, clearly, what White people think is significant to him. His notion of upward mobility means navigating that hostile gaze to gain acceptance. The perpetuation of negative images of Black people made his goal even harder to attain. Conversely, John's sense that his teachers suspect he can't write in SE also notes the hostile and judgmental gaze of those with power. Unlike Thomas, however, John thwarted the power of this gaze by refusing to write in SE. By refusing to attempt SE, he denied anyone the power to diminish his authenticity.

The sense that students were being judged, and judged harshly and immediately, by the way they spoke permeated most of the interviews. Language was a key site of assessment, and students were quite aware of its power. Delpit (2002) explains the power of this hostile gaze in coping with her own feelings of hearing her daughter using BL and her perception of the Black response to the Ebonics controversy in the late 1990s:

> The real issue was our concern about what others would think. We worried how, after years and years of trying to prove ourselves good enough, we might again be dismissed as ignorant and unworthy by those in power, by "the white folks." We worried that our children would be viewed, and subsequently treated, as "less than"—in schools now, and in the workplace later. Consequently, those of us who reach for or attempt to maintain middle-class acceptability work hard to stamp out the public expression of the language with which we enjoy such a love/hate relationship. . . .
>
> So, when my child's language reflects that of some of her peers, I feel the eyes of "the other" negatively assessing her intelligence, her competence, her potential and yes, even her moral fiber. (37–38)

This deep anxiety about being harshly judged by those with power informed language politics at Renaissance. Students who rejected the imposition of SE wanted to be free from that judgmental gaze in the classroom. They wanted it to be a space of self-expression, authenticity, and where they felt powerful. They did not want to be encumbered with the burden of the dominant idiom and be subject to the "eyes of the other" assessing them.

Language politics are not just about self-expression or the expression of aspirations beyond the immediate community; they are also about the ways power shall be used in the classroom and for what purpose. The anxiety about being judged that crossed the boundaries of language politics highlighted the ways dominant culture and the expectations of the powerful were always present in the classroom. Complicating the notion of self-expression that many teachers and BL supporters endorsed was the ways the classroom was a different space than the halls. It is a space where teachers present curriculum and evaluate students on their mastery of it, and thus it is always a space where judgment is passed. Those rejecting the imposition of SE were seeking to keep the classroom within the realm of the familiar—a less hostile place and perhaps one more connected to their social and historical experience.

Language politics highlighted the contested nature of classroom space. As noted in the last chapter, the use of BL in the halls reinforced those spaces as Black spaces connected to the local and street cultures familiar to students. However, the uncertainty that surrounded the language of the classroom particularly highlights its unstable qualities. Students did not see the classroom as an extension of hall space because they generally changed their tone and vocabulary, if not their entire dialect on entering the classroom. It did not seem that students wanted the classroom to be an extension of the halls. Students were also generally not opposed to code-switching, but students disputed which codes were most appropriate for the classroom. The tensions present in language politics between a vertical and horizontal worldview and the conflicting values of individual success or group solidarity would inform other struggles over classroom space as well.

These tensions also call attention to different strategies of resistance in which students engage. Some confront the hostile gaze of the "other" head on, as Shelly (HA) felt she could do, while John (Amb) chose to deny those eyes the opportunity to judge his linguistic competence. For both Shelly and John, there is always an audience eager to pass judgment, but each sees his or her relationship to that audience differently. At the heart of language politics are perceptions of how power should be distributed and mediated in classrooms. Should these relationships be more hierarchical in nature, as most students perceived the workplace is, or should they be more egalitarian relationships that do not establish distance between participants. I begin this discussion of the contestation over classroom space with the exploration of language policy because it richly demonstrates the nature of contact-zone struggles and the lack of consensus among students or teachers about what the classroom did or should represent. The nature of power in classrooms was unresolved at Renaissance. The next two chapters examine the problematic relationships between teacher authority and democratic school reform that further destabilized classroom cultures.

5

■　■　■　■　■　■　■　■

"You have to change your whole attitude toward everything"
Threshold Struggles and Infrapolitical Resistance

One day during lunch as I sat with a group of teachers in the staff resource room, a new teacher asked how we dealt with kids who didn't bring pens. We all laughed at the question because it was the kind of question that seemed so trivial on the surface and yet was such a serious classroom management issue. We talked through a number of tactics several of us had tried such as taking points off of class work or report card grades, which, we generally agreed, didn't work because, as one colleague noted, they "just don't care or don't believe you will take serious points off for not having a pen." Then, there was the tactic of charging a quarter and selling unprepared students pens. Some of the group used this method and felt it worked except that students would sometimes insist they didn't have a quarter, and one teacher explained, "that somehow gave them permission to not do any work." Another teacher said she just got fed up with battling her kids about pens. She decided to focus her energy on other things, so she just bought tons of pens and when students said they didn't have them, she simply gave them one. She preferred that they have no excuse to not do work.

At the time, my policy was that I would lend students pens if they gave me their student ID cards. They were not allowed in the building without them, so they had to have them, and this way I would know who had borrowed one. By doing this I had discovered that they often did have pens, and once they had to go in their bags for the ID, they miraculously found a pen. I only ended up lending one or two pens a period. "Most of the time," I observed, "they're scamming us."

Though at the time I only meant that students were scamming us when they claimed they had no pens and meant my comment humorously, in fact, students often misrepresented themselves. These "scams" were not major crimes—they were low-level confidence games in which their claims were credible. They also weren't trying to trick us out of property (the pens aside), but they were trying to steal back class time for themselves. They used a thousand little tricks—excuses, over-stated obstacles (I don't have pen, paper, a book, a partner, etc.), lateness, chatting, note-passing, taking the hall pass, foot-dragging, and so on—and though teachers might be suspicious of ulterior motives, we had no real way of knowing if students were telling us the truth. This was the brilliance of such tactics—though they frustrated teachers, they were always just believable enough, providing students with plausible deniability to escape any serious disciplinary action. The fact that a group of teachers spent much of their lunch period discussing just one of these tactics indicates how effective they were at frustrating our efforts without appearing serious enough to push us to really do something about them.

These "scams" were a form of what Scott (1985; 1990) refers to as infrapolitical resistance—resistance that flies under the radar because it does not directly confront authority and usually avoids serious sanctions. Teachers were unlikely to impose any severe penalty for not having a pen or coming in a little late, despite how much it bugged us and how much we groused about it among ourselves; such infrapolitical strategies effectively limited the amount of time students were required to give themselves over to our authority. Though overlooked in much of the scholarship on urban schooling, infrapolitical resistance offers valuable insight into the day-to-day engagement between students and schools. This chapter examines infrapolitical resistance that informs the threshold struggles that take place around the spatial and temporal shifts from hall space and "free" time to classroom space and a more industrial sense of time. In addition to bringing infrapolitics into the discussion of student resistance, this chapter also raises new questions about what resistance and oppositionality mean.

As discussed at length in the introduction to this book, the literature on student resistance, though rich and revealing, has been somewhat contradictory. Notably, resistance theorists have understood student resistance as a positive response to oppressive and at times demeaning school systems and practices (Willis 1977; Fine 1991; Kohl 1994; Grant and Sleeter 1996; Dance 2002). Conversely, scholars probing the concept of oppositional cultures have conceptualized resistance negatively, as a strategy that undermines academic performance (Fordham and Ogbu 1986; Ogbu 1988 and 2003; Flores-Gonzalez 1999 and 2002). However, urban students engage schooling in complex ways that belie the either/or parameters of these debates. I argue for a more nuanced understanding of resistance, opposition, and student identities by examining resistance that is widely deployed but rarely elicits severe correction from teachers.

According to Scott (1985) infrapolitical resistance, like infrared rays, is barely visible resistance that quietly seeks to limit the demands of the powerful. By examining the tactics students deployed to waste time, avoid or skirt assignments, and generally limit the demands teachers made on them, I want to call attention not only to the barely visible quality of these strategies but also to their politics. Infrapolitical tactics are often perceived as unorganized, individual acts to avoid the demands of bosses or those with power. As our conversation in the staff room suggested, teachers did not connect these aggravating tactics to any organized resistance or to any particular political stance. The lack of an articulated message makes infrapolitics effective—the tactics used do not appear dangerous or threatening and hence garner less policing. However, Scott (1985) emphasizes, as will I in this chapter, that such resistance is political and coherent. At Renaissance, it flourished in the gaps between school policies and teacher practices and called attention to the contradictions and inconsistencies in school authority and student relationships with school.

Threshold Struggles

Unlike hall culture, which is largely defined by students, classroom culture is a negotiation between teachers and school authority on the one hand and students on the other. Though teachers are recognized as authority figures in the classroom, their power is far from secure. Students test and challenge that authority constantly and ultimately determine whether they will respect it or not. Student efforts to reclaim classroom time and space for student-defined purposes compete with teacher efforts to control student activity and to increase time on task. The pen issue raised by the first-year teacher is one example of the seemingly endless power struggles between students and teachers.

Six educators noted in their interviews with me that the biggest challenges lay at the beginning of class. As one teacher, Alice, put it, "In the first few minutes when you walk into that room, you have a lesson planned. If you don't get started right away, don't worry because twenty minutes, thirty minutes, you're not going to!" The first few minutes of a class period were fateful in establishing teacher authority and in defining the work of the classroom. Importantly, much of the daily struggle around this crucial time was enacted through infrapolitical resistance.

Movement into classroom space requires that students not merely physically relocate from the halls but also psychologically move into a different psychic and bodily regime. Students go from the freedom of the halls where they can move around as they please, physically play with each other (wrestling, kissing, tag and flirtation games, etc.), and make any sounds they want (singing, screaming, swearing, etc.) to the highly structured space of the classroom in which they are expected to sit in seats, move and speak only with teacher approval, and attend to the teacher's agenda. In addition to the bodily restraints the transition requires, it also imposes a temporal shift from "free" time to structured time that is carefully measured and under the teacher's control.

Such transitions, not surprisingly, met a great deal of resistance, mostly infrapolitical, as many students sought to maintain their own sense of time and purpose within classroom spaces. These barely perceptible, often invisible, efforts to resist the imposition of what McLaren (1986) has called "the student state" are examples of infrapolitical resistance. Though enacted under the radar, infrapolitical student resistance undermines school efforts and highlights the ideological struggles that lie at the heart of student academic performance and resistance.

In his ethnography of a Catholic middle school for working-class boys, McLaren (1986) defines a number of "states" that students occupy during the school day. The two "states" of importance here are the "street-corner state" and the "student state." By "states," McLaren refers to "styles of interacting with the environment and with others which could, perhaps, be appropriately labeled behavioural clusters or complexes. . . . They consist of organized assemblages of behaviours out of which emerge a central or dominant system of *lived* practices" (86, emphasis in original). As students move from one state to another they change their behavior, the tone of their voice, their vocabulary and dialect, and the level of autonomy they exercise. When students are in the halls, school authorities have little control over them. They can yell, run around, and joke; in this unsupervised space for adolescent freedom, they are in what McLaren calls the "street-corner state," or in the Renaissance context, they are in the "hall state." When students enter the classroom, they must convert to the "student state," minding the rules of the teacher, complying with classroom protocols, speaking softly, and working nicely with their peers.

The transition from the hall state to the student state requires changes not just in behavior, but also in students' total way of being—not merely how they speak but also what they speak about, how they speak about it and what they think about. Thus, more than code-switching, or changing dialects in different contexts, transitioning to the classroom requires what I call "mode-switching," a visceral and significant reorientation of the body, desire, and purpose. Transition to the student state requires taking on more than merely outward behaviors; students must don the value system and way of looking at the world derived from the school and reflective of dominant culture.

Though students did not specifically use this language, they described being aware of these transitions from one state to another. Jennie (HA) describes,

> The hallway kids is, like, totally different from the students when you're in the classroom. 'Cause the hallway . . . you're like, all right, "I'm done with this class; I ain't got to do anything more," so you think about, you know, just talking with your friends and stuff, and you acting like a child. But then once you in your class, you know, you have to change your whole attitude towards everything.

For Jennie, transitioning to the classroom was not merely an external shift but also a mental one, altering her "whole attitude towards everything." In contrast to the changes she made when entering the classroom, Ricky (Amb) noted, "When they're in the hallway, they're loud with their friends and they talking, and they don't know the transition when you walk into the classroom to quiet down." He interpreted a lack of transition as a lack of cultural capital—students don't know better or they don't know how to make transitions. However, as debates about language choices among students suggest, students may be consciously resisting such transitions. In the student state, McLaren explains, students "lose their possession of time, space and street roles, transferring them over to the hierarchy and control of the school authorities" (95). It is precisely this shift of power that many students resisted at least to some degree.

Nina (HA), was rarely noticeably late but complained of the expected transitions,

> Yeah, it [talking in the hall] ends. Be like, "No talking!" "Don't do that!" "You can't do this!" "Get your books out! Do your work!" We know that, but sometimes, come on! Sometimes we not ready! We are not ready to get started. . . . They expect us when the bell rings, take out our books, start doing work, work, until the end of the period. Give us a break!

Nina draws a sharp contrast between the halls and the classroom, offering a barrage of commands to emphasize the loss of student autonomy. She is critical of the structure of school, which expects students to make a fast transition from talking to friends to obeying teachers. She uses the phrase "give us a break" both literally and ironically. Students wanted a break from schoolwork to talk at the beginning of class and she wanted a break from the unfairness of teacher demands.

The classroom door marks the threshold between the hall and student states as well as the physical and temporal regimes that support them. Because school authority and teacher control are more established in the classroom than in the hall, much of the resistance by students is infrapolitical. Despite its low profile, this resistance reveals the conflicted nature of classrooms and the instability of teacher and school authority.

Reading the Hat Rule

To begin this discussion of the logic of infrapolitical resistance, I begin with a case study of the "hat rule," which offers a window into the ways infrapolitics are deployed. Baseball caps were worn by many boys and targeted by a system-wide ban on hats in classrooms throughout the city. The principal, chancellor, and the media constructed the presence of baseball caps and do-rags as indicative of a school's nonacademic focus. The hat, in official discourse, is a symbol of the street and street culture and is inappropriate in the classroom. Thus, the principal aggressively enforced this district policy and required that teachers have students remove hats.

Though hats were confiscated during weapons scanning if they were not concealed and students were generally aware that hats were not allowed, they persisted in wearing them once they got into the halls. Symbolic of student dominance there, few school personnel challenged students over hats in the halls, and if they did, their commands were generally laughed off. When students entered classrooms however, teachers generally required, or at least requested, that students take their hats off. In my own classes only a few boys removed their hats after the first request, while most waited for a second or third appeal. Once removed, hats often popped back on heads during the lesson, demanding further correction. The quiet refusal to remove their hats is one example of student infrapolitical resistance. They did not openly refuse to comply but required that teachers ask several times in each and every class.

The struggle over hats, though tiring, rarely was considered a classroom management issue and was only occasionally openly challenged by students. Nonetheless, hats were a visible symbol of student-school conflict and suggest student resistance to leaving the hall state. The chancellor's insistence on their removal may have been to force this very point—that in the classroom, students must fully enter the student state. Enforcement of the hat rule fully asserts the primacy of the school's academic function.

The hat rule also reveals more subtle ways the classroom becomes a different environment for boys and girls. Many researchers have pointed out that school success requires a certain level of submission and passivity (Fine 1991), and thus girls who are socialized toward such behaviors do better (Tyack and Hansot 1991). The hat rule publicly, visually, and physically forces boys to submit to school protocols in ways that, though seemingly evenly applied, are not as abusive to girls. Though girls wore caps, they did so less regularly, often claiming they were having a "bad hair day," and thus, were more readily permitted to keep their hats on. Girls also tied scarves around their heads or wore more elaborate head wraps that were also forbidden and challenged at scanning but often overlooked in classrooms.

Some teachers perceived that the hat rule only applied to boys, echoing an old social code, "gentlemen must remove their hats," and did not require girls to remove any headwear. In her 2003 study of West Indian and

Dominican youth, Lopez found that this "boys only" interpretation of the rule was a common practice in the urban classrooms she observed. Other teachers applied the hat rule to baseball caps and do-rags but not to headwear they interpreted as cultural or religious. The principal sought to include these head wraps in the ban, but many staff openly rejected this construction. Many students and teachers perceived that head wraps, whether simple scarves or more elaborate wraps made of kente cloth, were specifically African forms of dress and refused to challenge them. Thus, girls were far more able to keep their markers of Black identity on in the classroom.

Boys, conversely, were required to remove a key marker of street culture and a symbol of their masculinity in order to enter the student state. The subordinate position of girls in the hall, their less-frequent use of caps, and their greater ability to evade the rule meant that girls had less at stake in the enforcement of the rule. The loss of status that classroom culture exacts from boys may inform their participation in it. Boys were far more likely to be class clowns and to openly attack teacher authority. Such activity may have been aimed at regaining status lost from the visible act of submission their entry into the classroom required. The universal resistance to removing caps (including among academically oriented and high-achieving boys) suggests that entering the student state was an emasculating experience for some young men. Warren's 2005 study of African-Caribbean young men noted that his subjects perceived the demand to remove their hats as a sign of disrespect. He argues that hats are part of the "cool pose" of young Black men, a survival strategy that secures respect. The practice of stripping boys of a powerful symbol of their local culture and masculinity places the requirements of academic life in a tense relationship with the identity of young Black men.

At the same time that the hat rule is an example of the ways school routines effeminize classrooms and structure the antischool identities of some students, it also reveals the conflicted nature of schools. Teachers did not universally apply the hat rule, and they did not enforce it the same way. The hat rule reveals teacher ambivalence to school- and district-generated mandates as well. In my classes, students ignored first and second requests to remove their hats but rarely verbally protested. When they did, they often pointed out that other teachers let them wear hats in their classrooms. Their reference to differing teacher policies highlights a significant fissure in school authority: teachers selectively enforce rules.

I often heard colleagues complain out of the hearing the principal that they thought the hat rule was "stupid," a "distraction," and a "waste of energy." Some refused to enforce it at all in their classes, and students in my classes reported that some teachers openly criticized the rule in class. Other teachers, however, strongly endorsed such a rule, insisting that students needed to learn to present themselves appropriately in different contexts. One Black teacher noted in an interview that she felt the lax enforcement of the hat rule was indicative of the low expectations that too many teachers held for students. Though teachers disagreed about the rule, the principal expended a lot of political capital on its enforcement, pressuring teachers to comply and constantly telling students to remove hats, even in the halls. Teacher disagreement over the hat rule, like their disagreement over almost every mandate and school practice, reveals conflicting ideological orientations toward teaching, students, and the purpose of school, as well as the official discourses of the state, district, and principal.

The hat rule is a useful example of infrapolitical resistance. Students quietly resisted the rule in several ways. They required that teachers ask several times before students removed their hats, and they also feigned compliance with the rule—removing the hat but putting it back on a few minutes later. In both cases, students required that teachers work harder at enforcement and, in fact, required that teachers actively enforce the rule. Though students were well aware of the rule, they refused to internalize it. Having to ask repeatedly and throughout class drained teachers' time and energy. This kind of quiet but relentless resistance enabled students to negotiate limits on the rule. In my own classes, I found that once hats had been removed, I paid less attention to them as they popped back on, despite my pretending this rule was out of my control as I noted in my "dictatorship rules" (see Introduction). Once I was in the flow of my lesson, I chose not to stop over hats, indicating my own ambivalence to the rule. Clearly, other teachers also came to some kind of compromise. The differential enforcement from room to room made clear to students that the rule was malleable, exposing the unstable nature of school authority. Resistance to the hat rule shows that students rejected, without openly protesting, the school's assault on local notions of masculinity and street culture. The opposition to the rule also demonstrates that infrapolitical resistance can be quite effective.

Infrapolitical Resistance through Lateness

The hat rule echoes the front-door cleansing ritual of scanning in that it asserts an appropriate style for classroom comportment. Like the scanning ritual, the hat rule requires that students alter their bodies as they move from one space to another. When passing through the threshold, students were also expected to transition from one notion of time, passing time, to classroom time. This temporal transition echoes transitions from leisure time to industrial time or being "on the clock" as opposed to off it. The use and control of time was one of the central sites of infrapolitical struggle as students sought to alter the nature of the classroom space through maintaining as much control over time as possible. Like twentieth-century peasants in Southeast Asia (Scott 1985 and 1990) and workers in nineteenth-century England (Thompson 1962), students used lateness as a way to whither away work time without directly confronting authority.

Being late to class not only enabled students to resist transitioning to the student state, but it also may have been part of a wider critique of schooling. In her 1986 study of the use of time among Black community-college students, Weis found that students used lateness and cutting class to resist the imposition of dominant notions of time. She argues that lateness was an oppositional aspect of student culture aimed at preserving Black solidarity and resisting White culture. Given the emphasis on group solidarity at the heart of hall culture, lateness was also used to affirm peer solidarity.

Lateness was one of the most significant discipline problems at Renaissance. According to teacher estimates from interviews, between 30 and 50 percent of students entered class after the late bell rang on a regular basis. At Renaissance, the passing bell rang to mark the end of each class period. Four minutes later, a second bell, the late bell, rang to note that the next class period had begun. Students, even some high achievers, typically ignored the late bell and did not rush off to class. As I stood in the halls during passing time, I often greeted students who warmly waved as they passed my door to their hall hangouts. They then entered my classroom several minutes after the late bell rang. Despite my noting that they had walked passed the room well before the bell rang, they simply shrugged. These students perceived their time in the halls as a right and my pleading was not going to interfere with it. Such behavior was typical, and few classrooms were full when the bell to begin classes rang.

More than merely coming a few minutes late, students slowed the beginning of classes by coming in at all different times. Though more than half the class might be present five minutes after the bell rang, the rest would drip in every minute or two, each interruption slowing the class down and causing small disruptions. Though the principal urged teachers to keep their doors open, many teachers, myself included, refused because there was too much noise from the halls. But closing doors meant that each late student had to knock and be let in, further interrupting the flow of class. Lateness was a powerful tool that served many student purposes while undermining classroom instruction and teacher agendas.

One way that lateness was a powerful infrapolitical tool was its effectiveness in enabling students to redefine the start of class time, particularly the meaning of bells. The use of bells in schools to mark time has its roots in the industrial model of public schools as they developed in the nineteenth and early twentieth centuries. One goal of these early public schools was to train students to rise on bells and move to the next activity. The use of bells and the moving of students from one subject to the next echoed the assembly line itself while it also reinforced an industrial discipline (Cohen and Mohl 1979; Spring 2001). Students recognized this industrial model in their understanding of class time as work time and hall time as leisure; a notion of time specific to industrialized societies. However, like workers during the Industrial Revolution, students used lateness to resist this notion of time and to push for a more intuitive and organic sense of time.

Though the principal sought to impose an industrial notion of time through significant emphasis on teaching "from bell to bell," student lateness complicated the execution of her mandate. Students successfully rejected the bell as a marker of temporal change and asserted alternative notions of when class begins and what is considered late. In particular, students focused not on the bell but on when the teacher begins the lesson as the marker of the beginning of class. Jennie (HA) explains,

Jennie: Most of the time I'm late to class. I know that for a fact, but . . .
MD: About how late? Do you have a sense of it?
Jennie: Yeah, I have a sense of it. I'm usually like three or four minutes late. I'm not, like, real tardy. Like those people who come at,

> like, the end of the class, I don't do that. I come to class about three or four minutes late. . . . 'Cause, when I come in three or four minutes late it's just that now everyone's just getting settled in and stuff like that. So, I kind of slip through, but it's like, I'm doing my work and getting prepared to do my work.

To Jennie, arriving at the end of class is unacceptably late, but her own practice of arriving a few minutes after the bell was acceptable because she hadn't missed any instruction and didn't interrupt it.

Such practices among students may have made it difficult to start teaching at the bell, but teachers also seemed to establish different standards for starting their lessons as well. Some of these practices encouraged students to remain in the halls. Laura (AO), who was rarely late, complained that some teachers wasted time at the beginning of class. Using one of her teachers as an example, she explained, "Okay, he have to give himself five or ten minutes in order to get students to quiet down in order to start the class. [Then] he doesn't want to start the lesson when he only has a handful amount of students." She was frustrated with this waste of her own time and felt that such practices only encouraged further lateness.

Beyond shortening class, lateness enabled students to resist boredom, abuse of power by teachers, and poorly run classes. Asked how long she usually waited before going to class, Andrea (Amb) answered,

> It depends on who I have. If it's a class that I really need or it's a class where the teacher is not bull-shitting with me, I'll be like, "dag, I got to go to class, I can only stand like five minutes." But if it's a teacher that I know get on my nerves it takes me like fifteen minutes on the radiator till I gotta go.

Andrea notes that some classes are more purposeful than others and that some of her lateness is informed by her refusal to have her time wasted with ineffective instruction or with teachers who annoyed her. If students can get the class work done in half a period, why should they give the teacher a whole period of time? Andrea indicated that the quality of the class determined whether she hung out for five or fifteen minutes, but, in either case, she was late. She suggests that students make tactical decisions about how late they will be and quality of instruction plays a role only to a point.

Andrea used lateness to protest quietly against boredom and lax teachers. When she arrived late she usually set to work. Her critique of her teachers and schooling, present in her own descriptions of her lateness, was not raised in the class. Students who discussed their lateness spoke about it as an individual decision contingent on specific factors. But the widespread practice of lateness created a collective protest. Students did not mobilize to formally renegotiate the start of class but through their infrapolitical actions, they nonetheless impacted classroom practice and reclaimed time for themselves.

Burn Time

Though students used intuitive measures to mark when a class had begun, they used scientific measures to note its end, watching the clock carefully and knowing, to the second, when the bell would ring. Sharon (AL) admitted, "Well, I see it this way, it don't matter if the class is fun, if the class is boring, or whatever; the bell ring and I'm up and gone." Regardless of their level of interest or immediate activity, the bell signaled the absolute end of class work. I thought of the time that was lost to instruction at the beginning and end of each class as "burn time." Like burning a candle at both ends to melt it faster, student efforts effectively melted down the time available for class instruction. Students used "scientific" measures to burn minutes off the end of the period by declaring class over before it officially was, in particular by packing up their bags and putting their coats on a few minutes before the bell. When I instructed packing students to finish an assignment, they protested, "but the bell is about to ring!" Shor (1996) refers to this phenomenon as the "students dismissing the teacher." Shor's description of this practice calls attention to the power inversion that takes place through such strategies.

Further, when bells were broken or out of sync because of changes to and from daylight savings time, students claimed it was the end of the period well before it was. Class clowns also enjoyed imitating the bell to send the class into a packing frenzy before class time was up. Students selectively recognize the bell insisting on its authority at the end of class though ignoring its significance at the beginning. Again, though these practices may have bothered teachers, they were effective. Though students were not politically organized, they collaborated in overwhelming the teachers' capacity to control all of class time.

In addition to burning time off each period, some students also melted down the school day. Many students, particularly ambivalent and alienated students, simply came to school late and left early. A few students I interviewed claimed that they often had to drop off siblings before school started or had to meet them when their school got out at the end of the day. Others who were late every morning admitted that they just slept too late to come to school on time and those who left early simply were tired of being in school.

Though shortening the day, they still valued aspects of school. Melissa (AL) explained, "I like school, but I don't like to stay all day. That's how I feel. I don't like to stay all day." The widespread cutting of class at the beginning and end of the school day, particularly among alienated students, indicates that these students resisted the total amount of time school consumed. The principal observed that right after lunch (sixth period) there was a roar from a group of students who raced around the school in a maddening frenzy and then left the building. She saw this daily occurrence as an "exit ritual" that marked the end of the day for a segment of what she termed "the hall crowd." The importance of lunch reflected both the intense social scene that prevailed in the cafeteria (all Renaissance students and teachers had the same lunch period), as well as the importance of free school lunch for some students. Fed, tired, and having participated in the major event of the day, these students simply left.

Resisting by Obeying

Lateness and burn time cut down the amount of time school authorities and teachers could direct student activity. Once in the classroom, students also employed foot-dragging strategies to slow the transition from the hall state to the student state. Teachers and students frequently drew parallels between school and work, often noting the similarity of school and workplace expectations, comparing teachers to bosses and grades to pay. Not surprisingly, just as workers on the shop floor conspire to maintain their autonomy, so, too, do students in the classroom. Thus, students are not only prepared to be workers by the official socializing functions of school, but they also learn strategies of worker resistance through the unofficial socializing functions of student culture.

One of the most powerful points of struggle on the shop floor is control over the rate of work. Entire fields of study, such as Taylorism and industrial psychology, have emerged to find ways of increasing worker productivity. In response to the dehumanizing practices of industrial production, workers on the shop floor often collude to control how much and how quickly they produce, punishing those who "break the rate" and socializing new workers into their cultures of resistance. Students too, seek to limit the rate of production in the classroom and to control the rate or amount of class work required. Though some of these strategies are more visible and disruptive than others, such as taunting students who are too eager to please, I want to focus on the infrapolitical strategy of "foot dragging" (intentionally slowing down the rate of work), which called attention to teacher discourse as culturally specific and exposed conflicted teacher attitudes toward authority while asserting the significance of student cooperation.

One widespread foot-dragging practice that students used was a work-to-the-rules strategy in which they took teachers literally even when they knew the broader meanings of teacher instructions. Several teachers complained that students often did what they asked but only what they asked and only when they asked. James, a junior- and senior-level math teacher explained his experience:

What I try to do as they enter the room, I stand at the door and I have a handout and I say, "Okay, do this right now." But they'll still go to their seats and talk because I'm busy at the door handing them out. So, I have to actually go to the front and say, "okay, it's past time, now get started" and ask them to be quiet. If I do not do that, they will sit and talk all day long.

James shared many struggles with Emily, a freshman Social Studies teacher. She said,

There's that first few minutes when they come in the classroom, and no matter what you have on the board as a "Do Now" or something to start with, it's perceived as what you do after the teacher yells at you to do it. Until the teacher says, " . . . why don't you have out your binder?" Or, "why didn't you put your homework in the bin yet?" It's not until you're called on to do it that it actually means you should do it.

As these teachers suggest, they established rituals to facilitate the transition from the hall state to the student state, such as "take out notebooks," "put homework in the bin" or "do a 'Do Now.'" Despite their consistency and predictability, each one was met with student resistance. Students corroborated teacher frustrations. George (AO), a junior, described how students insist on direct requests from the teacher as a means of wasting time:

> And they go in with their coat and their book bags still on their back and just sit down to waste some time until the teacher tells you to take out your book and get prepared for class. . . . While you're taking off your coat you could do it for a very long time. You go and you stand up there taking your coat off very slowly while talking to a student . . . you act like you're looking for something but you're not, you just want to kill time. You take off your bag, okay, now that you're prepared, okay, you take off your jacket, you put your jacket on the desk, what have you. Now you're sitting down with your book bag on your desk and . . . you're just talking and talking, to kill time. The teacher tells you, "Please stop talking and take out your books, you're very late." Okay, so you're taking out your book very slowly, while you're talking to your friends . . . and the teacher's gonna tell you, "Open your book!" You open your book, okay, you have everything down. And, the teacher's gonna tell you, "Where's your folder?" "Papers from yesterday?" "Take out your homework," and things like that. And then you go back in your bag looking for something, and, you know, kids know how to really waste time these days!

These kinds of activities—waiting for the teacher to tell them to stop talking or to tell them to take their books out—are efforts to control the shop floor. Students do not disrespect the teacher's authority directly but force the teacher to work much harder to get the class into the lesson while they themselves work less. Taking out a book when told but waiting to be told to open it, for example, is one way that students slow the lesson down. These tactics both highlight teacher dependence on student cooperation and limit the squandering of student energy and ingenuity on schoolwork.

George (AO) suggests that working to the rules allowed students to remain in the hall state even after they had entered the classroom and waste teacher time, thereby reclaiming it as student time. Without openly refusing to participate in class, the student described here wastes time, saps teacher energy, slows the transition to class work, and remains in the hall state, at least to some degree. He is obeying but not obeying in that he is doing what the teacher tells him to do literally but avoiding doing what the teacher actually wants him to do. The teacher asks him to take out his notebook but actually wants him to begin an assignment. He slowly does what the teacher asks, knowing that the teacher implied much more in the command. As he finagles the teacher's directions, he talks to his friends, thus remaining social and connected to his peers all the while.

The refusal to follow implicit directions plays on the nature of teacher discourses. Lisa Delpit (1995) has noted that White teachers, in particular, often use implicit commands that in their own cultures are clearly understood. Though Black students may know what the teacher expects, they also bring understandings of authority as explicit and direct. Students at Renaissance may have refused to understand their teacher's implicit expectations as a way of calling attention to cultural differences and of resisting adopting teacher norms.

In 1997, inspired by my reading of Delpit (1995), I tried an experiment. I usually began my classes with requests such as, "Would you please take out your notebooks?" One day, after being ignored, I sternly said to my seemingly inattentive class, "Scratch that. Take out your notebooks!" Students quickly complied, laughing. One said, "Miss, we was wondering how long it would take you to figure it out." As Delpit notes, some Black students see such power-evasive, discursive strategies (a command issued as a polite request) as an abdication of power or as weakness. My snickering students suggested that they had always been aware of my wishes, but that they felt my wishes did not match my words and actions. Their refusal to comply with the implicit commands in polite requests may have been a rejection of White, middle-class modes of speech. And like the many strategies that forced teachers to actively enforce rules students knew well, students demanded that teachers explicitly use their power. Such resistance exposed that some teachers were uneasy about exercising their authority, a condition students exploited to regain class time for their own purposes.

Liminality

The last set of strategies I examine here are those around "liminality," which refers to being at the margins of different spaces or cultural regimes.

Liminality is being outside and yet somewhat within a community or culture. At Renaissance, students sought to be in the classroom without being in it and developed several practices that enabled them to maintain their hall state while physically being present in the classroom.

Andrea (Amb) perhaps offers the clearest example of resistance through liminality. She was a very capable student who was focused on popularity and life in the halls. However, like many ambivalent students, she also wanted to graduate from high school and occasionally even thought about pursuing college and a professional career. At other times, however, she disappeared from class altogether because she was focused on what she termed "drama" in the halls. Andrea was a student of mine for a year. She did almost all her homework and completed all projects, but she often handed them in before school or placed them in my mailbox. She did not want her peers to know of her diligence. Thus, she sought ways to do homework and not do it. Several high-achieving boys also slipped work in quietly to avoid being seen as academically oriented while they still pursued high grades. Despite Andrea's willingness to complete assignments, she vacillated between being a serious scholar and a hall hanger and in this sense was always between these two identities.

Andrea also deployed strategies of liminality in class. The desks in my classroom were clustered in groups of four, but Andrea always pulled one chair all the way to the edge of the front door and sat there, hand on the doorknob throughout the lesson. She always did assigned work but rarely answered questions or participated in discussions unless I specifically asked her opinion. She never behaved inappropriately herself and often helped keep her more disruptive friends in line. At the same time, I would often catch her with the door open and with her head (and sometimes her entire torso) out in the hall engaged in an intense, though hushed, conversation. In this way she was literally and psychically inside and outside the classroom at the same time. She participated in class just enough so that I would tolerate her persistence in moving her seat so that she could maintain contact with the action in the halls. Just as the student George described earlier who was obeying the teacher and disobeying at the same time, so, too, do liminal strategies allow students to participate and not participate in class. Such strategies may have been attempts to have it both ways. Andrea admitted of her behavior, "I was trying to get my grades up and still be popular."

Though no other student of mine was ever quite so adept at literally being in the classroom and the hall simultaneously, many students used liminal strategies similarly to maintain possession of their agendas and resist transitioning into the student state. A popular scheme mentioned by several students was known as "dropping off the bag" or "dumping books," which enabled students to be both late and on time simultaneously. Students entered class before the late bell rang, greeted the teacher, left their book bags on desks, and headed back out into the hall. They returned after class had begun, often as late as twenty minutes into the period. When corrected for lateness, they claimed, "I'm not late, my bag is here!"

Interviewees who employed this strategy insisted that it was quite effective at enabling them to be late without getting punished. They felt they gained other advantages as well. Some teachers, having seen them walk in, marked the students present though they were not. Other students did not sit in the seats they had claimed with their book bags so friends could walk in late and the pair could still have choice seats right next to each other. Additionally, when teachers made groups, students whose book bags were present were often placed in groups because it was evident that they would be arriving. When they walked in late, they were able to join a group already in progress and get credit for the group's work. They gained the added advantage of being able to hang out in the hallway unencumbered by their heavy book bags and got everyone's attention when they came in. Tina (AL) dropped off her bag at the beginning of most of her classes and admitted, "I just like the attention when you walk back in the classroom and everybody looks at you." One of the pleasures of lateness is the opportunity to bask in the celebrity of being very late, and these attentions encourage future lateness. Tina also explained that not having to carry her bag and coat made it easier to cover territory in the halls.

Camille (Amb) also used inside/outside strategies to both resist and participate in school and to maximize her social status:

It depends, if you by yourself in the hallway, you come to class, you dump your books. But, if you see a whole bunch of people, and y'all talking, ya laughin', you come to class mad late, you know. At the door, yo, check this out. I used to do that. They open the door and I got one foot in the door and I'm still yelling to my friend [imitates herself], "A'right, A'right, Okay!"

Camille used a combination of dropping off her bag and returning to the halls and a more aggressive performance of yelling in the halls with her foot in the class. Like Tina, who enjoyed walking in late for the attention, Camille also enjoyed her entry performance, admitting guiltily, "it's kind of fun." Camille, like Andrea, was physically in and out of the room at the same time. In Camille's case, she also asserted that she was in the hall state by yelling to friends in the hall while her body was between the hall and the classroom.

As already noted, lateness itself opened up numerous opportunities to resist the student state and to gain status. Because it enabled students to enter after the class had begun, it also enabled students to be in the classroom without having yet settled in to a student frame of mind. Thomas (HA) described his classmate Louis, who disrupted all their classes together often through lateness. Here Thomas describes a typical example of Louis's behavior in a class where students regularly worked in groups:

> Thomas: Like today in global studies, [Louis] walked in the class late and he started talking about rappers, you know. He came in the class late and after that he had the nerve to start talking about rappers after he joined like everybody!
>
> MD: He went to every group?
>
> Thomas: He went to every group.

Thomas's description shows that Louis's liminality enabled him to resist entering the student state and to launch more aggressive assaults on school and teacher authority. Because he walked in after the class had divided into groups and begun working, he had no defined place or role in the class. He used this liminal position to redirect the class by talking about rap music, something students see as their own and not the teacher's. Thus, he changed the subject to something closer to him and his peers, usurping the teacher's authority and curriculum. He also moved from group to group looking for an audience and probably picking up answers to the class work along the way. Louis preserved his control over his time through the entire period and got attention particularly from his friends, which Thomas assumed was his primary motive. Such attention gives him fame in the class, which converts to popularity in the halls. He also attacks the authority of the teacher and the sanctity of the subject matter by changing it, even though he doesn't directly confront the teacher or openly criticize the curriculum.

Resistance and Oppositionality

In this chapter I have limited my examination to infrapolitical resistance enacted at the boundaries of classroom time and space—the thresholds. But by no means does this discussion exhaust the manifestations of infrapolitical resistance. Students described numerous other strategies for wasting time, such as sleeping in class, and refusing to do no more than enough to get a passing grade, for example. My interest was to explore some of the more widely used and less visible strategies of resistance that focus on avoiding or slowing the transition from the hall state to the student state. Such efforts complicate scholarly constructions of student resistance and oppositionality, which have emphasized the antiacademic nature of perceptively disruptive behavior.

Infrapolitics tests the limits of power but does not openly challenge it, suggesting that student resistance operates far more complexly. The use of infrapolitics by students across the academic spectrum calls attention to cultural tensions and student/school conflicts. Infrapolitics also suggest that students deploy different strategies of resistance in different contexts and thus move along a continuum of resistance rather than occupying a fixed position. Serafina, the high-achieving student arrested at scanning (see chapter 2), identified very strongly with academics but was also a vocal critique of school practices, as was Nina (HA). Similarly, Melissa (AL), who didn't like to stay in school all day moved between active participation in academic activity to dropping-out behaviors (leaving school early) within one day. When she was actively engaged in her classes, she was not resisting in a perceptible way, but when she left the building an hour later, she was. The wide use of infrapolitics that sits between the open resistance of Serafina taking back her highlighters and of Melissa diligently completing school tasks suggests that we need more nuanced frameworks for reading resistance that capture the ways student positions and identities change in different contexts and throughout the school day and year. Understanding student resistance as existing along a continuum ranging from academic identification and participation on one end to open critical resistance on the other enables us to understand more fully the complex and at times conflicted relationship of students and schooling.

Threshold struggles such as those examined here also clarify some of the identity shifts students must make throughout the day. The tensions over transitioning from the hall state to the student state calls attention to the ways the classroom is a site where two competing regimes meet—a contact zone. More than just shaped by different activities, classrooms and halls require different ways of being and relating to peers and teachers. In the previous chapter on language choice, the largely ambivalent and alienated students who opposed using Standard English did so because, among other things, they felt that using Standard English was inauthentic. They sought to maintain a sense of wholeness by refusing to become, as John (Amb) described, "a whole different person" in the classroom. Their refusal to use Standard English is another infrapolitical move aimed at refusing to enter the student state. At the threshold between the halls and the classroom, then, students are not simply avoiding the work assigned by teachers (which is certainly a target of their resistance) but are also resisting the fracturing of the self required by mode-switching into the student state.

Another powerful lesson learned from examining infrapolitical resistance is that it forces teachers to exercise their power explicitly. This resistance, like working-to the-rules and resisting by obeying, made the ideological conflicts among teacher ideals, school policy, and student perceptions of school and authority, visible. Teacher reluctance to enforce all school rules consistently underscores their conflicted position and the conflicted nature of reforming urban schools. Bourdieu (1989) describes "strategies of condescension" through which actors situated higher in the social hierarchy interact with those below in ways that deny the social distance between them in order to reap some benefit, such as student trust or legitimacy. Others have termed these strategies of condescension "power evasive" (Frankenberg 1993; Delpit 1995) in that they seek to mask or deny unequal power relationships. Infrapolitical resistance, particularly that which demands explicit use of power, exposes and rejects such strategies, forcing teachers to inhabit their positions of authority. Thus, through their infrapolitical resistance, students expose power relationships for what they are, reminding teachers that despite their democratic pretensions and their political alignments with communities in struggle that "*you* are not one of *us.*"

In their 2003 study of cutting class (another form of infrapolitical resistance) Fallis and Opotow note that student disengagement is indicative of latent conflict with school, but school responses to disengagement tend to address the problem individually (case by case) and in an ad hoc manner, ignoring broader meanings of student disengagement. Though taken together, student lateness and foot dragging did slow the imposition of class work, students did not organize to do this. Their resistance did not present an audible challenge to the way things are done at school. Similarly, all of the teachers I interviewed perceived these infrapolitical strategies as individual acts that had to be addressed on their own, as Fallis and Opotow found in their study. The broader critiques implicit in infrapolitical resistance, particularly the reluctance to transition to the student state, were not addressed by reform efforts. But, such is the nature of infrapolitical resistance and such are its limits—students don't demand change or create a movement to protest what they dislike about schooling. Students' strategies, however, limit the demands schooling can make on them.

Infrapolitical resistance, like infrared light, is invisible in some ways but gives off heat nonetheless; despite its low profile it has some impact. It clarifies the complexity of student relationships to schools, teacher ambivalence, and the fragility of school authority. Schools do not operate univocally; instead they present a cacophony of voices on how students should behave, the purpose of schooling, and how teachers should use their authority. Infrapolitical resistance amplifies these contradictions in school authority, as much of this resistance flourishes in the fissures between school policy and teacher practice.

In many ways, then, infrapolitical resistance operates not only like infrared light, but also like ultraviolet rays. Crime investigators use ultraviolet light to make visible traces of material and residues otherwise invisible to the naked eye. In the sense that infrapolitical resistance sheds light on the underlying contradictions between students and school and within schools themselves, the resistance helps expose those imperceptible residues. But student resistance is not limited to that which is barely noticed; it is also enacted out in the open. In the next chapter I examine student resistance enacted in the open to further understand the nature of student/school contradictions and conflicts through the impact of clowning.

6

▪　▪　▪　▪　▪　▪　▪　▪

"You know the real deal, but this is just saying you got their deal"
Public and Hidden Transcripts

One semester, while teaching about the democratic revolutions of the eighteenth and nineteenth centuries, I handed out the first page of C. L. R. James's *The Black Jacobins*, a historical classic that poses the Haitian Revolution as one of the most significant events in history. I also distributed an encyclopedia item on the event. In contrast to James's enthusiasm, the encyclopedia briefly noted that Haiti's Revolution was the most successful slave rebellion in history and placed greater emphasis on its subsequent economic and political failure as the poorest nation in the hemisphere. I asked students to read the two, after which we compared them together. I then asked them to write a paragraph about why they thought the representations were so different. Planning to use their theories to drive class discussion, I thought the lesson was going well. When we had compared the two texts, students were animated—some were fired up. But parlaying their verbal enthusiasm into writing was always a challenge, so when one student, Phil, began telling me his ideas aloud rather than writing them, I was not surprised. I politely cut him off and said gently, "Don't tell me, write it. You can share it with the class in a minute." Phil stopped talking to me when I urged him to write, but he did not start writing (as was fairly typical of him). Several students, like Phil, loved discussion, were good historical thinkers and articulate speakers but struggled to express their thoughts on paper and, consequently, didn't do so when asked.

After a few minutes, I asked for volunteers to share their writing as a way to begin discussion. Carl, a student sitting by the back door, eagerly raised his hand. No one else's hand was up so I called on him despite my suspicions he had not really written anything.

"Listen up, y'all, " Carl said, ruffling a paper and clearing his throat as if he was going to read something really important. When all eyes were on him, he began reciting a rap song loudly. I didn't know the song, but it was about White supremacy. Phil moved next to him and began banging out the beat on the desk and interjecting parts of the chorus. I quickly linked the substance of the lyrics to the content of the lesson. Taken by surprise and angry, I sternly told them to stop it and gave them my most severe teacher glare.

Carl responded by jumping on top of his desk and continuing even louder. Phil joined him and they chanted the words together. A few other students picked up drumming the beat for them. I stood at the front of the room unable to shout them down and feeling the whiteness of my skin as my face burned red hot. I heard a debate about the shade of my skin somewhere near me, "Is that what they call 'puce?'" As the rapping continued, my sense of helplessness increased. I felt like the Wizard of Oz as Toto pulls away the curtain revealing that the great wizard was really a fraud. My class was paying no attention to the "man behind the curtain" after the façade of my authority had been pulled away.

Unable to be heard, I walked up to them and hollered, "You have to stop! You can't do this anymore!" Phil, who had gone back to drumming on the desk shouted back, "You're silencing me!" and Carl began chanting, "Don't shut us down!"

"You're silencing everyone else!" I responded.

"NOOOOOO!" Phil yelled at me.

Having failed at diplomacy, I walked back to my desk and dug through my top drawer for a pile of small blue cards, recognized quickly by those nearest to me as dean's referrals. "Yo, she's writin' blue cards!" a student in the front called out, and the drumming began to die down. I kept writing as the class became so quiet I could hear my pen scratching against the rough surface of the cards. When I looked up, Phil was sullenly sitting in his original seat. Carl walked out the back door.

I tried to continue with the lesson as if nothing had happened. The students obliged me and read what they had written when asked, but the lively discussion I had anticipated was not forthcoming. Thomas, a high-achieving student I have introduced in previous chapters, uncharacteristically chided, "You shouldn't have gone there, Miss." Several students nodded in agreement. Soon after his summation, the bell rang.

In the previous chapter, I examined the quiet ways students sought to slow the transition from the halls to the classroom through infrapolitics. However, as this event suggests, at times, students more directly challenged teacher authority and openly contested the meaning of classroom space, in effect, inserting an alternative curriculum to the official one. This anecdote is revealing for my discussion of such open challenges to teacher authority because, like many clowning incidents (and I believe this incident qualifies), this event sets something on its head. In this case, Carl and Phil seized power. They inserted an interpretation of Black history that in content and idiom was close to student experience and culture and undermined my authority to teach about this subject. They clarified relationships within the room by emphasizing their solidarity with their peers through the lyrics and genre they used both to seize the center of attention and highlight my racial difference from the class. The students who playfully mocked my flushing skin picked up on this very theme—as Carl and Phil emphasized a shared Black culture and identity among students, my whiteness marked me as outside that community.

My decision to raise the profile of the Haitian Revolution actually departed from the standard Eurocentric curriculum. Though introducing content more relevant to my students, I still sought to maintain control over the curriculum through my planned activities, the materials I selected, and the tasks I assigned. Thus, when I insisted that Phil write before he could speak about how Black history was represented, I insisted on my control of who speaks, what they can speak about, and how they can speak about it. This incident suggests that inserting Black history into the official curriculum, which largely marginalized it, was not enough to change the relations of students to the curriculum.

I was standing in the front of the room to lead discussion and make notes on the board, in the teacher's power space (McLaren 1986), holding the chalk, poised to translate their discussion into the official class record—in apparent command of the props that signified my institutional authority. A student, Carl, sat in the back by the door, a marginal figure in the early part of the lesson. Phil was sitting with the class between where I was standing and Carl's place by the door. When Carl began rapping "truth to power," telling about Black history from a Black perspective, Phil moved to join him, siding with Carl's curriculum.

The notion of speaking "truth to power," asserting what those with less power know or believe to someone in power, is important in this consideration of classroom culture. In the two previous chapters, I argued that classrooms are highly contested spaces. They are marked by infrapolitical resistance that thrives at points of weakness or in moments of conflict between teacher and school authority. The ambiguity about language policy emphasized the contested nature of classroom space: some students sought to create a space for their dialect-based self-expression while others saw it as a space to use Standard English, a tool of upward mobility. Clowning, a form of speaking truth to power that students widely deploy in classrooms, draws on these tensions and brings them into the open, which is why clowning needs to be further examined. The infrapolitics discussed in the last chapter included political critique, but because it was cloaked in a veil of compliance, it did not pose any serious threat to classroom authority. However, when these critiques were made visible, they did disrupt business as usual and exposed the contradictions between students and school.

Scott's 1990 framework of "hidden and public transcripts" offers a useful way to understand how official discourses contended with the unofficial ones circulating boldly in the halls and fugitively in the classrooms. In this regard, the "public transcript" represents interactions of superiors and subordinates structured in a way that those in power would like them to be. Authority sets the terms of the public transcript and establishes how different groups are expected to speak, move, behave, and look when openly addressing each other. In contrast to this top-down imposition of order, the "hidden transcript" is a bottom-up discourse spoken off stage, out of the hearing of the powerful (though those with power often have a separate backstage transcript shared among themselves as well). The hidden transcript is performed by subordinates among themselves in a time and place separate from authorities and hence, secure from their authority. While the public transcript affirms the interests of those with power, the hidden transcript is performed for an audience of peers who share similar conditions. Though teachers endorse the essential value of schooling and typically support school policies, they often engage in their own hidden transcript that may be critical of the administration or of state dictates. In the relative autonomy of their classrooms, they may close the door and engage in a pedagogy or curriculum that runs counter to that endorsed by the principal or state. The principal may know this is going on but may be unwilling to police all classrooms in the name of state mandates. Wherever a hidden transcript of alternative teaching occurs or where a hidden discourse of student assertiveness emerges, resistance to the status quo maintains itself despite the official orderliness of the public transcript.

Hidden transcripts displace public ones in the furtive spaces of the subordinated. As already suggested in the discussion of the halls, students are expected by their peers to use the community dialect outside classrooms and to affirm their horizontal solidarity, and they are also expected to perform the public transcript when facing authority. Spaces dominated by the hidden transcript, such as the hallways, sanction those who perform the public transcript too zealously or who seek to achieve individual advancement through it. Thus, though students insisted that the classroom and the halls were not oppositional, many also noted that being "too into" school at the expense of building relationships among peers was not acceptable. In classrooms, one key role of the class clowns was to impose limits on the public transcript by affirming the hidden one that circulates among students.

Scott developed his theory from extreme cases of domination: concentration camps, American slavery, peasant/landlord relationships, and imperialist relationships between Europeans and conquered subjects. These cases of highly punitive authority led Scott to conclude that the occasions when the "frontier" between the public and private transcripts collapses are incredibly rare (Scott 1990, 202). In contrast, modern industrial societies permit more open opposition than did the premodern or penal societies Scott examined. Classrooms today are not sites of complete authoritarian control. Teachers are mediating agents promoting dominant culture and enforcing the public transcript, but they are inconsistent in doing so, as student infrapolitical resistance reveals (see chapter 5). Teaching is also complex work that requires cooperative teacher-student work relationships if in-depth learning is to occur. Teachers' work also involves developing mentoring, coaching, and care-giving relationships to enable such learning. They are easily caught in the middle, expected from above to enforce the public transcript and required syllabus and expected from below to affirm their commitments to students. Such contradictions make conflict inevitable in the classroom. This conflict was apparent in the Haitian Revolution incident in my class.

Thomas's concluding comment in class, that I should not have "gone there," specifically noted that there was a territory owned by the students' hidden transcript that I had appropriated into the public transcript of the lesson plan. The subject matter I put on the table—the Black revolution in European-enslaved Haiti—opened the hidden transcript. Once I had breached that boundary, students, led by Carl, aggressively used hip-hop to reject my academic lesson plan and to assert their control over the hidden transcript, in this case Black history usually marginalized in the public transcript of the state curriculum.

Inside the public transcript, subordinates mask their hidden agendas so as to reassure the authorities that they believe what those in power want them to believe. Those in positions of power wear masks as well, performing their own scripts of power projection. Carl's hip-hop performance caught me by surprise and so completely seized the lesson plan from me that I felt compelled to retreat to a position of authority. I put on the mask of school authority (a mask I tried to alter all the time) and took up the tools of command (my blue cards). I generally taught as if my class and I were a community and rarely sought outside help for classroom management. That day, I was unable to catch up to events as my students reminded me that my perception of the class as a community was an extension of the public transcript—the class as I wanted to constitute it. They recognized hierarchies and power differentials that divided us. With no other ideas about what to do to stem the hip-hop rebellion, I raised the profile of my official position—I had the authority to refer them to more intimidating forces than myself. The public transcript made me the classroom authority, and this student-led disruption made me look weak. I wrote up blue cards to intimidate the whole class not just Carl and Phil. Carl and Phil forced me to play my role in the school hierarchy, throwing into relief the coercion that maintained the terms of our relationships.

My mistakes that day stick with me. I should have let Phil and others talk more before insisting they write, because they had something to say that mattered. Though realizing my own miscalculations and my inability to figure out how to incorporate hip-hop in that moment, I handed the blue cards to the dean to preserve their legitimacy as a tool. I had written them out in front of the class and thus I had to follow through or I would have been a fraud. As a White teacher in an urban high school, I had much on-the-job learning to do about how and what to tinker with in opening the classroom to subjects centered in student culture. Just as there was an unspoken script about what was acceptable curriculum, there was also a script on legitimate authority and the boundaries between students and teachers. I had to silence the hidden transcript in my class (for example, the hidden transcript that doubted my right to teach certain subjects) because these transcripts undermined my work.

Clowning performances, such as that of Carl and Phil, often sought to flip the script by seizing classroom space—the space designated for the dissemination of the public transcript—to promote hidden transcripts. Such actions challenged the substance of the curriculum and the legitimacy of schooling and enforced a peer and racial solidarity. In this chapter, I examine hidden transcripts lurking within public ones in student discourse about schooling to ground an analysis of the ways clowning brought those transcripts into the open. The interaction of hidden and public transcripts suggests the limits of current debates on reproduction and resistance in urban schools.

Public and Hidden Transcripts at Renaissance

Samuel (AL) offered one of the clearest articulations of public and hidden transcripts. When asked if education was important to them, most students roundly endorsed it, but Samuel was more cautious. He first said that school was not important but then reconsidered:

> Samuel: Wait, some real classes I like is, like, English, 'cause when we read, even though we have to read all them books, but when we discuss it, you understand it. That makes you feel good when you understand that you know the book. That's what I like about English. History is cool because I learn a lot of stuff. I learned a lot of stuff in that history. Sometimes, you just go outside and people be just talking about history, even though they say school teach you the wrong history, which I think is true sometimes because I can go and read a next book and find something else. You know, like, school's a bunch of lies, but, you know, you got to get your school for this, so you have a place in society, something like that.
>
> MD: What do you mean? That you have a diploma?

> Samuel: Yeah, then, in your street, you can get your street knowl-
> edge off the real street. You know the real deal, but this is just say-
> ing that you got their deal and that you can get pay high, and you
> could still have your real deal, your real street. You see, as I'm get-
> ting older, I see that I'm trying to get mad knowledge. I'm not just
> trying to get school knowledge, I'm trying to get the top knowl-
> edge. Try to better myself.

Samuel draws a distinction between school knowledge and street knowledge, "their deal" and the "real deal." He does not fully reject school
knowledge, though he sees it as less true than what he learns on the street,
particularly from the older men who sit on stoops on his block. Rather, he
sees school knowledge as useful because it authorizes him to "have a place
in society" so he can earn decent wages. "Their deal" includes understanding dominant ideology and being able to perform the public transcript—
their "bunch of lies." The street deal offers a counter-narrative—the hidden
transcript. According to Samuel, school knowledge is not pointless—it
is very useful in navigating "their" world. It simply does not have a mo-
nopoly on truth. He even admits he learns things in history and English
that are useful or interesting despite his awareness that the information
may be "wrong" according to the street. He has developed a strategy to get
"mad knowledge," the "top," which involves drawing on both school and
the street as sources. His recognition of these multiple regimes of truth
may have enabled him to hang on to graduate, despite his alienation from
school, since he could place schooling into a broader context that did not
negate his cultural identity and his knowledge.

Samuel's recognition of multiple transcripts was unusual in its ex-
plicitness. The awareness of multiple ways of seeing the world implicitly
emerged in many of the interviews despite the surface production of dominant discourses. When students espoused the centrality of hard work and
self-reliance and criticized failing peers as lazy, they clearly articulated a
public transcript. But, when they were asked to discuss their own behavior
or performance, they sometimes employed alternative discourses—that
the curriculum is boring or that poverty impedes academic achievement,
for example. The individualist discourse pervasive in schools emphasizes
individual accountability despite obstacles and ignores such issues. Samuel appears to be very aware of the mask he wears when demonstrating

that he knows "their deal." Though other students were aware of multiple explanations, it is much more difficult to determine what they had internalized.

Many scholars have noted the seeming contradiction of resistance to schooling commingling with the production of dominant discourses and have suggested that despite this resistance, students are absorbed into hegemony (Willis 1977; Fine 1991; Grant and Sleeter 1996). However, once we conceptualize these dominant discourses as the public transcript, we cannot take students' reproduction of them as adequate evidence that they have been reproduced. That remains the knotty problem—to what extent do students believe the official discourses in which they participate? In Scott's terms, to what extent have their faces grown to fit the mask?

The individualist discourse at the heart of the public transcript offered in schools emerged in many interviews and had specific and consistent elements: everyone can succeed, people fail because they make bad choices, and there are no significant obstacles to success. Many students, particularly high-achieving and academically oriented ones, insisted that everyone can do well if they are willing to do the work assigned. Nina (HA) explained,

> It's really a good school, but if you come here, hang in the halls or whatever, that's you. If you come here to do your work and stuff, that's what you're gonna do. If you make a decision to come and work and get good grades and get out of school, then that's what's gonna happen. But if you come here with a mind that, oh, I'm not gonna come, then you not gonna do any work, then therefore, you not gonna do very well.

Thomas (HA) put it more bluntly, "It's about the student. You can't force them to learn. You know it's up to them. They wanna be bums, let them be bums." Other students echoed this sense that the school's reach was limited and that ultimately students make choices, even to "be bums." Richard (AO) explained, "It has to come from the student, but the schools can only help." Darrell (AO) also felt that the students were responsible: "I feel everybody has a fair chance at opportunity in this school."

In Chapter 4, I noted that students who endorsed the use of Standard English in the classroom were predominantly academically oriented or high-achieving students who stressed the importance of increased opportunities through schooling. Given this pattern, it is not surprising that students who were making steady progress toward graduation perceived that they have made good choices and that their success is a testament to both their hard work and their abilities. Fine (1991) also found that students who she termed "stay-ins" (those who graduated from high school, as all of those quoted above did), also embraced this individualist discourse and perceived that the system was fair and their failing peers had no one to blame but themselves.

Interestingly though, ambivalent and alienated students also echoed this ideology, sometimes in more extreme terms. Camille (Amb), who managed to complete her high-school education on time, explained her own choices:

> Camille: Look, don't care about nobody else! Care about yourself! I'm speaking for myself, me. . . . You gonna be in night school for another year? Do what you gotta do. Forget about those who don't want to come to school and all that, even though that's your boys and stuff like that.
>
> MD: Is it hard to turn your back on your boys?
>
> Camille: Some guys, it is. Some guys, I mean, like the true ones . . . it's kind of hard. Some of them who have their head on straight, they're like, "I ain't staying up here with you. I'm going on, I am leaving. I don't want to stay in [Renaissance] for another year." . . . I'm saying because I have many friends who'll be in here for another year and I'm not gonna stay with them. I'll be like, "No! You did you your deed, you had your classes."

Camille defined herself as a "recovered hall-walker" and was one of the most useful informants on hall culture because she was so experienced in it. Though she tended to go to her classes regularly, she was usually quite late and at times entered classes disruptively, as she herself acknowledged (see chapter 5). However, though she was very peer oriented, in the end she insists one must not "care about nobody else." She also directs her advice to a male audience when she speaks of leaving "your boys" (your friends, support network, etc.) suggesting that these tough decisions were harder for boys. A high-achieving girl in a focus group comparing her experiences to those of her brothers concurred that peer pressure was a greater obstacle for boys.

Despite the difficulty of the choices schooling demanded of students, Camille asserts an extreme version of the individualist discourse as she insists that you must literally leave your friends behind. At the same time, the fracturing of her self—speaking as both a boy in the hall speaking to other boys and as Camille speaking to me—offers a hint that she is creating a persona for me. She was very animated throughout her interview, taking on the voices of different participants and at times even acting out parts of her story. She was performing throughout the interview (typical of her social behavior in general) perhaps to make her performance more believable, particularly about her endorsement of individualism over peer relations. She articulates the public transcript, but elements of her recital, particularly its exaggeration, suggest that she was literally performing and telling me what she assumed was the only legitimate discourse on the importance of schooling.

The Meaning of Laziness

In affirming individualist discourses, students frequently blamed their own laziness or the laziness of the less successful for their failings. The construction of a wide-range of student behavior as "lazy" defines the individual as a failure, not the school or the broader system. Melissa (AL), who frequently skipped school and cut classes, defined her behavior as "laziness." She said she valued education "because I know without it, I'm going nowhere. I know that I'm gonna be nothing. . . . I'm gonna be in the streets." When I followed up with a question about her inconsistent attendance, she explained, "I'm hard-headed, Miss; I don't listen. 'Cause it's [school] for my own good." Melissa did complain that she had some classes she felt were useless. She also talked about some classes in which she had worked very hard because she was interested in the work, explaining, "I didn't do that project because I had to. I did it because I wanted to." Thus, Melissa's own academic record suggested that she was not always "lazy" and that her alienation from school in fact may be partially related to her feeling that some courses were not relevant or interesting. Further, when asked about what she did when she wasn't at school, she explained she went back to bed. She would leave for school in the morning and wait until everyone was out of the house and then return home to sleep. She interpreted this behavior as laziness, when it might signify much more serious problems such as depression, illness, or hopelessness that remain unexamined and illegitimate within the prevailing discourses on individual accountability.

Tashona (HA) felt she couldn't do better than an 84 percent average because of "the stresses of life and me bein' lazy." Though acknowledging the "stresses of life," she sees her reaction to them as laziness, taking the blame for issues beyond her control. Interestingly, she was one of the few students who acknowledged "stress" as a factor informing her school performance, even though so many students led stressful lives but didn't cite the issue. Tashona answered my questions thoughtfully:

> MD: Do you think that most students have the attitude, "I want to improve and excel in school?"
>
> Tashona: The majority, but maybe it gets in their way, obstacles and then . . .
>
> MD: What kind of obstacles?
>
> Tashona: Maybe they have family problems, or, you know, money problems, or maybe they just don't have a lot of self-esteem or a lot of will power to get ahead. They want it, but they can't bring themselves to do it.
>
> MD: And that's why people hang in the hall?
>
> Tashona: Yeah, 'cause they weak-minded. Cause they let they friends control them.

Tashona names many of the problems students faced from family crises to poverty. She also identified an important phenomenon—wanting to do well but not being able to do it. This desire may have been widespread but was rarely discussed. Such anomie is often simply defined as laziness when Tashona suggests it may be grounded in the sadness and distraction of family problems and poverty. This "laziness" may also be one of the insidious ways oppression operates—that it saps the young of confidence, energy, and ambition, and leaves them believing that they are to blame. When I asked if this sense of futility may push students into the hall, she returns to the public transcript and defines such behavior as "weak-minded." Her abrupt shift from being very sympathetic to student (and her own) struggles to being critical is a hint that the problems she defined are not legitimate within the public transcript.

Tashona described a sense of hopelessness that she may have felt at times or assumed other students did when she links family problems, poverty, self-esteem, and will power. Hopelessness is not a manifestation of laziness but of the socio-economic issues she raises. Laziness frequently became a catchall phrase to explain school failure and a key term of the public transcript that erases structural inequality and replaces it with individual accountability. Though Tashona consistently returns to the public transcript, she draws on hidden transcripts as well, offering a concrete example of the ways the hidden transcript was ever present though submerged within the public one. Nonetheless, it is very difficult to gauge the extent to which Tashona believed laziness was her primary barrier. Her statements certainly point in that direction. Here is an example that forces the question, although she is aware of hidden transcripts, to what extent is she absorbed into dominant ones?

Switching Transcripts

Further evidence of the circulation of multiple transcripts are the transitional phrases that students used to announce a switch from public to hidden transcripts. For example, Ricky (Amb) described the ways students tested teachers and did as little as possible:

> Ricky: Well, sometimes, I feel that as I long as I put something on paper I should get credit for it. And then, there's other times when you gotta put some work into it. Some teachers won't accept garbage.
> MD: And there are some who will?
> Ricky: Yeah. Kids know which teachers they can get away with stuff with. And if I can just write down anything on the paper and give [it] to the teacher, I would. I'm not even gonna lie. But if I know I have to put my heart into it for a teacher, then that's what I'm gonna do.
> MD: And yet you said education is important?
> Ricky: It is, but there's time when you slack off because you know the teacher doesn't expect much, so if you know this, you're automatically gonna slack off.

Ricky's admission that he gave his teachers as little as they would accept was an infrapolitical strategy widely used at Renaissance and on shop floors everywhere—part of the work-to-the-rules strategy described in the last chapter. However, he emphasizes that this is not the way he is supposed to behave, by clarifying that he is "not even gonna lie" about it. His added emphasis on his candor highlights that he knows that his attitude is not sanctioned within the public transcript and that he should be lying to me in this situation. By signaling his earnestness here, he alerts his listener that he is departing from the expected performance of the public transcript.

In the class I described in the introduction to this book, Andrea (Amb) also noted she was departing from the public transcript when she prefaced her demand for access to the hall pass with the phrase, "I'm gonna keep it real with you." In using this introduction, she suggested that there was something more true than what was being said at the moment. She made a tactical decision to expose the hidden transcript in order to secure greater freedoms, using the phrase to indicate her "real" and usually hidden intentions. Such phrases like "keepin' it real," "I ain't gonna lie," and "I'm not gonna front," which popped up in student talk are transition phrases from the public to the hidden transcript that alert the listener to the change.

The quiet circulation of hidden transcripts amid performances of public ones alert us to ongoing tensions between schools and students. Whether they are as conscious as Samuel (AL) about "their deal" and the "real deal" or not, students move between these transcripts with some degree of aplomb. Were the insertion of the hidden transcript always at an infrapolitical level—at a barely audible decibel, we could conclude that school authorities were always in control of the classroom. However, the public transcript also came under direct attack as students sometimes openly asserted the hidden transcript, as Carl and Phil did in my history class. Such performances taxed the authority of teachers and the school itself, undermined academic efforts, and placed the contradictions between school authority and student identity on the table. Clowning, or mocking the class work or the teacher in some way or creating an inversion of power, brought the hidden transcript into the open while reinforcing peer solidarity and asserting limits on performances of public transcripts.

Clowning

The pervasiveness of class clowns in most schools suggests that clowning is an invasion of the public transcript with the hidden one to create a carnivalesque disruption of the order. Though clowning can be very disruptive, it straddles the line between infrapolitical and open resistance. It is infrapolitical insofar as class clowns play "the harmless fool" who wittily or good naturedly interrupts the teacher (a trespass eased by the comedy in it) and puts the teacher on the defensive. Daring the teacher to clamp down on an amusing disruption, class clowns compel teachers to behave in an authoritarian manner or to surrender some control to the clowns, which puts the teacher between a rock and a hard place. Class clowns test the limits of the pubic transcript and teacher authority by cloaking their intentions in playfulness. Humor is a vehicle through which power relationships can be made visible by subordinates because such performances are not *intended* to be taken seriously. Joking or teasing acts as a shield so that when the hidden transcript is made visible, its meaning is ambiguous. It is, after all, merely play and therefore limits how those in authority respond, because who wants to be known as someone who can't take a joke?

Anderson (AL), a self-identified class clown, described his clowning, "We still kids right now. So we like, growin' up, we still makin' fun of people, we doin' things we not supposed to be doin' but we know it's wrong, but we tryin' to have a little laugh, a little fun, while being relaxed." Such a description denies any subversive intent to his actions. However, in chapter 4, I cite his story about using youth slang with his teachers as a form of disrespecting them. Their seeming ignorance or "slackness" as he referred to it, opens up this opportunity to mock them by drawing on the subtleties of coded discourse, clear to students but opaque to teachers, which allows his furtive enunciation of resistance. His friends who started laughing as he told the story suggested that his sassing the teacher was not so innocent or naïve. This is an example of the way humor protects the speaker from punishment as he or she inserts the hidden transcript that challenges teacher authority. Though it could be laughed off or dismissed, clowning is a successfully disruptive disguise for students who want to confront the teacher in the classroom. In this way, it is generally more disruptive than infrapolitics using humor as a mask for its cultural work.

Though readily dismissed as "just having a laugh," clowning challenges the meaning of schooling and the authority of teachers in general. One of the most common features of clowning at Renaissance was the way it mocked teachers and the curriculum. A social studies teacher described a frustrating day with one of her ninth-grade classes. She asked for a volunteer to read a primary source document aloud. A student, who was frequently very disruptive but seemed to be making an effort to be more cooperative lately, raised his hand. Eager to encourage his positive participation, she called on him. He began reading normally but as he progressed he began altering his voice so that soon he was reading in what she referred to as "burp voice"—literally belching out the words of history in a grotesque mockery of the seriousness of the material. The class, needless to say, found the performance brilliantly funny. She congratulated him on his interpretive reading and tried to move on with the lesson despite her humiliation.

In culling through my journals for incidents of clowning, I find similar stories. One day, I was using an overhead projector to show pictures of art from the Renaissance and the Middle Ages so we could compare the ways the two periods differed. Seeing me struggling to take notes on the board and manage the pictures, a student, Mark, offered to help. I asked him to place the picture students were talking about on the overhead so that as we spoke about it, the class could see it. Meanwhile, I took down their ideas on the board. Once the class finished discussing the first set of pictures, I directed Mark to show the first picture from the next pile of overheads, which was Michelangelo's David. The class became excited by the nudity (the photo was of a copy with fig leaf in the appropriate place, but the students got the idea). After they got over the initial thrill, they discussed this work that many of them had seen elsewhere (in cartoons, magazines, etc.) and made comparisons to the art we had just examined. Still writing on the board, I directed Mark to show the next overhead, a picture of a Rafael Madonna. The class roared with a thrill greater than that which had greeted David. Surprised that the painting had created such a stir (the Madonna was fully clothed), I turned to see what was on the screen. Mark had turned the light of the overhead so it created a spotlight, and was performing a mock strip tease in it, much to the delight of the class. Trying to stem the flood, I returned the projector to its correct position and thanked Mark for his help as I invited him to return to his seat.

Historical texts were not the only targets of such performances. Jennie (HA) tried to describe an incident in a recent class that she found hilarious. As she retold the story (the names are changed here), she giggled so much she had trouble getting it out:

> "Mike" is like the class clown. Mike sits there . . . I mean you could be doing your work, trying to, um [laughs], you know, concentrate on your work, and then Mike [laughs] will just come up [laughs]. Like, in math class, Mike came up and had some toilet tissue. He just started playing with the toilet tissue, it was funny, but it was immature, but it was funny. And Mike makes the class fun and stuff. Other people makes the class fun, not necessarily me and stuff so when Mike cracks jokes and be in the classroom . . .

Though she could not convey clearly what he did (I guess you had to be there), it had been very funny to students in the class. Whatever his specific actions, he supplanted the math lesson with his toilet paper antics. I suspect that part of the hilarity was the fact that his medium was toilet paper, something that contrasted earthly bodily functions to lofty academic matters. In all of these stories, a key aspect of the clowning is the inversion that reduces the sacred curriculum to ridicule.

Interestingly too, though Jennie thoroughly enjoyed the events in class, she inserts a judgment from the public transcript when she calls the clown "immature," protectively distancing herself from clowning by noting that "other people makes the class fun, not necessarily me." She seems a bit uncertain about her audience as she shifts between reveling in the low-humor and dismissing it as a teacher or adult might (as immature). She also clarifies her bona fides by claiming that she does not do such things herself. Within her story, we hear the voice of a student caught between the allure of the hidden transcript and the authority of the public one.

In all three cases here, students seized an opportunity to displace the curriculum brought in by the teacher—a primary source document, pictures of great art, mathematics—with low, bodily humor mocking the syllabus and the teacher. By sabotaging the formal lesson, clowns assert the hidden transcript as primary and compelling. These behaviors rallied students to their carnival antics and situated the teacher outside the joke or as the butt of it. Such actions reconfigure classroom discourse and polarize teacher-student relations because they sever the teacher from the potential community by installing an aggressive adolescent solidarity. Typical of Saturnalia or Carnival rituals, they invert power relationships so that the bottom is on top: students define the activities and take control of the class until the teacher puts his or her foot down and restores order.

By hijacking the class, at least briefly, drawing the class together is another key element of much clowning and a crucial aspect of the cultural work clowning consolidates. Shelly (HA) described an incident that seems like a textbook case of clowning (if there could be such a thing) that notes not just a curricular reorientation but also a reorientation of student attention:

> When I had U.S. history, the class was big, first of all, you know, and there were a few clowns in there. But, like, when Ms. [teacher] set the class to work, everybody used to be working. I feel like they need attention in a way, 'cause then, like, the class would actually be quiet, everybody's working. You would hear somebody say something stupid and everybody laughs. The joke just gets taken all the way and the focus is just thrown on them and they feel happy, you know. It's like, that's another thing, I think class clowns, they just want focus, you know, they feel like nobody's paying attention to me, I gotta say something. I gotta do something, you know . . .

Shelly's frustration is that just when the class seems to be intensely focused on the curriculum—"quiet, everybody's working"—a class clown makes a joke that pulls the class off task and reassembles attention elsewhere. Shelly is quick to dismiss such antics as merely a need for attention. However, the readiness of the class to enjoy the joke and extend it suggests their complicity with the clown who is setting popular limits on academic demands. In halting class work with a joke, the clown essentially rallies the rank and file in a temporary strike against the teacher.

Changing the subject was a key aim of much of the clowning described. Jeanette, a teacher, offers the public transcript on a clowning incident she noticed when she conducted a peer observation. She describes a student (names are changed) seeking to change the academic subject at hand to popular culture such as hip-hop and television to supplant the day's lesson with something closer to students' everyday lives:

Jeanette: "Steve" came into that class having been there four times. He doesn't know a word of Spanish. He was cool though! He sat down right next to his girlfriend, or his friend, and got her to write down his answers for him. Once that was done, he felt like he had done his part. So the whole rest of the lesson was about trying to start conversations and get more people off-task because he was. He started talking about television and stuff. And he didn't want to be alone. And so if you don't get what's going on and you're bored, you want somebody else to be there with you. . . . It's that peer pressure thing.

MD: Did he just start talking to people in his group?

Jeanette: Kept bringing up subject after subject to get them on with him. . . . And so the whole group got off task and engaged with him. . . . He was insulting other kids, teasing them.

In this instance, the student was indirectly confronting the teacher by offering his peers topics of interest to them in place of the curriculum. More than this, though, Jeanette observes that he turns to "insulting" and "teasing" other kids so as to provoke them off-task if they were persisting in the assignment. Jeanette insists that he was behaving this way because he was bored and didn't know the work. Though her analysis of his aptitude in Spanish may be accurate, his actions have political meaning as well. He was not only displacing the formal curriculum, he was also punishing those students who remained focused on it rather than the peer-oriented one he offered. He was forcing disruption on students as well as on the teacher. As in Shelly's story, class clowns assert limits on how focused students can be on school matters and insist on the solidarity of the peer group.

Scott (1990) notes that subordinated groups often protect the hidden transcript by insisting that community members adhere to it. Such enforcement historically has been a survival technique of oppressed people. For example, workers must maintain control of the rate of work or be worked to exhaustion. Scott explains:

The subordinate moves back and forth, as it were, between two worlds: the world of the master and the offstage world of subordinates. Both of these worlds have sanctioning power. While subordinates normally can monitor the public transcript performance of their subordinates, the dominant can rarely monitor fully the hidden transcript. This means that any subordinate who seeks privilege by ingratiating himself to his superior will have to answer for that conduct once he returns to the world of his peers. . . . Social pressure among peers however, is by itself a powerful weapon of subordinates. (190)

Class clowns invade the public transcript of the classroom with the hidden transcript of the halls. In doing so, they polarize social relations in the classroom—"us" (the students) versus "them" (the teacher, the school)—daring students to publicly choose "the enemy" over their peers. This puts all students on the spot as potential traitors, so it's crucial for teachers to interrupt the bullying inherent in clowning.

Shelly (HA) described such patrolling via bullying in her further discussion of clowning. She complained, "In my U.S. history class they used to do the same thing to me 'cause I used to use big words, like a few idiots in the back would be, like, 'I didn't understand what you said, could you speak English?' I was like, 'I spoke English!'" The "idiots in the back" no doubt, knew she was speaking English but were mocking her and calling attention to her choices to use academic language instead of a shared vernacular. Shelly found such teasing infuriating and grew angry as she told the story. In such examples, the class clowns are enforcing group norms of peer solidarity and punishing those too readily identifying with school.

More than just patrolling the limits of academic engagement, clowns also implicitly coded classroom space and academic identification as feminine. Willis's 1977 study of counter-school culture among working class British boys finds that "the lads" (the boys who resist) frequently mock their teachers and make sissies of the young men who buy into the mission of the school. According to the lads, boys who are oriented toward school success, "ear'oles," were effeminate, and through their taunting the lads exacted sanctions against those who too willingly complied with the public transcript by diminishing their masculinity. Class clowns at Renaissance operated in a similar way. Like the lads, notorious class clowns at Renaissance were overwhelmingly academically-alienated young men who implicitly constructed classroom space as female through both the bravado they sometimes used in making fun of their teachers or the content and the ways they teased academically-oriented boys, though, clearly, they did not only tease boys. Oliver (AO) offers an instructive case. He seemed to admire the very disruptive group of clowns in his class and vacillated between wanting to be accepted by them and being harassed by them. He explained,

> Oliver: If you make a joke, they're gonna get this big image that you're popular or everyone knows him. So, I guess they try to fit in or something like that.
>
> MD: When you make jokes you are trying to fit in?
>
> Oliver: Yeah, I would say, like, sometimes I make a joke, sometimes I overdo it, sometimes I try to be accepted. Or sometimes, like, every time they bother me, I think that if I make jokes they'll leave me alone.

Oliver attempted to gain acceptance by participating in the joking, but his willingness to participate in teacher-led activities made his efforts ineffective, targeting him for more teasing:

> MD: Does that work [making jokes]?
>
> Oliver: Well, yes and no. Sometimes it does, for a period of time. Sometimes they just, when they're not doing anything, when they're just talking with each other, and I'm doing my work, they throw things at me. And, you know I just don't bother with them. . . .
>
> MD: Why do they throw things at you?
>
> Oliver: I think it's just to get respect from everybody else. Like, if I'm throwing paper at somebody, everybody's laughing because I'm doing it.
>
> MD: So, getting the laugh is a way of getting respect?
>
> Oliver: Yeah, it's like, if you amuse somebody, he's cool, although he doesn't do his work.

Like the 'ear'oles, Oliver was bullied because he refused to go along with the group that was not doing work. The class clowns he encountered publicly punished him by throwing paper at him. His attempts to affirm his solidarity with them by joking back were unsuccessful because he continued serious academic work. Oliver also observed that they only threw paper at boys who were doing their work, so the polarizing intent of the clowns is apparent. Humor and academic disidentification mark the work of boys in his class and the few boys who don't participate in the clowning are physically and socially punished. Though girls were not immune from teasing, the clowning students affirmed a masculine challenge to feminized classroom space thus exacting a higher price for academic participation on scholastically oriented boys.

Though class clowns in the public transcript disguised their politics behind humor, they had a consistent agenda. In enforcing the hidden transcript, the clowns, as Oliver suggested, gained status among peers for such classroom behavior. Jamal (AL) was explicit about the importance of getting recognized, a key to popularity. Admitting that he used to be a class clown, he explained,

> I just yell out stupid answers to get the teacher mad. . . . Yeah, it was fun, and people laughed at you and they made you feel better because you figure you funny now. You're recognized for something. 'Cause everybody in this school is recognized for something, everybody.

The rewards for clowning are important because they demonstrate the ways that the classroom and halls were always in contention. Clowns disrupted the classroom and reintegrated it as student space, and then these disruptions in class enhanced the status of the clowns in the halls. Florence (AO) also suspected that class clowns were "smart" but,

> They think it's better to be, like, the class clown. . . . . 'Cause they want to be funny, they don't want to be known as a geek. I'd rather be known as a geek, getting a scholarship, doing good, and then everybody else will envy me instead of sitting up there making a fool of myself.

Florence embraces the public transcript of success against the choice of a peer-group alternative. The general quickness with which many students and teachers waved off clowning behavior both protected class clowns from more serious punishment and blunted the thrust of any critique they voiced. Herein lies the strength of clowning and its limits—clowning performances enable students to insert the hidden transcript into classroom space, but the clowns do not have to be taken seriously and do not make explicit demands. It is an indirect assault on authority that disrupts but does not change the public transcript.

Reconsidering Reproduction Theory

Clowning contests the curriculum and enables students to bring the hidden transcript into official school space. Clowns also serve as representatives of hall culture by enforcing general limits on students' performance of the public transcript. Further, they can challenge the official curriculum by insisting on subject matter that is closer to student experience—like popular culture. More than this, they simply challenge the legitimacy of schooling by not only changing the subject but also by debasing the official curriculum. Despite the indirect and masked nature of each individual act of clowning, the regular presence of class clowns and the consistency of the thrust of their jokes comprise a clear critique of the formal curriculum and the nature of relationships in the classroom. They affirm the more collectivist values of the halls that emphasize group solidarity over individual advancement.

Student/school contentions are summarized by the phenomenon of clowning. Through clowns, hall culture invades classrooms. The propensity for class clowns to be young men heavily identified with hall culture and not academics, especially those whose clowning is very public, indicates what is at stake here. Through their clowning they remind their peers of the significance of their horizontal solidarity and therefore occupy an oppositional location on the continuum of student resistance. Clever and quick, clowns rally their peers to their disruptive game, at least temporarily. Students lured or cajoled into resistance may enjoy the joke at the teacher's expense, but they often find their way back to the public transcript once the performance is over or the teacher stops it. Clowns represent one pole on the continuum of classroom resistance and the teacher represents the other pole by embodying the official functions of school. Many students may move between these two poles throughout the lesson—enjoying the joke and the break from work it offers but then refocusing on academic tasks shortly thereafter. We cannot assume that any one position they occupy along this continuum is more authentic than another. Debates on the relationship of oppositionality and academic identification have often polarized these positions though such a construction misses the dynamics of classroom cultures.

Though clowns expose the hidden transcript in public space, these hidden transcripts, though masked, are familiar to most students and are already lurking in the public space. As was subtly evident in interviews, many students were always mindful of alternative ideologies despite their performances of public transcripts. Many scholars have argued that the primary function of the public schools is the reproduction of the status quo and the dominant ideology that supports it, even if such reproductive work is not ever explicitly acknowledged (Bowles and Gintis 1976; Bourdieu and Passeron 1977; Anyon 1980; Apple 1990). However, though students widely endorsed dominant ideologies on the agency of the individual and the significance of schooling, they also hinted that they were wearing a mask, saying the lines they assumed were required in the conversation. Hidden transcripts lingered within and alongside student productions of dominant ideology, which raises questions about the extent to which they had internalized the values they espoused.

Scott's 1990 framework of hidden and public transcripts helps make seemingly contradictory positions coherent because it recognizes that we all perform roles in disparate social arenas. Applied to student discourse at Renaissance, these transcripts offer us an opportunity to understand student resistance more clearly. Reproduction theorists have assumed that student readiness to articulate dominant discourses indicates that even resisting students are ultimately absorbed into hegemony. However, framing these loyalties as performances for the public transcript, which coexist with robust participation in hidden transcripts, shows that hegemony is fighting for compliance and is rarely complete. Subordinate groups engage in a hidden transcript that supports their autonomous agency and their aspirations against dominant discourses. At Renaissance, students move between these transcripts regularly. Hidden transcripts emerge in the classroom, suggesting the struggle over space that is ever present at Renaissance bleeds into the curriculum as well.

Alternative agency in alternative times and spaces (the hidden transcript) survives despite the powerful messages circulated by schools and society. However, materially, many of the students in this study and their peers grew up to occupy very similar social and economic locations to those of their parents, though there are notable exceptions. In arguing that students are incompletely absorbed into the dominant system, I am not denying that social reproduction is also a by-product of formal schooling. Rather, I am correcting the theory to argue that social reproduction in schools is not complete and this incompleteness offers both hope and raises serious dilemmas for the future of urban students.

■ ■ ■ ■ ■ ■ ■ ■

7

A Eulogy for Renaissance

Looking Forward

In June 2007, on the restored green lawn of the Old School campus, Renaissance High School graduated its last class. Failing to significantly improve student outcomes, it met the same fate that the original Old School had thirteen years earlier. This book chronicles Renaissance's school reform effort and offers insight into why the student-centered and democratic model failed to bring about the hoped-for changes. Having worked doggedly for four years to make those reforms work and even more time analyzing, reflecting, and revisiting them and the substantial student resistance they met, Renaissance's closing leaves me with mixed feelings.

I am disappointed that the vision of a democratic and student-centered school was not realized at Renaissance. We really wanted to make a difference, we worked long hours and pushed ourselves to our limits, but all the hard work couldn't make up for the huge gaps between school discourses and those of students. We also worked against great odds, given that the school was far too big to be a small school, had little control over curriculum, and had to address the systematic and historically poor academic preparation that students brought to the classrooms. We dealt with all this also while the school was grossly underfunded by an unjust school finance system that left us short on resources, understaffed, and overworked. The declaration of the school as a failed project doesn't acknowledge these structural obstacles. More than this, it negates the significant human effort that was made there. I loved my students and many of my colleagues and for all the harshness I report in these pages, there was also a lot of warmth and friendship that made Renaissance humane at least some of the time. So though I believe its closing to make way for newer, smaller, and better conceptualized schools is in the best interest of students, it is still worth noting that the failure of Renaissance was not for lack of effort or commitment.

The second wave of restructuring that replaced Renaissance took a distinctly different form than the first and represents the significant development of small schools and school-reform agendas over the last decade. When Renaissance was created, Old School had simply been divided into three smaller units with all teachers in the building guaranteed a job at one of the new schools and all students being evenly distributed among them. These schools began as smaller versions of Old School and had to forge new identities without a clean slate. In this second wave of restructuring, Renaissance and its two sister schools were phased out over four years by not admitting any new students. At the same time, six new schools were phased in, admitting a new ninth grade each year. This next generation of schools are truly new schools with new staff and new students and are much freer from the history of Old School itself. They also have had the opportunity to grow into full capacity rather than having to "build the plane while flying," as the former principal of Renaissance described the reform effort there. Further, when Renaissance was created, the small schools movement was relatively young. Over the last decade, this movement has matured and these new schools will benefit from its accumulated wisdom.

These new schools are no larger than 450 students (at least, that is their design), whereas Renaissance enrolled twice that many. I suspect the smaller scale will change the nature of spatial formation and perhaps establish a less-formidable hall culture and a less contradictory classroom culture. Perhaps, too, these schools are more coherently designed and some of the contradictions that undermined student academic engagement at Renaissance will diminish. And perhaps the schools will be considered less violent so that the scanning rituals will be loosened to further reduce the kinds of student-school conflicts that Renaissance's reform effort was unable to resolve.

These new schools operate in a very different policy context as well. Since 2001, the New York City school system has been radically reorganized twice—first dissolving the community school boards and consolidating the nearly forty local superintendencies into ten, and second, disbanding those ten superintendencies and giving principals far more autonomy in running their schools. Today, principals, particularly, and schools in general are far more accountable on more measures. In addition to the usual indicators, such as test scores, reading levels, four-year graduation rates, and attendance rates, schools and principals are now rated by parents and teachers, and schools must administer more formative assessments to track student growth. The consequences are greater as well because a principal can be fired if his or her school doesn't meet targets. At the same time, principals have more control over most things that occur in their schools, and they have greater control over their budgets. Though principals face more curricular constraints, the increase in control at the site may enable their schools to address the kinds of issues that emerged at Renaissance. I conclude this book that explored the contradictions between student culture and school reform at Renaissance with a message to the new schools at the Old School campus and those opening in cities everywhere. I hope they can learn from Renaissance and build schools that not only enable students to reach higher standards but also offer students an education that matters to them.

By examining how several pivotal spaces were culturally produced at Renaissance, we gain a more nuanced and complex view of both schools and student resistance. The findings here significantly challenge current understandings of student resistance and oppositionality and suggest new directions for urban education.

One of the limits of much of the literature on urban schooling is the tendency to conceptualize schools as one-dimensional. Scholars have largely focused on classroom interactions—a logical choice—because, as I note, they are the most intense sites of student/school engagement. However, an emphasis on classrooms alone too often overlooks not only the significance of halls and other student-dominated spaces in shaping student academic identities, but a classroom emphasis also ignores situations like school entry rituals that also condition student-school relationships. The focus on classrooms has also emphasized what schools do to kids, but a broader reading of spatial formation reveals that student-school relationships are more dialogic, with students seeking ways to transform school experiences and to preserve local knowledge and hidden transcripts. Focusing on how spaces are culturally produced reveals the ideologies and value systems informing everyday experience.

Though classrooms are rich sites of student-school conflict and negotiation, a spatial analysis reveals the multiple and conflicting discourses
that are generated in different sites and that inform classroom negotiations. Renaissance was disturbingly incoherent in the sense that students received so many conflicting messages. The contrast between the
scanning ritual and the student-centered pedagogies attempted in some
classrooms offers perhaps the clearest example of this incoherence. Every
single morning students were subject to an invasive and visceral scanning process that denied academic identities and assaulted some cultural
identities. In classrooms, conversely, students were urged to be serious
students and sometimes the content was drawn from their cultural experiences, which were supposed to have been left at the door. Though
it is useful to recognize the ways the classroom and the scanning site
were very different spaces, they were both sites of official school policies
and practices and, as such, were also part of the same institution. Which
voice should students believe?

Beyond this obvious contradiction, there were many more subtle ones
as well. Students were encouraged to value peer solidarity in the halls,
urged to work collaboratively in classrooms, and expected to embrace individualist ideologies that atomized their academic efforts and urged them
to focus on their own advancement. In addition to contradictory ideologies that presented dilemmas for students, school authority was also inconsistent. Students knew that different teachers would tolerate different
levels of inattention, require different levels of effort, and enforce school
and classroom rules with different levels of gusto and consistency. Not
only did students move between the entry scanning, the student dominated halls, and the teacher convened classrooms, each with a different
set of protocols and expectations, but they also moved from one class to
the next, each one somewhat isolated from the others and having a different set of expectations. Such is the cacophony of urban schools: there is a
level of discord that is made visible by the infrapolitics that exploits these
problematic gaps in school authority.

This spatial analysis of Renaissance also helps reframe debates about
student resistance. In the literature on oppositional culture, oppositionality
is conceptualized as a fixed position in which Black students reject school
achievement (Diamond, Lewis, and Gordon 2007). Ogbu's (1988) original
formulation of oppositional culture held that it was a cultural adaptation

of Black people that rejected assimilation into racist systems. This oppositional culture meant that Black students constructed academics as something belonging to White people and academic success as a betrayal of the group. According to Ogbu, oppositional culture was cultivated in the Black community and brought into schools. Close exploration of the exclave culture students installed in the halls of Renaissance challenges these constructions. First, before students arrive in the halls, the school itself, via its aggressive scanning, assaults various aspects of Black culture, targeting boys sporting street and hip-hop styles and stripping girls of beads and head wraps clearly not linked to gang affiliations. Further, the school constructs students as inherently nonacademic by confiscating many ordinary school supplies. Through such practices, the school constructs students as oppositional and nonacademic by insisting that aspects of their self-presentation are unacceptable and by denying them the right to carry some of the tools of academic identity. Oppositionality in schooling must be seen as a position that is co-constructed by students and schools—it is not a fixed identity created outside.

Once in the halls, students created a derivative of local street cultures, but this too, is an adaptation to school structures; it is not a direct import from outside. The concept of an exclave calls attention to the connection to the outside locale but also to the ways students modified local street cultures within the enclave of the school. This student-generated exclave culture was also not an oppositional culture, though it contained oppositional elements. It was rather a thirdspace (Soja 1996) that contained dualities but was not entirely defined by them. Thus, many students insisted that the halls and classrooms were somewhat irrelevant to each other, to a point. Over-identification with academics at the expense of the peer group was going too far. The exclave of the halls presents a student culture that asserts an alternative to school identification but does not entirely reject academic achievement.

In noting that a fixed oppositional culture did not exist, it is a mistake to discount oppositionality altogether. Class clowns at times occupied such a space, as did some students who strongly identified with the halls and often the streets. Even some high-achieving students identified with the halls when they protested school routines. Student resistance operates along a continuum; students move along this continuum throughout the day and their academic careers.

Conceptualizing student resistance as a continuum rather than as a fixed identity better captures the complexity and nuance of student identities. It also recognizes that students are not unchangeable, a crucial facet of my hopefulness for the new schools at Old School. Students identified in this study as alienated were designated so because they were significantly behind in credits, may have been disruptive in class and/or expressed their alienation from school in some tangible way. However, alienated students such as Samuel and Jason managed to pass enough state exams and classes to graduate (though the others in this category did not). Melissa (AL), who did not finish high school, nonetheless put significant effort into some of her school assignments though she cut many other classes and eventually disappeared from school. Though she passed few classes, she did engage in some school activities. She cannot be fixed as a staunch resistor because of her occasional willingness to cooperate with her teachers. Similarly, Serafina (HA) identified as a serious student but nonetheless refused to cooperate with SSOs when they assaulted both her cultural and academic identities. At other times, too, she challenged individual teachers and school policies. Assuming her academic ambitions mitigated her strong critique of the school, racism, and sexism would be a gross misrepresentation. She moved in and out of oppositional stances throughout her Renaissance career.

Recognizing that students move along a continuum between oppositionality and accommodation more accurately captures student engagement with schooling. Shifting our attention to the factors that inform why and how they move along this continuum (rather than assessing where they are at any given moment) may prove to be more helpful in improving academic outcomes for Black students and closing the achievement gap.

Spatial formation at Renaissance further highlights the ways the classroom is the most contested site in the school. Students largely controlled the halls, and the SSOs controlled the entryway through scanning, but classrooms were a site of ongoing contention between students and teachers. The struggle over idiom and the nature of classroom space calls attention to some of the contradictions noted above that exist in classrooms. In particular, the tension between the idiom that should dominate verbal classroom exchanges emphasized multiple interpretations of classroom space—that it is a culturally relevant space for student self-expression and that it is a space of social reproduction inculcating cultural capital students need for upward mobility. In this sense, classrooms are clearly contact zones—sites of asymmetrical struggles whose outcomes are indeterminate. Infrapolitics and the insertion of hidden transcripts into public space are also part of these contact-zone struggles. The spatial formations in the halls and at the front door condition the nature of these contact-zone struggles, but the classroom itself is where the struggles are most intense.

The fate of the new schools at the Old School campus, as well as many other urban schools, will largely lie in their ability to resolve these contact-zone struggles in ways that affirm student identities and perspectives while also engaging them in the formal curriculum. Educators and activists who seek more just and meaningful schools for all students must address two key dilemmas. The first dilemma is that of the conflicted messages and discourses produced by schools. School leaders, reformers, designers, and teachers need to pay more attention to the ideologies they draw on to frame their work and they need to pay attention to the ideologies that are either passively or actively, intentionally or unintentionally circulated in schools. As part of this first dilemma, they also need to attend to consistency across the school community and in the broader school. Educators have spent too little time considering the contradictory messages that schools generate and the ways those messages imperil student achievement. Meaningful urban school reform must make these institutions more coherent and coherent in a way that also is more humane and respectful of student identities.

The second dilemma is the unfinished conception of the pedagogy of the contact zone. This pedagogy must draw on student historical and cultural experience in meaningful, rigorous, and consistent ways. The sporadic insertion of culturally relevant content at Renaissance was met with student suspicion because a largely cosmetic inclusion of such material doesn't inspire students. The pedagogy of the contact zone must close the chasm between school and student discourse, draw on local idioms and knowledge to build academic competence in standard English, and be grounded in a coherent ideology that supports solidarity and community struggle.

Contact-zone pedagogies should also address the contact zone itself. They should include explorations of the local community and sites within the school drawing on ethnography and other tools of social research. Another way of making schools more responsive to students is to develop a public transcript that does not negate structural issues that frame students' lives. Rather, these issues should become legitimate parts of the subject matter. Engaging students in critical explorations of their society and of their own subcultures may enable students to develop productive frameworks, like Samuel (AL) did, that enable them to navigate among multiple discourses productively. It also may enable them to recognize oppressive structures not just in dominant society but also in the local and youth cultures in which they participate.

Last, pedagogy of the contact zone is ever mindful of the ebb and flow of student resistance and also explores the factors that may push students one way or another. Such pedagogy then, also employs an iterative process through which teachers explore and address the ways students engage or refuse academic work. It uses the construct of a continuum of resistance to be vigilant that no student is out of reach and that resistance is often a reasonable response and therefore important to explore.

The failure of progressive school reform at Renaissance was not merely a failure of instruction or vision, but was also conditioned by the intense contradictions that informed many levels of school life. More than just contradictions, there were problematic gaps among teachers, school policies, and students. The future hope for urban schools lies in the abilities of educators and students to find ways to bridge these chasms and contradictions.

Notes

■ ■ ■ ■

Introduction

1. West Indies refers to countries in the Caribbean that are former colonies of Great Britain. Jamaica, Trinidad and Tobago and Guyana were the most widely represented nations at Renaissance, though almost every nation in the West Indies was represented. Additionally, a noticeable and highly marginalized Haitian population also attended the school.

2. It should be noted that high achievers are overrepresented in this study because, not surprisingly, such students were more likely to volunteer. They represent 25 percent of the interviewees but made up only 10 percent of the student body.

Chapter 1

1. In 1898, New York City consolidated and the previously independent cities of Brooklyn and Queens became boroughs of New York City. At that time, their public schools were turned over to the city but with some strings attached. The expansion of Old School was one such string.

2. Though they were referred to as "schoolmen," many decision-making educators were women such as Ella Fladd Young, the superintendent of Chicago schools, and Julia Richman, the superintendent of Manhattan schools.

3. I have met other alumni who also said they went to "the other Old School," which suggests that students may have used this phrase when they attended the school.

4. It is important to note that this practice of dividing existing student populations into new schools has generally been abandoned. Now, the common practice of reorganizing big schools is to phase out the old school and open up new schools with one grade only, adding new grades and new schools as space becomes available.

Chapter 2

1. It should also be noted that the first time debaters were allowed to bring their lawyerlike accordion files to and from school, and they often told me that the SSOs had praised them at scanning. Debaters often were eager to show off their trophies

to the guards when they brought them to school after a tournament. Though on this day the SSOs hassled Serafina, they were also some of the team's most ardent supporters. While they are enforcers of these problematic policies, they are also adults in the school who try to positively impact student lives.

Bibliography

■ ■ ■ ■

Aggarwal, R. (2000). "Traversing Lines of Control: Feminist Anthropology To-day." *The Annals of the American Academy of Political and Social Science* 571: 14–29.

Ainsworth-Darnell, J. W. and D. B. Downey. (1998) "Assessing the Oppositional Culture Explanation for Racial/Ethnic Differences in School Performance." *American Sociological Review* 63(4): 536–53.

Akom, A. A. (2003). "Reexamining Resistance as Oppositional Behavior: The Nation of Islam and the Creation of a Black Achievement Ideology." *Sociology of Education* 76 (October): 305–25.

———. (2007). "Free Spaces: Excavating Race, Class, and Gender among Urban Schools and Communities." *International Journal of Qualitative Studies in Education* 20(6): 611–16.

Anderson, E. (1999). *Code of the Street: Decency, Violence, and the Moral Life of the Inner City.* New York: W. W. Norton.

Alim, H. S. (2007). "'The Whig Party Don't Exist in My Hood': Knowledge, Reality, and Education in the Hip Hop Nation." In *Talkin' Black Talk: Language, Education and Social Change.* Edited by H. S. Alim and J. Baugh, 15–29. New York: Teachers College Press.

H. S. Alim and J. Baugh, eds. (2007). *Talkin' Black Talk: Language, Education and Social Change.* New York: Teachers College Press.

Anyon, J. (1980). "Social Class and the Hidden Curriculum of Work." In *Rereading America: Cultural Contexts for Critical Thinking and Writing. 3rd ed.* Edited by G. Colombo, R. Cullen and B. Lisle, 45–60. Boston: Bedford Books.

———. (1997). *Ghetto Schooling: A Political Economy of Urban Educational Reform.* New York: Teachers College Press.

———. (2005). *Radical Possibilities: Public Policy, Urban Education, and a New Social Movement.* New York: Routledge.

Apple, M. W. (1990). *Ideology and Curriculum.* New York: Routledge.

Archibald, R. C. (1999). "Schools in New York Area Reassess Safety for Students." *New York Times.* A18. August 13..

Arriaza, G. (2003). "Schools, Social Capital, and Children of Color." *Race, Ethnicity and Education* 6(1): 71–94.

Astor, R. A., H. A. Meyer, and R. O. Pitner. (2001). "Elementary and Middle School Students' Perceptions of Violence-Prone School Subcontexts." *Elementary School Journal* 101(5): 511–28.

Behar, R. (1995). "Introduction: Out of Exile." In *Women Writing Culture*. Edited by R. Behar and D. Gordon, 1–31. Los Angeles: University of California Press.

Berger, J. (1991). "To Avoid Jail-Like Atmosphere, Principal Spurned Metal Detectors." *New York Times*. B2. November 26.

———. (1992). "Bitter Debate on Scanning for Firearms." *New York Times*. 2; Column 6; Metropolitan Desk.

Board of Education, City of New York. (1987). *The Chronicles of _____ High School, 1937–1987*. New York: New York City Board of Education.

Bourdieu, P. (1989). "Social Space and Symbolic Power." *Sociological Theory* 7(1): 14–25.

Bourdieu, P. and J.-C. Passeron (1977). *Reproduction in Education, Society, and Culture*. London: Sage.

Bowles, S. and H. Gintis (1976). *Schooling in Capitalist America: Educational Reform and the Contradictions of Economic Life*. New York: Basic Books.

Brodkin, K. (1998). *How Jews Became White Folks and What That Says about Race in America*. New Brunswick: Rutgers University Press.

Brumberg, S. F. (1986). *Going to America, Going to School: The Jewish Immigrant Public School Encounter in Turn-of-the-Century New York City*. New York: Praeger.

Buterbaugh, L. (1993). "Teen Gun-Toters Elude Detection." *Chicago Sun-Times*. 21. October 15.

Carter, P. L. (2003). ""Black" Cultural Capital, Status Positioning, and Schooling Conflicts for Low-Income African American Youth." *Social Problems* 50(1): 136–55.

Casella, R. (2001). *"Being Down": Challenging Violence in Urban Schools*. New York: Teachers College Press.

Chisholm, S. (1994). From "Unbought and Unbossed." In *The Brooklyn Reader: Thirty Writers Celebrate America's Favorite Borough*. Edited by A. Sexton, A. Wyatt, and L. Powers, 43–52. New York: Three Rivers Press.

Cohen, R. and R. Mohl (1979). *The Paradox of Progressive Education: The Gary Plan and Urban Schooling*. Port Washington, NY: Kennikat Press.

Conchas, G. Q. (2001). "Structuring Failure and Success: Understanding the Variability in Latino School Engagement." *Harvard Educational Review* 71(3): 475–504.

———. (2006). *The Color of Success: Race and High-Achieving Urban Youth*. New York: Teachers College Press.

Dance, L. J. (2002). *Tough Fronts: The Impact of Street Culture on Schooling*. New York: Routledge.

Davis, M. (1990). *City of Quartz; Excavating the Future in Los Angeles*. New York: Verso.

Delpit, L. (1995). *Other People's Children: Cultural Conflict in the Classroom*. New York: The New Press.

———. (2002). "No Kinda Sense." In *The Skin That We Speak: Thoughts on Language and Culture in the Classroom.* Edited by L. Delpit and J. K. Dowdy, 31–48. New York: The New Press.

Devine, J. (1996). *Maximum Security: The Culture of Violence in Inner-City Schools.* Chicago: University of Chicago Press.

Diamond, J. B., A. E. Lewis, and L. Gordon. (2007). "Race and School Achievement in a Desegregated Suburb: Reconsidering the Oppositional Culture Explanation." *International Journal of Qualitative Studies in Education* 20(6): 655–79.

Dickar, M. (2004). "Words Is Changin' Everyday: Language and Literacy in the Urban Contact Zone." In *Teaching English Today: Advocating Change in the Secondary Curriculum.* Edited by B. R. C. Barrell, R. F. Hammett, G. Pradl, M. Mayher, and J. S. Mayher. New York: Teachers College Press.

Dickar, M. and W. Klann (1997). *The Great Sweater Girl Riot of 1996: Critical Pedagogy, Horizontal Violence and Urban Schooling.* The Pedagogy of the Oppressed Conference, Omaha, Nebr.

Dillon, S. (1993). "Years of Neglect Raise Cost of Restoring a High School: Repairs to _____ at $78 Million. *New York Times.* B37, B44. November 7.

Doyle, L. (1992). "Lessons in Death at NY Schools." *The Independent* (London) 18. March 18.

Du Bois, W. E. B. (1903). *The Souls of Black Folk.* New York: Library of America.

Eckert, P. (1989). *Jocks and Burnouts: Social Caterfotires and Identity in High School.* New York: Teachers College Press.

Eliade, M. (1961). *The Sacred and the Profane: The Nature of Religion.* New York: Harper & Row.

Epp, J. R. (1996). "Schools, Complicity, and Sources of Violence." In *Systemic Violence: How Schools Hurt Children.* Edited by J. R. Epp and A. M. Watkinson, 1–24. London: Falmer Press.

Epp, J. R. and A. M. Watkinson, eds. (1996). *Systemic Violence: How Schools Hurt Children.* London: Falmer Press.

Fallis, R. K. and S. Opotow (2003). "Are Students Failing School or Are Schools Failing Students? Class Cutting in High School." *Journal of Social Issues* 59(1): 103–19.

Ferguson, A. A. (2000). *Bad Boys: Public Schools and the Making of Black Masculinity.* Ann Arbor: University of Michigan Press.

Fine, M. (1991). *Framing Dropouts: Notes on the Politics of an Urban High School.* Albany: SUNY Press.

Fine, M. and S. McClelland (2006). "Sexuality Education and Desire: Still Missing after All These Years." *Harvard Educational Review* 76(3): 297–338.

Fine, M., L. Weis, and L. Powell. (1997). "Communities of Difference: A Critical Look at Desegregated Spaces Created for and by Youth." *Harvard Educational Review* 67(2): 247–84.

Flores-Gonzalez, N. (1999). "Puerto Rican High Achievers: An Example of Ethnic and Academic Identity Compatibility." *Anthropology and Education Quarterly* 30(3): 343–62.

Flores-Gonzalez, N. (2002). *School Kids/Street Kids: Identity Development in Latino Students*. New York: Teachers College Press.

———. (2005). "Popularity Versus Respect: School Structure, Peer Groups and Latino Academic Achievement." *International Journal of Qualitative Studies in Education* 18(5): 625–42.

Foley, D. E. (1990). *Learning Capitalist Culture: Deep in the Heart of Tejas*. Philadelphia: University of Pennsylvania Press.

———. (2005). "Elusive Prey: John Ogbu and the Search for a Grand Theory of Academic Disengagement." *International Journal of Qualitative Studies in Education* 18(5): 643–57.

Fordham, S. (1996). *Blacked Out: Dilemmas of Race, Identity, and Success at Capital High*. Chicago: University of Chicago Press.

Fordham, S. and J. Ogbu (1986). "Black Students' School Success: Coping with the Burden of 'Acting White.'" *The Urban Review* 18(3): 176–206.

Frankenberg, R. (1993). *White Women, Race Matters: The Social Construction of Whiteness*. Minneapolis: University of Minnesota Press.

Gagen, E. A. (2000). "Playing the Part: Performing Gender in America's Playgrounds." In *Children's Geographies: Playing, Living, Learning*. Edited by S. L. Holloway and G. Valentine, 213–229. New York: Routledge.

Gendar, A. and N. Bode. (2002). "Metal Detectors Testing Patience." *New York Daily News*. 3: Suburban. November 20.

Gibson, M. A. (2005). "Promoting Academic Engagement among Minority Youth: Implications from John Ogbu's Shaker Heights Ethnography." *International Journal of Qualitative Studies in Education* 18(5): 581–603.

Gilroy, P. (1993). *The Black Atlantic: Modernity and Double Consciousness*. Cambridge: Harvard University Press.

Giroux, H. A. (1983). *Theory and Resistance in Education: A Pedagogy for the Opposition*. South Hadley, Mass.: Bergin & Garvey. Repr., Westport, Conn., 2001.

Goodnough, A. (2001). "The Ruling in the Schools: The Overview: State Judge Rules School Aid System is Unfair to City." *New York Times*. A1. January 11.

Gordon, T., J. Holland, and E. Lahelma. (2000). *Making Spaces: Citizenship and Difference in Schools*. New York: St. Martin's Press.

Grant, C. A. and C. E. Sleeter (1996). *After the School Bell Rings*. London: Falmer Press.

Hammock, F. (1997). "Ethical Issues in Teacher Research." *Teachers College Record* 99(2): 247–65.

Hancock, L. (1992). "Halls of Shame." *New York Daily News*. 1. February 16.

Harvey, D. (1990). *The Condition of Postmodernity: an Enquiry into the Origins of Cultural Change*. Cambridge: Blackwell.

Haymes, S. N. (1995). *Race, Culture and the City: A Pedagogy for Black Urban Struggle*. Albany: SUNY Press.

Haynes, B. D. (2001). *Red Lines, Black Spaces: The Politics of Race and Space in a Black Middle-Class Suburb*. New Haven: Yale University Press.

Hemmings, A. (2002). "Youth Culture of Hostility: Discourses of Money, Respect, and Difference." *International Journal of Qualitative Studies in Education* 15(3): 291–307.

———. (2004). *Coming of Age in U.S. High Schools: Economic, Kinship, Religious, and Political Crosscurrents*. Mahwah, NJ: Erlbaum.

Holloway, S. L. and G. Valentine (2000). "Children's Geographies and the New Social Studies of Childhood." In *Children's Geographies: playing, living, learning*. Edited by S. L. Holloway and G. Valentine, 1–26. New York: Routledge.

Horvat, E. M. and K. Lewis (2003). "Reassessing the 'Burden of Acting White': The Importance of Peer Groups in Managing Academic Success." *Sociology of Education* 76 (October): 265–80.

Katz, M. B. (1971). *Class, Bureaucracy and Schools: The Illusion of Educational Change in America*. New York: Praeger.

Kohl, H. (1994). *"I Won't Learn From You" and Other Thoughts on Creative Maladjustments*. New York: The New Press.

Kohn, A. (2000). *The Case against Standardized Testing: Raising Test Scores, Ruining the Schools*. Portsmouth: Heinemann.

Kozol. J. (1991). *Savage Inequalities: Children in America's Schools*. New York: Crown Publishers.

Krinsky, H. (1987). "Architecture at _____." In *The Chronicles of _____ High School: 1937–1987*. Edited by R. Rush, 19. New York: Board of Education.

Lamont, M. and A. Lareau (1988). "Cultural Capital: Allusions, Gaps, and Glissandos in Recent Theoretical Developments." *Sociological Theory* 6: 153–68.

Landmark Preservation Commission (2003). _____ High School. New York: City of New York.

Lazerson, M. (2005). "The Education Gospel." *Education Week* 24(36): 38, 48.

Leander, K. M. (2004). "Reading the Spatial Histories of Positioning in a Classroom Literacy Event." In *Spatializing Literacy Research and Practice*. Edited by K. M. Leander and M. Sheehy, 115–42 New York: Peter Lang.

Leander, K. M. and M. Sheehy, eds. (2004). *Spatializing Literacy Research and Practice: New Literacies and Digital Epistemologies*. New York: Peter Lang.

Leavitt, P. (1992). "Arms-Checks Begun at 5 NYC Schools." *USA Today*. 3A. March 2.

Lee, P. W. (1999). "In Their Own Voices: An Ethnographic Study of Low-Achieving Students within the Context of School Reform." *Urban Education* 34(2): 214–44.

Levinson, B. A., D. E. Foley, and D. C. Holland, eds. (1996). *The Cultural Production of the Educated Person: Critical Ethnographies of Schooling and Local Practices: Power, Social Identity, and Education*. Albany: SUNY Press.

Lewis, A. (2004). *Race in the School Yard:*. New Brunswick: Rutgers University Press.

Lipman, P. (1998). *Race, Class, and Power in School Restructuring*. Albany: SUNY Press.

Lipman, P. (2004). *High-Stakes Education: Inequality, Globalization, and Urban School Reform*. New York: Routledge-Falmer.

Lopez, N. (2002). "Race-Gender Experiences and Schooling: Second-Generation Dominican, West Indian, and Haitian Youth in New York City." *Race, Ethnicity and Education* 5(1): 67–90.

———. (2003). *Hopeful Girls, Troubled Boys: Race and Gender Disparity in Urban Education*. New York: Routledge.

MacLeod, J. (1995). *Ain't No Makin' It: Aspirations and Attainment in a Low-Income Neighborhood*. Boulder: Westview Press.

Makin, K. (1994). "Class Conflict: A Look at School Violence." *Globe and Mail* (Toronto, Canada). May 21.

Massey, D. B. (1993). "Politics and Space/Time." In *Place and the Politics of Identity*. Edited by M. Keith and S. Pile, 141–61. New York: Routledge.

———. (1994). *Space, Place, and Gender*. Minneapolis: University of Minnesota Press.

McCormick, J. (2004). *Writing in the Asylum: Student Poets in City Schools*. New York: Teachers College Press.

McLaren, P. (1986). *Schooling as a Ritual Performance: Towards a Political Economy of Education Symbols and Gestures*. New York: Routledge.

Medina, J. (2006). "School Aid: Meet the New Math, Same as the Old." *New York Times*. B1. March 31.

———. (2007a). Police Arrest a Student, Then Her Principal, Too. *New York Times*. B3. October 10

———. (2007b). Safety Agents Are Defended after 2 Arrests at City School. *New York Times*. B2. October 11.

Metz, M. H. (1978). *Classrooms and Corridors: The Crisis of Authority in Desegregated Secondary Schools*. Berkeley: University of California Press.

Monkman, K., M. Ronald, and F. D. Theramene. (2005). "Social and Cultural Capital in an Urban Latino School Community." *Urban Education* 40(1): 4–31.

Noguera, P. A. (1995). "Preventing and Producing Violence: A Critical Analysis of Responses to School Violence." *Harvard Educational Review* 65(2): 189–212.

Oakes, J. (1985). *Keeping Track: How Schools Structure Inequality*. New Haven: Yale University Press.

Obidah, J. (2000). "On Living (and Dying) with Violence: Entering Young Voices in the Discourse." In *Smoke and Mirrors: The Hidden Context of Violence in School and Society*. Edited by S. U. Spina, 49–66. Lanham, MD: Rowman and Littlefield.

Ogbu, J. (1988). "Understanding Cultural Diversity and Learning." *Educational Researcher* 21(8): 5–14.

———. (2003). *Black American Students in an Affluent Suburb: A Study of Academic Disengagement*. Mahwah, NJ: Erlbaum.

Olmstead, L. (1993). "Mayor to Announce Plan for Putting Police Officers in All New York Schools." *New York Times*. 1:48. September 19.

Pollock, M. (2004). *Colormute: Race Talk Dilemmas in an American School*. Princeton: Princeton University Press.

Pratt, M. L. (1986). "Fieldwork in Common Places." In *Writing Culture: The Poetics and Politics of Ethnography*. Edited by J. Clifford and G. E. Marcus, 27–50. Berkeley: University of California Press.

Rich, A. (1986). "Compulsory Heterosexuality and Lesbian Existence." In *Blood, Bread, and Poetry: Selected Prose 1979–1985*. New York: W. W. Norton. 23–75.

Scott, J. C. (1985). *Weapons of the Weak: Everyday Forms of Peasant Resistance*. New Haven: Yale University Press.

———. (1990). *Domination and the Arts of Resistance: Hidden Transcripts*. New Haven: Yale University Press.

Shor, I. (1996). *When Students Have Power*. Chicago: University of Chicago Press.

Smitherman, G. (1977). *Talkin and Testifyin: The Language of Black America*. Detroit: Wayne State University Press.

———. (1998). "Black English/Ebonics: What It Be Like?" In *The Real Ebonics Debate: Power, Language and the Education of African American Children*. Edited by T. Perry and L. Delpit. Boston: Beacon; Rethinking Schools.

Snyder-Grenier, E. (1996). *Brooklyn: An Illustrated History*. Philadelphia: Temple University Press.

Soja, E. W. (1989). *Postmodern Geographies: The Reassertion of Space in Critical Social Theory*. New York: Verso.

———. (1996). *Thirdspace: Journeys to Los Angeles and Other Real and Imagined Places*. Cambridge: Blackwell.

Solomon, R. P. (1992). *Black Resistance in High School: Forging a Separatist Culture*. Albany: SUNY Press.

Spears, A. K. (2007). "African American Communicative Practices: Improvisation, Semantic License, and Augmentation." In *Talkin Black Talk: Language, Education, and Social Change*. Edited by H. S. Alim and J. Baugh, 100–14. New York: Teachers College Press.

Spina, S. U. (2000). "Introduction: Violence in Schools" In *Smoke and Mirrors: The Hidden Context of Violence in School and Society*. Edited by S. U. Spina, 1–39. Lanham, MD: Rowman and Littlefield.

Spring, J. (2001). *The American School, 1642–2000*. Boston: McGraw-Hill.

Stanton-Salazar, R. D. (1997). "A Social Capital Framework for Understanding the Socialization of Racial Minority Children and Youths." *Harvard Educational Review* 67(1): 1–40.

Tatum, B. D. (1999). *"Why Are All the Black Kids Sitting Together in the Cafeteria?" and Other Conversations about Race*. New York: Basic Books.

Thompkins, D. E. (2000). "School Violence: Gangs and a Culture of Fear." *Annals of the American Academy of Political and Social Science* 567(January): 54–71.

Thompson, E. P. (1962). *The Making of the English Working Class*. New York: Vintage.

Tuan, Y.-f. (1977). *Space and Place: The Perspective of Experience*. Minneapolis: University of Minnesota Press.

Tuan, Y.-f. (1990). *Topophilia: A Study of Environmental Perception, Attitudes, and Values*. New York: Columbia University Press.

Turner, P. V. (1990). *Campus: An American Planning Tradition*. New York: The Architectural History Foundation; MIT Press.

Tyack, D. B. (1974). *The One Best System: A History of American Urban Education*. Cambridge: Harvard University Press.

Tyack, D. B. and E. Hansot. (1991). *Learning Together: A History of Coeducation in American Schools*. New Haven: Yale University Press.

Valenzuela, A. (1999). *Subtractive Schooling: U.S.-Mexican Youth and the Politics of Caring*. Albany: SUNY Press.

Venturi, R., D. B. Brown, and S. Izenour. (1997). *Learning from Las Vegas: The Forgotten Symbolism of Architectural Form*. Cambridge: MIT Press.

Warren, S. (2005). "Resilience and Refusal: African-Caribbean Young Men's Agency, School Exclusions, and School-Based Mentorship Programs." *Race, Ethnicity and Education* 8(3): 243–60.

Waters, M. (1999). *Black Identities: Immigration and West Indian Dreams*. Cambridge: Harvard University Press.

Watkinson, A. M. (1996). "Suffer the Little Children Who Come into Schools." In *Systemic Violence: How Schools Hurt Children*. Edited by J. R. Epp and A. M. Watkinson, 173–90. London: Falmer Press.

Webber, J. A. (2003). *Failure to Hold: The Politics of School Violence*. Lanham, MD: Rowman and Littlefield.

Weis, L. (1986). ""Thirty Years Old and I'm Allowed to Be Late": The Politics of Time at an Urban Community College." *British Journal of Sociology of Education* 7(3): 241–63.

Wilder, C. S. (2000). *A Covenant with Color: Race and Social Power in Brooklyn*. New York: Columbia University Press.

Willis, P. (1977). *Learning to Labor: How Working-Class Kids Get Working-Class Jobs*. New York: Columbia University Press.

Winter, G. (2002). "Decent Education, Figured in Dollars." *New York Times*. B8. October 2.

Index

■   ■   ■   ■

About the Author

■　　■　　　■　　　■　　　■

Maryann Dickar is Assistant Professor in the Department of Teaching and Learning at the Steinhardt School of Culture, Education, and Human Development, New York University. She received her doctorate in American Studies from the University of Minnesota. She has served as the project director for the NYU-Community School District 10 Alternative Certification Initiative and conducts research on urban school cultures.